www.thesavvylandlordbook.com

"Due diligence always pays off."

the
savvy
LANDLORD ™

A Common Sense

Approach To

Real Estate Investing

Steven VanCauwenbergh
with Walter B. Jenkins

THE SAVVY LANDLORD:
A Common Sense Approach to Real Estate Investing

International Standard Book Number: 978-0-9859805-0-4

Published by Teflon Publishing,
8 NE 48th Street, Oklahoma City, OK 73105
The Savvy Landlord name and logo are trademarks of Teflon Publishing
Library of Congress Cataloging-in-Publication Data
is available from the publisher

Interior design by Garowski.com
Printed at Jerico, LLC
Edited by Thomas Womack Book Ox www.bookox.com
Cover design by Elizabeth Hunt with Gorilla Media Group
www.gorillamediagroup.com

To my mother,

for years of hard work and labor

in raising me.

When faced with the many trials

of being a single mother—you carried on.

I am forever grateful.

Contents

Finding Freedom

"Everybody wants to go to heaven, but nobody wants to die." Everyone has a life they dream of, but the sad reality is that many people won't put in the work or live with the discipline required to make it happen.

I read a shocking statistic once. It said more than 90 percent of people who open a book will never finish reading it. Many of them won't make it past the first chapter. This has nothing to do with how well the book is written or what it's about. Most people aren't willing to put the effort into building better lives, even if that means reading only a few chapters.

Change is never comfortable. People want to stay in the safety and security of what they know. They aren't willing to fight through the discomfort of change, or they allow themselves to become distracted by the disappointing routines their lives have become.

This book can be a powerful tool—if you read it, learn its lessons, and apply those principles in your life. If you're not willing to do all three of those things, this book is no more useful than a clump of dirt or a pile of rocks.

This book isn't really about real estate. That may sound strange, considering the word *landlord* is in the title, and we talk about things like how to draft a lease and where to buy locks for rental houses. But this really isn't a book about how to manage property.

What *is* it about? This book is about freedom. What is freedom? Freedom is time and money. Freedom means you have time to do what you want when you want. You're not chained to an office, a desk, or to someone else's schedule. You have enough money to pay off your debt, and you don't have to worry about how you'll pay your bills every month.

This book is a template to help you create residual and passive income streams to live the life you've always wanted, and it's designed to empower you. When you learn and apply the lessons between its covers, you'll take control of your life and have the ability to improve your lifestyle.

Each of the lessons in this book has been proven to work in a variety of places. Your success won't depend on your race, creed, religion, or education. There's no reason why you can't build wealth and income using real estate. Freedom will soon follow.

You don't have to be a genius or have any special talents to make these techniques work for you. When I started investing in real estate, I didn't know anything about the industry, and I wasn't highly educated. I wasn't born with a silver spoon in my mouth. I was as blue collar as they come (and still am). I only had the dream to build a better future than the one I'd been born into. And I was willing to work to make that dream come true.

These pages contain some of the most powerful life lessons you'll ever read. Notice the overall themes that I give repeated emphasis to, and absorb them into your thinking.

I've also included detailed accounts of mistakes made by me and other successful real estate investors as we transformed ourselves from newbies to seasoned owners of multimillion-dollar portfolios. It's not easy for me to talk about my own shortcomings in such a public fashion, but I knew I wanted to help others avoid falling into the same traps that have snared me. The best way to do that was to surrender my pride and be honest about the things I've done wrong. So learn from the mistakes of others, and you'll shorten the time it takes to change your life.

Those of us who've walked before you are happy to share the lessons we've learned along the way. It's only by helping others that we become truly successful and significant. When you experience failure or setbacks, remember that these are only steps everyone must take to grow and move forward. Failure is one of the most powerful ways you can learn. Hopefully, you'll spare yourself some pain by learning from the mistakes of others.

I'm excited to share what I've learned. I know how this information has transformed my life and the lives of others who've applied it. Many people are unhappy with their lives and want to change. A few of them take the time to read and learn ways they can improve their options. But even fewer have the discipline to apply what they've read with an intense, long-term approach of improving their circumstances.

Don't let this opportunity pass you by. Today is the time to change your circumstances and take back your life. Work past your fear, and read this book so you can change your mindset and your life.

PART ONE

Beginnings

All successful people men and women are big dreamers.
They imagine what their future could be, ideal in every respect,
and then they work every day toward their distant vision,
that goal or purpose.

Brian Tracy

Looking at my early life, there's no reason you'd expect me to achieve any level of success. And you'd never imagine I could build wealth in real estate.

I wasn't born into a rich, powerful family. In fact, it often seemed that my family situation closed as many doors as it opened. That's one of the reasons I get so excited when I start teaching people how to use real estate to create freedom. If *I* can overcome all the challenges I faced and build positive cash flow…I know anyone else can too.

I was born in Dover, New Jersey, the second son in what seemed an average family. My father was a plumber, and my mom worked a lot of odd jobs, such as being a server in a restaurant and the person who put up displays for greeting card companies. We never had a lot of money, and we weren't getting invitations to the country club to discuss high-level business deals.

When I was two and my older brother was eight, our father left our family. I don't know his reasons or who was to blame. I don't remember him living with us. I do remember my mother working whatever odd jobs she could find to keep food on the table, with no support from anyone else. Some of the jobs she took meant she had to travel or work on weekends, and I didn't get to see her as much as I would have liked. But that's the life of a single mother. She even tried real estate at one time, but never took it to a high level.

Life was tough for us. We couldn't afford nice places to live. One of our apartments was a cockroach-infested place in a bad part of town. We had to move after one of the tenants shot a gun. About a week before that, someone had stolen the battery out of our car. It's a good thing I wasn't born with a silver spoon in my mouth, because it probably would have been snatched from me and pawned.

I did the best I could in school, but I had a learning disability, which left me six years behind in many of my classes. I eventually taught myself to read with the Hardy Boys books. I enjoyed those stories, and reading them was the only way I could make sense of words on paper. Socially, I wasn't doing much better. It wasn't easy for me to make or keep friends. I was always a loner, which is tough for kids.

My brother didn't handle it much better than I did. He had a lot of trouble dealing with our dad leaving us, and he became too wild and out of control for my mother to handle. By the time I was nine, he was placed in a foster home. I don't know how my mother dealt with his leaving, but somehow she managed to carry on.

She and I moved into a one-bedroom apartment. I didn't know it at the time, but as I look back she was always sacrificing for me. She slept in the living room on the couch and allowed me to have the bedroom. And that's the way it was for most of my childhood.

I started to dream of living in a house. It was never anything fancy, but I knew any house would have to be better than an apartment where my mom was forced to sleep in the living room.

When I was fourteen, my mom made a major life change. She decided to move us from New Jersey to sunny Southern California. She felt it was bound to change our luck, and we would have a better life on the West Coast. We had vacationed in San Diego a few times and enjoyed it, so we thought it would be a great place to live.

We packed up our belongings and headed west, just like Daniel and his mother in the movie *The Karate Kid*. We were both hopeful things would improve once we reached the end of our journey. We knew things couldn't get any worse.

Things did get better for a while, but eventually we found ourselves in the same position we were in before, although we did have better scenery.

It didn't take long for my mom to realize she wasn't equipped for the competitive work environment in San Diego. It was as tough to be a single mother in San Diego as it was in New Jersey. Before long, we were in dire straits, and welfare became our only viable option to stay afloat.

We couldn't afford to buy furniture and were renting the few pieces we had. But even that didn't last long. I'll never forget the day the company came and repossessed virtually every stick of furniture in the house. They carried it outside and placed it on a truck. While they were carrying the couch, one of the men let his end slip and it plopped into a mud puddle. As they walked back into our apartment to retrieve the last of our furnishings, one of the men shook his head and muttered,

"Why are we taking this? These people have already paid for these."

So Mom and I were left in a one-bedroom apartment with almost nothing to sit on, in a place where we didn't know anyone or have any support.

Not long afterward, we were eating dinner on a square folding table. It was one of the few things we still owned. We didn't know what we were going to do or where we could turn for help.

Mom did whatever she could to make sure I was fed and clothed, and she wasn't going to let me go hungry, even if it meant she had to swallow her pride. She turned to the only person who came to mind. She did the unthinkable and called my father. I can't fathom how desperate she must have felt, but I do know it must have been painfully humbling for her to reach out to him.

He was living near San Francisco in the East Bay area and reluctantly agreed to let us stay with him in his three-bedroom apartment. We sold almost everything we still owned to travel north to the East Bay.

I wasn't happy about the move. I'd never really known my father, and once we moved in, he started issuing rules. I've since forgiven him for leaving my mother, but when I was younger I was too headstrong and proud to understand that his reason for leaving had nothing to do with us and everything to do with him. The situation was made worse by the fact that he always had plenty of money for another of his ex-wives but could never support my mom.

We had nowhere else to go, however; we had to make it work.

We lived there until my dad decided to move back to New Jersey nine months later. My mom and I were abandoned again, and we had no idea how we would survive. Mom found a better job and a smaller place to live.

When I turned eighteen, I left California and went to a small college in Oklahoma where I studied business and lived in a dorm. But I had no idea what I was going to do as a career. The only dream I had was one I carried from my childhood: I wanted to live in a house instead of an apartment.

Two of my college friends and I rented a three-bedroom house. My dream had finally come true. One of the guys talked about actually buying the house, but I wasn't ready to understand what he was talking about. He was thinking about his financial future and was speaking a language I hadn't learned yet.

Over the course of the next few years, I made some bad decisions. I was in the music business and focused on that instead of on building wealth. I met the wrong woman and eloped with her.

By the time our marriage was nearly over, I was fifty pounds overweight and sleeping on my couch. Some friends from Tulsa gave me a copy of *Rich Dad, Poor Dad*. I read it from cover to cover, and it changed my life forever. I literally sold everything I owned and started doing real estate the next day.

Not long after reading that book, I was living in a rental home. The owner of the house next door posted a sign in the yard that read "Auction Today." The timing couldn't have been better. I was fired up about my real estate career and wrote down the web address of the auction company. I went online, read about the houses they were selling, and decided to drive down to see one of them. The auction was happening later that day, and the house wasn't available for viewing. But I did as thorough an inspection as I could. I walked around the exterior of the house, peeked in the windows, and that was it. I couldn't see anything, but decided to go to the auction anyway.

I drove to the auction, excited that I was beginning my new career, but completely ignorant of how naive I was. I didn't know what I didn't know. When I arrived at the auction, the room was filled with chairs and people. The main auctioneer stood at the front next to a video projector. Two other auctioneers patrolled the left and right aisles of the room. Though I didn't know what to expect, I knew this was where I was supposed to be.

The auctioneer banged his gavel on his desk, and everyone quit talking. Moments later, the first house was up for sale. I was caught up in all the action as people bid for that house. Looking back, I wasn't paying enough attention to the details of the auction. I got excited and didn't learn as much as I could have.

The house I was interested in, 620 NW 31st Street, was the second house for sale. I was ready when the auctioneer announced it was up for bidding. *This is the way you build wealth,* I told myself, as I tried to stay calm. *You buy assets.*

The bidding started at $10,000, quickly went to $11,000, and reached $13,000 when I raised my hand. When it was almost halfway up, I thought, *What am I doing? I don't know anything about this house or real estate.* But I cleared my head. *How can I go wrong? This house costs less than a lot of cars, and I want to be a real estate investor.*

Moments later, the gavel came down, and I won the auction with a bid of $14,500. I was ecstatic. I'd set a goal and achieved it by purchasing my first investment property. I knew I was on my way to financial independence.

Once the excitement subsided, reality slapped me between the eyes. I realized I was going to have to pay for the house. How would I find the money for it? The auction required me to put down 5 percent of the purchase price when the auction was over. So I wrote a check for $725, though I had no money in the bank. I told myself, *I have twenty-four hours to come up with $725 dollars—I can do that.* I smiled, walked out the door, and headed for my house.

The next day I pawned everything I could to get my hands on $725. I deposited the money in my account and was thrilled to know the check would clear.

But I wasn't out of the woods yet. I had thirty days to come up with $13,775. *That shouldn't be a problem. I could go buy a car that costs more than that.*

The banks were quick to let me know this wasn't going to be easy. I couldn't get a loan anywhere. The main problem was that I was self-employed, which was a real taboo in 1999. On top of that, I was a mobile disc jockey. I played at parties and weddings and had built a pretty good business. But most bankers had no idea what a DJ was, or if it was even a profession.

I spent a week calling every bank willing to listen to me, and none of them would give me loan because I had no proof of income. I worked for myself and couldn't bring in a stack of pay stubs, though I was making money.

I was desperate and saw my dream slipping away from me. With no other options, I turned to the one person who could help me. I called my mom in California and explained I just bought a house at an auction and needed her help to get a loan. She said she would check into a few things and get back with me.

In a few days she called back with great news. She procured a loan from Bank of America. They couldn't believe she was buying a home that cost only $14,500. I would have the money in time to pay for the house.

When I got off the phone with my mom, I felt a huge sense of relief and accomplishment. I was on my way.

That was the start of my real estate investing. I had a limited education, no money, and virtually no one who could help me, but I was still able to buy a home, which I sold for a profit.

I now own forty-seven units. And I accumulated that by investing in real estate on a part-time basis. I've owned other businesses, and I've only recently made the change to doing real estate full-time.

If I can overcome the challenges I've faced in my life—if I can start with nothing and build a multimillion-dollar portfolio on a part-time basis—*you can too.* It may not be easy; it certainly wasn't easy for me. But it was worth it.

Momentum

In 1999, I was twenty-six, had done one real estate deal, was pumped to invest, and wanted to be a landlord full-time. I looked everywhere to get my hands on the next deal. It made sense to me that most millionaires acquired their wealth in real estate. I couldn't stop thinking about being wealthy and creating a retirement for my future family and myself. I became obsessed with building my portfolio.

I read every book I could find about real estate investing. Some were written by experienced, successful investors and were very good. But others were obviously written by people who had no experience, and that bothered me. When I decided to write this book, I didn't want there to be any doubt about my credentials. I'm including this detailed account of my story so you'll know I'm the real deal. I'm not some wannabe who has never put a deal together. I've fought the same battles you have. I've looked bankers in the eye as I tried to get financing, tenants have lied to me about paying rent on time, and I've felt the victory of holding a check from the equity I earned at closing. The proof is in the pudding, and here's my story, warts and all, to prove what I've done.

One day not long after I closed on my first deal, I was looking in the paper and found a house listed as an owner carry. The seller wanted $35,000 for the house and required $5,000 down. I called the number and met a gentleman named Bill Billings who was selling the house for one of his clients. The property needed a lot of work.

Bill took a liking to me, told me he was retiring, and suggested I take a look at one of the rental properties he owned. I was delighted and a little nervous because I didn't know what to expect and wondered why he offered his own rental home so quickly.

I followed him over to his rental property at 1424 Maple Drive in Midwest City and was wowed. It looked like a great opportunity. One of the property's selling points was that the backyard abutted the high school. I was super excited and wanted to add that house to my portfolio. That deal was burning hotter than a twenty-dollar bill in my pocket.

Bill was the original owner, and the tenant had lived in the property for over ten years and was on Section 8. I asked him why he was selling the property, and Bill said he just wanted the consistent payment and was tired of dealing with tenants. He told me he would sell the property for $35,000 with $5,000 down, and would finance the balance for eight years at 8 percent interest.

This was soon after I'd bought my first house at the auction, and I didn't have much money. I'd already pawned almost everything I owned. I figured I could come up with $2,000 and asked Bill if he would take that as the down payment.

He shook his head. "No. Do you have anything else?"

"I have a six-foot enclosed trailer." Somehow that trailer hadn't made its way to the pawnshop along with all my other stuff.

Bill took the trailer, credited me $600, and gave me a second note for the balance of the down payment. After the deal was done, I paid $300 for the first mortgage and an additional $100 a month for the second.

After I did that second deal, it hit me: *I'd officially started my career as a real estate investor.* It took a while for that to sink in, and I thought about all I'd overcome. I thought about my broken family and the poverty I had to endure when I was growing up.

That deal gave me the confidence that I was going to become wealthy and make an impact in this world. My rough childhood and lack of education weren't going to stop me from doing anything. I pressed on because I wanted to change my legacy.

From that point on, I had only one thought: *Where can I find the next deal?*

I went back for another auction at the auction house where I bought my first property, and I walked out having bought my third property for $23,000. It was a small, two-bedroom, one-bath frame house on corner lot with a large garage/shop in the back, located at 2344 Westlawn Place.

Despite my experience, I had the same problem with this property that I'd had with the first two: I didn't know how I was going to pay for it. I knew, however, that buying income-producing assets was the right thing to do. I tried getting a loan at Countrywide Mortgage and used my bank account as proof of income because I was still self-employed. That's how little I knew about how banks work and the importance of accurate financial documents. The bank denied my application, but I came up with plan to get the loan in my mom's name. I called my mother and asked if she would take out a loan with Countrywide Mortgage.

She was a little reluctant, and couldn't understand how the home prices were less than a tenth of what they were for a decent home in California. I told her I won another auction and was committed to the purchase. If she didn't help me, I would lose the earnest money I'd paid at the auction.

"Let me call the bank and see what they say," she told me. When she called me back, she said the bank had approved her for the loan.

Let me pause here and tell you about my mother's situation at this time. She lived in Concord, California, in a single-wide trailer she purchased for $16,000. She commuted every day to Oakland for her job as a tax collector for the IRS in the small businesses division. My mother dealt with all kinds of squirrelly business owners who didn't pay their taxes, and when I called her about purchasing a rental property for such a low amount, she became suspicious. But I kept raving about creating wealth and having a future in real estate, and she knew I was serious about it.

At that point in my life I was advocating for people to take control of their finances, and I can't give you an accurate account of how many copies of *Rich Dad, Poor Dad* I purchased and forced on friends. I wanted people to know they could change their lives for the better and create a prosperous future. I was pretty zealous about it, and my enthusiasm must have given my mom the courage to take out that loan.

Once the loan was approved and I owned my third property, I felt I was on fire and could change the world. I wanted to push even harder, knowing I was on the right track. However, I had to come to grips with the fact that I needed down-payment money and a bank to keep the momentum rolling. I was working as a mobile disc jockey on the weekends and didn't do much during the day, so on paper I was a self-employed person with no steady income. I wasn't the ideal customer most banks look for, so I had to find owner-finance opportunities.

I searched the papers and called all over the place for owner carries. Anytime I saw a For Sale by Owner (FSBO) sign in front of a house, I would jot down the number and call as soon as I could. I was naive, and it didn't bother me that people thought I was a little strange for asking them to carry the note. The naysayers will tell you it can't be done that way, but I didn't know any better, so I just did it. I made calls and asked people if they would like to sell me their home for $2,000 down. I knew all I had to do was twenty DJ gigs (which paid me

$100 each), and after the twentieth gig I would buy a house. It seemed simple to me.

During my calling frenzy, when I was looking for anyone to sell me a piece of real estate, I met a savvy landlord named Scott Smith. He took a liking to me and became my first mentor in the business. As I look back, the word *mentor* is a not the right term for him, because I was buying rental properties from Mr. Smith at 10 percent interest, which was a lot higher than I should have been paying. I didn't know what I was doing, and Mr. Smith loved that I kept coming back with $2,000 down to buy a few small pieces of his huge empire. I was really inspired by Mr. Smith because he'd been my age when he started in the 1980s building a portfolio worth more than $8 million in less than twenty years. I was so impressed with what he'd done, I didn't do any due diligence on the deals we did together.

I bought several properties from Mr. Smith in one year. I was inspired by the fact that he owned an entire block. I was super motivated to be like him, so my plan was to buy those houses from him one at a time until I owned the entire block. Those properties were, in an area called Paseo, which was near the first house I bought. It's an older neighborhood and has a reputation for being trendy and hip, with several art studios and some great restaurants. I bought 537 NW 30th with $2,000 down from Mr. Smith, and I told him I also wanted the abandoned house next door.

After I got the keys for the house, I started doing the cosmetic work to get the property ready to rent. One day I heard a commotion next door (it sounded like beer bottles breaking), and I looked outside to see what was happening. Several undesirable men were working on the house next door, which I saw as my future investment.

I was shocked and let down at the same time. I thought, *Mr. Smith sold the property to a bunch of punks.* I was pissed and angry because he didn't honor his word. So I drove down to Mr. Smith's office and demanded my money back. He just looked at me and said, "I can give you another house."

I paused (remember, I was naive at the time) and asked, "What house, and where?" The house was 309 E. Harmon in Midwest City, with a tenant already in the property who had been on Section 8 for over five years. *At least I don't have to get the house ready to rent,* I thought. I did a quick inspection, and everything seemed fine.

A week later we filled out the paperwork. I learned a tremendous amount from Mr. Smith—mostly that I was doing all the work for him, because he was cash-flowing a lot and I was cash-flowing a little. I also learned that 50 percent of "contracts for deeds" (or owner carries) fail, and he had no risk. I learned the power of mortgage interest, and I learned that I was on the wrong side of the deals I was doing. I wanted to be on the other end.

I earned my stripes and lost $10,000 on a different house I bought from Mr. Smith, but you can't get mad when you don't know what you're doing and the other party is in business to make money. The house I lost $10,000 on was 1720 NW 19th, in a well-established and desirable neighborhood called Gatewood, and I lost the money because I didn't do my due diligence. It was a *real* money pit. There was concrete in the sewer line, no gas line to be found in the house, and a slew of other major issues. I learned a lot from that mistake—in fact, I feel like I earned a college degree from the amount of money I spent and the stress I endured.

Mr. Smith has become a great friend and wonderful adviser over the years and has encouraged me to think bigger and acquire some wonderful deals, like a fourteen-unit apartment building. I no longer own any of the properties I bought from Mr. Smith in 1999 and 2000. When I went through my divorce a decade ago, I just gave all the houses back. There was no way I could keep them. I still remember what he told me: "When the divorce is over and the dust settles, I can deed the houses back over to you." I wasn't thinking clearly at that time (I was an emotional wreck), but I wanted to walk away and start fresh. I knew more about real estate than I did when I started, and I thought I could get back in the business when I was ready. Plus, those houses weren't great deals, but they helped get me into real estate, and I'm glad I went through the intense training. I wouldn't be where I am today without that experience.

The Fuzz

By February 2001, my mother had moved to Oklahoma. Somewhere along the way, my passion for real estate had rubbed off on her. When she saw how much money could be made, she was as excited as I was to find new deals. She and I would troll the streets looking for FSBOs and anything we considered a deal. We stumbled upon a warehouse in a rundown part of Oklahoma City called Plaza District. It's close to downtown, an area that has been booming the last few years, but when we looked at this property I didn't see any of this promise.

A sign on the side of 1705 NW 16th said the property was for sale for $600 down and $600 a month for ten years. I'd done a few deals and thought I knew what I was doing, so I called the number.

The owner was Gary Armstrong, a super laid-back CPA. I offered him $1,000 down and $450 a month. He accepted the deal, and I bought my first commercial property.

The main reason I wanted to own a commercial property was to open a club/rock venue to host bands. To no one's surprise, I was in way over my head. If I tried telling you all the reasons this venture failed, I'd have to double the size of this book. But I don't want to disappoint you, so I'll share a few things I learned. The first problem was that the building didn't have door access. The only way in was through a bay door in a ground-level garage. That wasn't a problem unless you don't pay your electricity bill and your garage door opener doesn't work. I learned that the hard way.

Another fascinating tip is that when you host a concert, be sure you have fire extinguishers, smoke detectors, and restrooms. I didn't think of these things, but I soon learned they were very important to other people. In the middle of a concert I was hosting, the police shut the place down and demanded to know who the owner was. I was so proud that I'd bought the place and had put this event together, and I immediately stepped forward and enthusiastically announced to the police, "Here I am!"

An officer looked me in the eye and ordered, "Turn around and put your hands behind your back. You're going to jail for failing to have proper safety measures. You can't operate a concert venue like this." So I spent the night in jail.

I was also paying too much interest on the loan. I still hadn't grasped how important the interest rate was, and I was paying 10 percent. I'd been paying on this building for three years, but I had no equity because the interest rate was so high.

After three years, I went back to Mr. Armstrong, who asked if I wanted to cash out. I responded, "Would you give me a concession on what I owe you?" Mr. Armstrong discounted the balance by $5,000. After all the headache, drama, confusion, and incarceration, I may have broken even.

While I was paying on this nonproducing investment (some call them "alligators"), I met another investor by the name of Eric Williams. He owned sixty properties in a really rough area, where many landlords carried guns to give themselves confidence while knocking on doors to collect rent.

Mr. Williams was a dominant player in the subprime lending frenzy and made a lot of money during that time. He would leave town for the summer, and one year he asked if I would manage his properties for him while he was gone. I thought it would be a great opportunity to learn. But this unpaid part-time job became a full-time, overpowering, losing proposition. At first I was green and thought, *This isn't a big deal. All I need to do is collect the rent, send Mr. Williams his mail, and deposit the checks in the bank.* Little did I know I would have to be a traffic control wizard to maintain his demanding tenants, who knew about their MIA landlord.

It took three weeks for the tenants to acknowledge my existence, and when they did, they would play the game, "I already spoke with Mr. Williams." If they were late with their rent and I asked them about it, they would say, "I already spoke with Mr. Williams."

After about two months of living hell, I called Mr. Williams and said, "I can't do this for free any longer." He offered to pay me, and I respectfully declined. I was ready to get out of there.

The following winter, Mr. Williams needed cash because his over-leveraged empire was heating up. Many of his deals were 110 percent LTV, no-doc loans, and had adjustable rate mortgages (ARM). Interest rates were increasing, and his cash flow was declining so quickly he couldn't service the loans. Mr. Williams suggested I purchase a solid, two-bedroom, brick property at 2129 Cashion for $30,000.

"I don't have financing," I told him, "but would you do an owner carry?" He agreed, and I gave him $5,000 down and paid $300 a month.

Several months later, Mr. Williams was trying to dump all his properties in a hurry because the loose-lending bubble burst. I considered buying his properties, but he was too leveraged to make any decent proposal that would benefit both parties, and I didn't have any financing to close the deal.

Foundation

In the spring of 2005, I purchased 4006 Dogwood Drive in Midwest City. It's a three-bedroom, one-bath home, and I bought it for $30,000 from 1-800-2-Sell Homes (RAK Properties). I thought I made a good deal, but I was still a rookie. Soon after I signed the papers, I realized that RAK Properties had purchased the property from someone who was behind on his property taxes, and they paid much less than I had. It was a sweet deal for them, but it sucked for me.

About thirty days later (when I was still stinging from realizing I'd overpaid), I got a call from an investor named Dan Ward. He saw my number on the "For Rent" sign in the yard and asked if I wanted to own another rental property in the neighborhood.

I was little taken aback, and thoughts flooded my mind: *Who is this guy? Why's he calling me? Is this for real?* I gathered my thoughts. "Yes," I said. "What do you have?"

"I have a three-bed, one-bath on 932 Locust Lane, just five houses down and across the street from your property, for $24,000."

I didn't have to think about my answer. I was hungry to build my empire. "Okay. When can I see it?" I drove over, and after speaking to Mr. Ward, I was amazed and a little frustrated. I was really learning the real estate game the hard way. Mr. Ward got the house under contract for $20,000 and was flipping it to me with a $4,000 profit. I'd bought a house across the street for $6,000 more and hadn't seen a penny.

The good news was that I had the new house rented in two weeks, and it has been rented consistently for seven years now. Not only did I buy a great investment, but I also found a lifelong friend in Dan Ward. Dan was and still is an asset in my real estate business because he introduced me to the investment bank that I deal with on regular basis. That relationship has given me the ability to acquire more investment properties and build my portfolio.

By early 2006, I had a solid reputation as a real estate investor, and I tried my hand at flipping a property, 3301 N. Maloney. I thought, *How can I go wrong? Everyone else is doing it. Why not me?* Wrong. If you ever think you can do something just because "everyone else is," sit down, take a breath, and call your mentor. No good will come of you acting on that thought.

Dan Ward's friend knew a family who was downsizing and needed money to move into a retirement community. Dan called to tip me off about the property. The owners wanted $50,000, but the house appraised for nearly $95,000.

The numbers sounded great, so I got the financing and the fix-up money from a bank Dan introduced me to. It was really that easy. The bank I use loans at 70 percent of the appraised value so I took out a mortgage for $60,000, walked out of closing with $10,000 working capital, and started working on the property the very next day.

Now this sounds like every investor's dream. I bought a property with no money down and got a big, fat check at closing, but I was out of my element. It was my first bank loan and my first retail rehab. The home needed higher quality craftsmanship, more attractive fixtures, and more repainting than any of my rental properties. When you're selling a home, you have to make sure every detail is perfect. You want the buyers to feel at home and don't want them to have any doubts. I had no trade skills or experience in working with contractors at that point. To put it bluntly, I had no idea what I was doing.

I was able to keep everything under control for a while. The poop hit the ceiling fan when I was in the middle of class (I was trying to go back to school) and I received a text message from the gal I hired to help me. The message said there was a major crack in the foundation of the house. And I mean *major*. It was ten feet tall and six inches wide. I almost crapped my pants and went into panic mode because I hadn't seen this issue in my inspection, and I'd never worked on foundation problems before. Just writing this story raises my body temperature and makes me nervous.

I hired a good foundation repair service that gave a lifetime warranty in writing (so I could pass it along to the new owners), and found an awesome bricklayer who removed the brick from the back part of the house and repaired the damage.

I learned many hard lessons through this project, and here's a quick summary: I wasn't focused and trusted someone to take care of the details, which only delayed the project and increased my holding costs and created errors and omissions. The worst mistake (and one that still burns) was the listing. The Realtor asked what I needed to net on the sale of the house. It was listed for $110,000, I had $75,000 invested, and had to factor in the Realtor's commission. I needed $82,000 to break even, and that's what I told him. The Realtor had a contract for $82,000 before I knew what happened.

I was super bummed and frustrated that nine months of work didn't yield me a cent while everyone else made money. The bank made interest and fees, the contractors got paid, and the lovely Realtor made his commission, while I financed the operation. All I got out of the deal was a bad taste in my mouth about flipping properties.

Being an investor isn't about funding other people's lives. It's about turning a profit on your investment, whether it's your time, your cash, or your relationships. Watch out for other people's hidden agendas.

Lovely Realtor Continues

After my failed attempt at flipping, I jumped back into rental properties. I had such a good relationship with the investment bank, I felt like a kid in a candy store with an unlimited amount of cash. I got busy trying to find deals and was working with an investor Realtor (a Realtor who also invests in income-producing property). At this time I couldn't really find any good Realtors who had the same mindset I had. None of them wanted to acquire property to become wealthy. Most of the Realtors I met were "Avon ladies with big hair" who were motivated only to get a listing and sit on it.

I was lazy, and reached out to the only investor Realtor I knew, explaining that I had the green light from my bank and was ready to buy. It was the same Realtor who sold my first flip. He turned me on to a house that was supposedly "turnkey." He told me it was ready to rent and only needed a roof.

I rushed over to see this "turnkey" deal at 1444 NW 99th Street and was impressed. It had all the cosmetic stuff done. There were nice wood floors, great tile, and excellent appliances, and it was painted with contemporary colors. It looked ready to roll.

I did a little negotiating, bought the property for $48,000, paid $3,500 to get the roof done, and was ready for the first tenant to move in. Then I discovered one small detail. The plumbing wasn't hooked up. It was a complete facade. While I was scrambling to take care of the plumbing, I realized the wiring was out of code. After I took care of those problems on my "turnkey" deal, I crunched the numbers. The deal was too skinny, and I would cash-flow only $25 a month. Then the only AC window unit in the home crapped out, and I had to replace that monster unit, which cost another $500. After factoring in that expense, I wouldn't make any money on the property for twenty months—one year and eight months of hell. The most painful lesson I learned was to not trust what someone says, but to verify, verify, and verify.

I also overpaid for the house, which was close to a desirable area but not in it. I bought at the height of the market, didn't understand investment cycles, was in rush, and got sold instead of buying. That house taught me the term "blow and go," which is what lousy contractors do when they're covering up shoddy rehab work.

I realized that the other investor got me. I almost wanted to call the seller, shake his hand, and congratulate him for being able to sell the property. Now I'm stuck with this house in a down market playing a waiting game. My tenants are paying down the debt, and I can cash out in fifteen years. The city even lowered the assessed value of the property, which makes it even more difficult to dump this trial by fire.

The real beauty of this deal was that the previous investor bought the property for $28,000 and sold it to me for $48,000. Six years later I still own the property, and it's a monthly reminder that success is about what you know, and that you're responsible for your lack of education.

There's a bright spot in this story. In nine more years I'll have a cash flow of $600 a month. Maybe I'll throw a party and celebrate, unless the air conditioner goes out again.

California Cash Investor

I was feeling a little wounded from my last purchase, so I called my mentor, Scott Smith, and asked him about the market and if he had any insight. He always makes me feel better because he's positive and has his finger on the pulse of the city and knows what's happening.

He told me he just looked at a "beast" of deal in Mesta Park at 300 NW 21st, and suggested I take a look at it. I called the listing Realtor, drove over, and did a stupidly quick inspection. When I looked at the house I started seeing cash falling from the sky.

I really thought I knew what I was doing. I'd suffered and learned so much on the last deal and was certain this was my opportunity to get in the multifamily game. The listing price had been close to $200,000 several months earlier when it was under contract, but that contract was busted, and it was back on the market. The price was lowered several times as it had been in probate, and the family wanted to get rid of it—or at least that was my understanding. In reality there was an inspection done on the property, and after it was completed the buyers walked away from the deal.

The house was listed at $168,000 and the city assessed its value at $300,000. After viewing the property and getting the inspection report from the Realtor, I called Scott to chat about the deal and asked him what I should do.

"Offer them $110,000," Scott said.

I ran the numbers and told him I should offer $150,000 because I really wanted this property and offering $18,000 less than the asking price sounded like a decent lowball offer to me. I couldn't comprehend a $58,000 drop. I thought it was borderline disrespectful.

"If I get it for $110,000," I told him, "I'll give you $1,000 just for giving me the balls to offer such a low amount." I dropped my pride and thought, *What's the worst thing that can happen? They give me a counteroffer, and we have to negotiate.*

I was baffled when the seller quickly accepted my offer of $110,000 for this beast. After closing, I begin rehabbing the property cosmetically and addressing all the issues I knew about. There were two tenants left from the previous owner, and I thought they would give me some sort of income, but they turned out to be a challenge. Plus, the units were underrented, and one of the tenants was such a downer he made Negative Nancy look like Norman Vincent Peale. That guy complained more than two rival candidates in a political debate. He gave me a headache in the first degree, and I avoided him as much as I could. That was extremely difficult, because I spent a lot of time on the property meeting with contractors, getting supplies, and making work orders.

I learned a lot about dealing with crappy tradesmen when I had to replace a shower pan in the upstairs unit, and it wasn't installed properly. The leak caused costly damage and more repairs in other units. Of course, my lack of experience continued to surface when I didn't notice foundation issues throughout the property and didn't do the right calculations to make the investment profitable.

During the process of rehabbing, I was working a full-time job and had to evict a jerk of a tenant from one of my other properties after he beat the front door down with a hammer when he locked himself out. I thought, *What will happen when I serve this guy a five-day notice?*

Things really started heating up at the Beast when I called the city to set up trash and water service. They wanted a $250 deposit for each unit. *That's just the cost of being a big bad multiunit landlord*, I thought, and I paid it.

Then things went from bad to worse. My friendly new acquired tenant called and told me there was something wrong with the hot water and I needed to fix it. "Man! Now I have to get a new water heater." I drove down to the property to assess the problem, and it was even worse than I thought. The gas line hadn't been split. There was only one meter for the entire property, which meant I had to pay the full bill. I called the gas company, and they told me the average bill was $500 a month. That completely destroyed my cash flow and turned my world upside down.

I slumped down and tried to come up with some options. What

was I going to do? *Holy smoke, what are my choices? Do I have to raise the rents? Find new tenants? Or should I just dump this beast?* I figured it was better to bail out while the ship was sinking than to go down with the *Titanic.* That sounded a lot better than trying to ride out three months of hell while the problems got solved.

I called Scott Smith and told him about my situation. He'd heard of a great Realtor named Rick Colbert who had just sold a duplex in the same neighborhood. Scott suggested I give him a call to see if he could sell the property.

Sixty-five days after closing, I had the Beast back on the market, and twenty-five days later it was under contract with some wonderful California investors who came to Oklahoma with big pockets buying up as many properties as they could get their hands on. They couldn't sign the paperwork fast enough for me. I couldn't wait to get out from under the holding costs and expenses I had to endure.

This is how it played out. It was the same song, second verse. I barely broke even after paying the Realtor's commission and my holding costs. I was grateful the endeavor was over.

I hope you learn and take away a great deal from my experience. I don't want anyone else to endure what I went through trying to become the Savvy Landlord. Regardless of what I did, I couldn't make a silk purse out of sow's ear.

Can't Close an REO?

It took almost a year for me to heal and even think of buying another investment property. I wasn't sure I wanted anything to do with it again. In late June 2007, I got a random call from Lovely Investor

Realtor who was in a bind because one of his clients couldn't close on a HUD REO. He called to see if I was interested, and as I look back I was probably the last guy on his list.

I entertained the opportunity and drove to the property at 4817 Casper Drive. I was amazed that the other investor couldn't close on the deal because the property was under contract for $33,000 but was worth $65,000. As I looked at that house, all the dreams I had about building wealth through real estate started coming back to me.

"I want the property," I told Lovely Investor Realtor.

"Great," he said. "There's only one catch. We have to close within ten days." He said it without batting an eye.

Thank goodness I had a working relationship with my bank, and they were willing and able to move quickly and help me get the deal closed. I couldn't have done it without their help.

Let me give you some thoughts about my bank. The majority of this bank's business is loaning on investments like rental properties, churches, and even funeral homes. In the beginning of my investing career the bank thought I was hot stuff because I paid off two properties (including more than $100,000 on the Beast, which I sold in less than ninety days). The bank didn't know that the investment was intended to be a hold and not a flip, even though it looked like a flip on paper.

The banker who was handling my transactions at that time saw my skill at getting things done quickly, and he had the impression I knew what I was doing. But the bank really didn't care if I made a profit or loss; they only thought I was knowledgeable as an investor and expected to be paid back. To be honest, I thought I knew what I was doing, too. But that wasn't always the case.

I reflect back to the lending craze, and as I write this in 2012 the main question people ask me is, "How are you getting bank funding while we're in a countrywide recession?" They remind me how highly regulated banks are now, with their hands tied when it comes to lending money.

But it's always possible to borrow money. You have to build a relationship with a bank and learn the business of borrowing. It's not as easy as walking in with a paper sack and asking them to fill it up. You just have to learn the right way to do it and be vigilant about it.

Now back to the deals I've made. In order to close the deal within ten days, the bank had me do a drive-by appraisal. We closed, and I acquired almost $30,000 of equity. It cash-flows like a soda pop machine, with more than $200 a month.

Later that same month I was driving down a busy road and a FSBO sign caught my attention at 6608 SE 15th in Midwest City. The sign offered the three-bedroom, two-bath house with a large shop in the back for $52,000.

I called the number and inquired about the property. "How did you come up with $52,000?" I asked.

The lady who answered the phone said, "It's worth it. A Realtor friend told us we could get that."

My first thought was, *Then why didn't your Realtor friend list it?* But I didn't say that. I didn't want to come off as a smart-ass when I was trying to make a deal.

"I'm a real estate investor, and that seems high to me," I told the lady. Then I paused and waited for her to respond.

After a few moments, she finally asked, "Well, what's it worth to you?"

I knew I had my chance. "I've bought and sold a few properties similar to the one you're trying to sell. I didn't pay over $40,000 for any of them." I paused to see if she would start negotiating with me. After a pause, I told her, "Good luck. But if you can't sell it, give me a call back. Have a good day."

About a week later she called me back and started asking a few questions. She was motivated to sell, and after talking to the whole family I got the property under contract for $45,000.

I was a little nervous about that deal because it was only the second time I worked without any outside help. I had to find a suitable contract, do the negotiations, and secure the financing by myself. When investors have a question or feel anxious about a deal, they should reach out to an investor they trust. I followed that advice when I bought this house.

I vividly remember calling a friend and making sure this was a solid deal and that I wasn't missing anything. We double-checked my numbers, my exit strategy, and the condition of the property. I've made it a policy to invite an investor friend to lunch and have him walk the property with me before I do a deal. It helps to have a different set of eyes view a house.

My friend gave me the confidence to sign off on the deal, and it closed within three weeks of the previous deal. I was on my way to building my future with another $200 a month in cash flow.

I learned two lessons from acquiring this property and leasing it out. The first was that being in a better school district will attract more, highly qualified tenants and will allow you to charge higher rents. I also learned I could make more money with better tenants in more upscale properties, because they created less damage, and there was less turnover and fewer headaches. Up to that point, I usually went for lower priced properties that rented for about $500 a month and usually had mortgage payments of $250 to $350. I would cash-flow $150 to $250 a month, but I had to invest a lot of time and expense to make sure they were occupied.

Since I started buying investment properties worth at least $50,000, my cash flow has stayed about the same, but I have better tenants in the homes. They stay much longer and don't create as many problems. I'm coming out ahead in the long run. I currently have one tenant who has lived in the same property for over three and a half years.

Freebies

There's a gold mine in looking at and calling on FSBOs. If you aren't doing this, your business will never grow as quickly as it could. I was driving to one of my properties and came across 804 N. Midwest Boulevard. It had been about four months since I'd done a deal. Timing can play a big part in getting a great deal, and this property was a perfect example. It was November 2007 and getting close to the holiday season. Real estate usually slows down during this time of year.

When I called the number, the gentlemen who answered sounded surprised. I could sense he was motivated. I found out he and his family didn't want to be landlords and had inherited this property as part of an estate.

I walked the property with the owners and pointed out issues that seemed major to them, but were cosmetically simple to me. I offered $20,000 and started negotiating, making sure I told them I could close quickly. We agreed at $23,000, and there was a bonus. The deal included a 1970s pop-up camper trailer that was parked under the carport. I signed the contract on the hood of my truck in the middle of the driveway.

I'll never forget that deal because it was so cold outside. I had little experience with contracts, and I didn't want them to change their mind, so I had to act like I knew what I was doing. I learned how to fake it till you make it. I also found a hidden opportunity by taking care of the pop-up trailer the previous owner left behind. The following Saturday I sold the pop-up on Craigslist for $500. I actually made money before the deal was closed at the title company.

Six months later, in early summer 2008, I was pretty jazzed about real estate and had my properties under control. I wanted to expand my music production company (which was my daytime job) and needed more space. Our office at the time wasn't meeting our needs. I had a burning desire to find a commercial property to house our offices and to warehouse the tools and equipment needed in doing rehabs.

Finding a commercial property with a maximum budget of $150,000 was extremely difficult, and at times seemed impossible. I finally met a driven commercial real estate agent named Michael Raff who turned me on to a slightly rough 3,000-square-foot property nestled in the heart of Oklahoma City, near the major crossways of I-44 and I-235. It was near downtown and had great access. Within minutes you can be anywhere in town.

Michael took me to the property, and during the first viewing I felt like I was on the TV show *Hoarders*. The tenant operated an upholstery business and had stacked everything from floor to ceiling. There was furniture, fabric, supplies, and virtually anything else you can think of.

This building was a fire hazard waiting to be ignited. But I had a vision for the property and could see its unlimited potential because of the location, the way the building could be used, and the land it was on.

I had my reservations because the asking price was retail, and negotiating alone wasn't working to make the deal work. If I bought the property, I would have to evict the tenant, and it would cost close to $2,000 to remove all the junk. Then I would need to invest $10,000 to build walls and update the interior.

I called my mentor, Scott, and ran the deal past him. As usual, he provided great insight. He told me I'd have to pay for what I wanted or needed, and to make sure I had an exit strategy. I ran the numbers, viewed the property several times, and even paid for an inspection, which I normally don't do. I felt comfortable and ran with my gut on this opportunity, so I signed the contract and called my investment bank.

They were quick to pump the brakes. Because it was a commercial deal, they needed better financials from me. I thought, *Why is my bank giving me static? I'm putting $50,000 down, which is close to 40 percent on the purchase price of $134,000 This is a no brainer!*

You may ask where I came up with $50,000. I refinanced two of my first three properties, which taught me another valuable lesson. The fees I had to pay to get to my equity were outrageous.

The loan officer expressed that he needed a current financial statement, and that he had some concerns about my tax returns. I had just jumped through several hoops to get the $50,000 refinance from Bank of America, and my local bank was scaring me with the threat that I might not be able to buy the commercial property because of my unorganized bookkeeping.

I pleaded with my banker. "Why is there so much drama when I'm making a large down payment, and I've done no-money deals before?"

He told me he was being scrutinized because my financials were so sloppy. They were going to discuss my loan in the next board meeting, and I knew I had to fix the problem or I could kiss the building good-bye.

So I got my butt in gear and put together a financial statement with a few clicks of the dummied-down Quicken software (that was the only financial software I owned). That was the only way I could provide a profit-and-loss statement of my businesses at the time.

A few days later my banker called back to say he fought for me in the meeting, and they had approved the loan. But it was going to be the last one if I didn't provide them with more professional documents. I needed to hire an accountant to get my stuff together and to package myself in a more professional manner before I applied for another loan.

I closed on the deal but had to get rid of the tenant before I could move in. I drove down to the building and presented him a thirty-day notice. I was a little apprehensive because I didn't know what was going to happen. I was afraid I was going to be stuck.

The tenant was a little put out but respectful, and asked for some time. In the same breath I said, "Yes" and "I need your rent." It was stressful for me because I knew I'd just told him he had to move his business, and I didn't like being in that position.

About forty-five days later the tenant moved out, and I was anxious to see what he'd left behind. I really dreaded going to the building and started calculating the number of man-hours it was going to take to get all that junk out of my property. To my surprise, the whole building was cleared out and broom cleaned. I learned to not take anything for granted, to have all your ducks in a row, and to keep jumping the hurdles even when you haven't stretched.

After getting the new office built out and running smoothly, I was building relationships with investors who were working in a hot trend, wholesaling. Wholesaling seemed like the new money maker for real estate, and everyone was trying to flip assignable contracts and call themselves wholesalers. I got the bug and bought my first deal from a wholesaler in December 2008. I was alerted to a deal at 1404 NW 102nd, a three-bedroom, two-bath house with a two-car garage that I closed on for $43,000.

That deal was my first double-closing. I actually bought the property through a third party who got it under contract for $34,000 when the property was worth $70,000. When I saw those margins (fifty cents on the dollar), I knew those were the kind of deals I wanted to make.

Let me break down how this deal happened. An investor got the property under contract for $34,000, then another investor (a wholesaler) placed it under contract from him and flipped that contract to me. We did a double-closing (the first investor transferred title to the wholesaler who transferred it to me). The beautiful thing was that the wholesaler got paid, and he was just a mediator. He had little risk of not getting paid and made money with just a few minutes of his time.

After I realized there were some crazy deals out there, I knew I wanted to be the one that bought the property for $34,000. I didn't

46

want to be further down the food chain picking up the crumbs other investors left behind. I still had so much to learn about this powerful business of creating wealth, and I was struggling to understand how wealth could be created out of thin air.

I was still trying to grasp the wholesale concept and was trying to learn the ins and outs of how to find deals where I made 50 percent. Out of the blue, the wholesaler I'd just double-closed with called and asked if I was ready to buy another property for $15,000.

"Of course," I told him. I didn't have any idea how I would pay for it. But you often have to give the impression you can close. You learn to say yes even when you can't finance, because if the deal is right, the money will always be there.

He told me he had a four-bedroom, one-bath property at 1005 Holly Lane. "Do you want it, or do I need to call another investor?" I knew he meant business by the way he asked.

"I'll be right over." I wasn't going to let this deal slip away. I was building some real momentum and wasn't going to let it stop.

After viewing the property, I knew it needed about $7,000 worth of cosmetic repairs and a roof. I tried to posture myself and offered a lower price, but the wholesaler made it very clear this was a super deal. There weren't going to be any negotiations.

He quickly educated me on what a real wholesaler did. The goal for a wholesaler is to move every deal very quickly and leave room for the investor to make a profit. If there's no profit for the investor, they won't trust you when you call them. Wholesalers don't want investors thinking too much about the deals they bring, they just want to get the deal done and move on to the next one.

You may be asking yourself, "Why doesn't the wholesaler just keep the deals for himself?" I asked the wholesaler that, and he said he would if could, but he didn't have the funds to do the $7,000 rehab.

After the deal was closed, a friend I was mentoring in investment told me he thought this wholesaler ripped me off because he got the deal for $7,000 and sold it to me for $15,000. "That's not right," my friend said, "and that guy's a jerk."

"Hold on a minute," I told him. "We just bought a home worth $55,000 for $15,000 and will cash-flow over $300 a month. I wasn't ripped off at all. It was a good deal all the way around."

The point is, we shouldn't get mad at someone who's doing something better than we are. We should learn from them so we can improve. I'm close friends with that wholesaler and still buy deals from him. I truly am amazed at his skill and how he finds deals and creates income with minimal capital, or at times no capital at all.

Some people say you can't make money without spending money. Yes you can, and I know people who do it all day long. Education is the key. The more you know, the more you make. Make yourself savvy and increase your profits by doing what you set out to do at all costs, even when you don't know what you're doing. When you're willing to learn, you'll get it done.

The Big House

Two months later I got a call from our lawn care guy, Delton Brown, who told me a duplex was for sale in our neighborhood. This was the first time I got a deal from a bird dog, and it was one of the proudest moments in the ten years I'd been in real estate. The brick property at

2814 N. Coltrane had 3,000 square feet, four bedrooms, two bathrooms, two living rooms, and a two-car garage. It sat on a large lot on a cul-de-sac, and I bought it for $150,000, which was a steal. The spectacular part was that it came with a duplex—each side had two bedrooms, one bathroom, and a one-car garage. It easily had the potential to bring in more than $900 a month in revenue.

For a moment I couldn't believe this opportunity fell into my lap. My initial goal was to rehab the "Big House" and retail it so I could recoup my fix-up money. Then I could keep the duplex for free. That was a lofty goal, but if I was going to dream, I was going to dream big.

My first issue was the duplex. I figured I could get the units up and running to generate cash flow and cover the interest-only loan that I took out from the bank. I signed that kind of loan because I was going to flip this house. One side of the duplex had a long-underrented tenant who had been living there for over ten years. He claimed he was doing maintenance on the property, but that seemed farfetched, based on its condition. We immediately raised his rent to $475 a month, which was more in line with the value of the property.

The other side of the duplex had been empty for a long time and needed to be rehabbed. That didn't seem difficult until I started tearing into it. I quickly realized we had to replace the whole outer wall because untreated termites had destroyed it. I also remodeled the kitchen and bathroom. This rehab set me back about $5,000.

After I finished the duplex and rented it, it was time to tackle the Big House, which hadn't been updated since the home was built in 1960. "Retro décor" was an understatement. A huge bar in the middle of the living room had to be removed, as did the built-in dining room table and mirrored wall. And then there was the hideous green shag carpet.

The Big House was the largest project I'd ever undertaken, even more so than the Beast. Everything needed attention. I spent $4,000 on new carpet, turned an office into a laundry room, and relocated major plumbing in the walls. I was burning through cash with no end in sight, and realized I had to put the property on the market to get paid back. Things were so tight I put most of the repairs on my credit cards.

When I was working out the budget I didn't factor in remodeling the kitchen, which was a dumb decision. I was trying to cut corners and thought I could get away with attractive walls with bull-nose corners to give it a high end look, but I had to skimp on the kitchen appliances and it looked dumpy. Looking back, I can see it was idiotic.

After showing the property to several investors and Realtors for help and advice, the consensus was I had to put another $10,000 into the kitchen. This meant I had $45,000 of my own money in the deal. When it was over, we owned a beautifully remodeled home during the worst real estate market in history.

I did everything I could to get rid of that property. I tried using a neighborhood Realtor, but that yielded only two showings. The house sat empty for over nine months, burning even more of my cash while I tried to keep hope alive. I finally got a great couple to do a lease purchase for $2,500 down and $1,350 a month. They left fifteen months later, and the property is currently being rented for $1,400 a month, which is just shy of covering insurance and taxes. I'm cash-flowing because of the duplex in back, but it remains to be seen if and when I'll receive the $45,000 I have in the deal.

I would prefer to sell the Big House, but in this down market and with the tight lending restrictions, I'll have to hold on to it for a while. But that experience taught me how to do a lease purchase contract, and it introduced me to the pain contractors cause when they don't get their jobs done on time. I had to fire the painter in the middle of the project and finish the job with another guy, which made the job drag on and increased the costs. I also learned to always double-check your numbers and projections. Staying within your budget can be a dream, but you should always be diligent to stay on course.

The Big House hasn't turned out to be the great deal I thought it would be, but I try to stay positive and see the light at the end of the tunnel. In fifteen short years the note will be paid off, and I'll cash-flow at almost $2,000 a month.

The Big House kept my focus for almost a year, and it prevented me from being able to purchase another investment property. If every project took that long, I would never achieve my goals and dreams.

In May 2010, I got a call from my wholesaler friend, and he had a brick, three-bedroom, one-bathroom house with a one-car garage that assessed at $55,000. It's located at 3104 SE 51st, which is further south than most of my properties. I overlooked the neighborhood and focused on the solid structure and amenities of the house and saw the cash-flow potential. I bought it at another double-closing. The wholesaler had it under contract for $29,000 and flipped the deal to me for $31,500. The property didn't need too much to get it ready to rent, which was an attractive part of the deal.

It was difficult to rent the property, which didn't surprise me, because the neighborhood was less then desirable. I was a little worried, but I pushed on, and in six weeks I had a Section 8 tenant under lease. The property is still going strong with $200 a month in cash flow. I learned you must take the distance of every property into consideration and prepare for some vacancy losses when renting in a rough neighborhood. This turned out to be a great deal, and I'm building up equity over time and cash-flowing now.

Ms. Hoarder

A month later I closed on a duplex it took me three years to buy. An investor friend of mine was in a partnership with two other investors, and together they owned five properties. They were friends with different personalities and goals, and they each handled the business of real estate in a different way. I was on the sidelines watching this partnership unravel from day one until it completely dissolved three years later.

Investor number one was just the money man and didn't want anything to do with property management. He contributed the seed money for the down payments and had his Realtor's license. Investor number two was a seasoned investor who owned more than thirty units at the time and was focused on growing his empire and was attending to his personal development. His goal was to borrow a million dollars as soon as he could. He figured the three of them would make enough cash flow after debt service that paying it off wouldn't be a problem. I don't know what happened to him, but I tried calling him on his mobile phone recently and discovered it was disconnected.

My friend, investor number three, wanted to be in real estate because he ran an insurance office and was in regular contact with several investors. He saw the power of building wealth with real estate and wanted to be part of it. I bought life insurance from his office to protect my wife if something ever happened to me so she wouldn't have to worry about the real estate debt.

My friend told me he and his two friends got a smoking deal on a 2,220-square-foot, two-story duplex at 1123 NW 30th for $50,000. Each unit had two bedrooms, two baths, and a double garage. I was shocked. I know that area really well, and I comb the streets there looking for deals because it's so desirable. It's close to downtown and has access to all the major freeways, and it's near schools and shopping areas. The duplex had to be worth at least $100,000.

When my friend closed on the property, I asked what his plan was. They were going to remodel the downstairs unit and raise the rent or replace the tenant upstairs. They didn't know at the time that the upstairs tenant was an all-star hoarder, the worst I've ever seen. She'd been renting the upstairs duplex for almost twenty years, and it seemed like her clutter had become attached to the structure.

She had newspapers stacked from floor to ceiling. They filled in every inch of space. I walked through the unit once and couldn't see where I was going because her stuff blocked any light from the windows. The only place I could step was the narrow trail she hadn't covered with junk. When her stuff was finally removed, you could look at the carpet and see the outline of where she'd placed her "treasures." A few small tracks were worn in the carpet, and those were the only places people could negotiate around the obstructions. The rest of the carpet had been covered for years, never walked on, and looked brand new. Had I been thinking, I would have taken a camera with me and started a reality television show.

Nine months after my friend bought the duplex, I checked on him to see how everything was going. He said, "We're working on it," and that's the only response I got. Six months later I asked again, and he said, "Not too good. I'm doing all the work, and I'm not getting any help from the other two investors." He was thinking about selling because they weren't making any money but still had their monthly expenses.

Six months after that, they had the property for sale, which gave them a lot of buzz, but the asking price of $80,000 had any potential buyers walking away. Every so often I would express interest and even walk the property, but I would offer only $50,000 because it needed a rehab and still had the crazy tenant upstairs. The property sat for eight months until they finally had it under contract with another investor and thought they had it sold. After waiting two more months, the investor was unable to finance the deal, and it folded.

My friend had to put the property back on the market, but now it was looking rough. None of the regular maintenance had been done, and the surrounding trees and shrubs were overgrown. I connected with my friend, said I was interested, and told him I could close quickly, in part because their mortgage was held at the same bank I deal with.

They owed a balance of $45,000. After speaking to the most seasoned investor of the three, we settled on $53,500, and I called my banker to ask if I could assume their loan. To my surprise he said I could. I showed up at the closing with the difference in a cashier's check, and it was a done deal.

I was super happy because I thought you couldn't assume any loans after the S&L craze of the 1980s when banks started putting acceleration clauses in mortgages. I immediately went to work to get the bottom unit ready to rent and served the top tenant a thirty-day notice. She was underrented, had created a fire hazard, and there was no lease in place.

I knew this lady had some issues, and I didn't want to just throw Ms. Hoarder out on the street. My office assistant spent hours researching potential new homes and making appointments for her to see them. She even spent a full day driving Ms. Hoarder to several properties, but nothing seemed to fit her fancy. After fifty days, Ms. Hoarder found a new home, and she's now rebuilding her newspaper collection in someone else's investment.

We finally finished the duplex, and it rented as quickly as I expected. By staying in the loop and having patience I was able to purchase a property that grosses $1,200 a month.

Location, Location, Location

Things were starting to happen quickly. In November 2010, I got a call from a rookie wholesaler who said he had a deal for me. He offered me 2105 NE 27th—a 1,276-square-foot, brick, three-bedroom, one-bath house—for $13,000.

That sounds low for a brick house, I thought, and I looked up the neighborhood. It was in a rough part of town, but I figured for $13,000 I couldn't go wrong. I called the rookie back and was talking to him about the property when he spilled the beans. He told me it had a tax lien, and several thousand dollars were owed on the property.

He was up-front and explained he had it under contract for $9,000 from another investor who specialized in tax sales/liens, and we settled on a fee of $2,000 for him to assign the contract to me. I did my quickie inspection, called the rookie back, and said, "Let's make it happen."

He said he would give me the contract and put it in my name, and at the closing I could write him a check for his fee. For two months I babysat the deal because there were several title issues caused by multiple city liens and back taxes. For some reason, having to work out those details made it a thrill to get the deal done. I got caught up in the game of getting the deal and wasn't thinking about the return on my investment.

I paid $11,000 for the property and $1,000 for closing fees, and I wanted to spend about $15,000 for the remodel, which would bring my total investment to between $27,000 and $30,000. My goal for the rent was $700, and after taxes and insurance I would cash-flow $600. I paid cash so I didn't have to worry about paying a mortgage. It would take about four years to get my investment back, and I would cash-flow 100 percent thereafter.

You have to love real estate.

Just after the closing I began the remodel process, but this time I wanted to be less involved because the margins were so large. I decided to use a contractor to accelerate the remodel and to free me up to look for other deals. I ran into issues right off the bat. The next-door neighbor kept parking in the driveway of the property, which caused issues for the contractor's vehicles. I spoke to the neighbor, and she assured me she wouldn't park there anymore.

But within a few days she had amnesia, and I had to walk back over and put my foot down. I went back to the office and wrote a letter to her landlord expressing the difficulties I was having with the tenant. I realized this one wasn't going to be easy, but I wasn't going to roll over and just take it. I started worrying about it so much my mind started playing tricks on me, and I began to think I bought the wrong house. In spite of all the challenges, I sucked it up and started listening to motivational CDs. And best of all, or so I thought, I let the contractor deal with the not-so-friendly neighbor.

About six weeks into the remodel I dropped in to check on the work that had been done. I was shocked to see how sloppy the contractor's work was. I was eager for him to finish so I'd never have to see him again. It was really that bad.

After I got that dog manicured and ready to rent, I was slapped into reality when people started calling about the property. After I told them where it was, there was always a pause when they started thinking about the location. "Hell no! I don't want to rent in that area!" was a typical response. So I did what any "smart" landlord would do. I lowered the rent from $650 to $600, and when that didn't work I threw myself off a cliff and lowered it to $500.

The house sat empty for almost a year until I called my stud Realtor friend and said, "I need your help. Can you market this rental for me?" My friend is a gifted online marketer, and in a little over a month he'd screened twenty applicants. He called me one day and told me to check my e-mail. "I have a nice couple that wants to lease your property." I don't know if I've ever heard sweeter words in my entire life.

I couldn't believe he was able to find renters so quickly. In fact, I'd even thought of donating the property to charity because I was so deep into the deal and I couldn't see a way out. Somewhere along the way, I called on a FSBO sign, and I spoke with a lady who owned a house around the corner. She let me know the neighborhood property values weren't nearly as solid as I thought.

I asked her what the asking price was for her house, and she said, "It's a four-bed, two-bath with CH&A for $24,000. My name is Trina, and I run this area." My heart sank, because her house looked solid enough from the outside. I thought it would rent for at least $900 a month on Section 8. But her property trumped my $30,000 headache.

My new nice tenants wanted to move in thirty days, but my Realtor said there were some issues I needed to address before I could start cash-flowing. "Whatever it takes to get this ready," I told him. "Just send me the punch list." I didn't care what he wanted. I just needed to have someone rent the place.

There weren't just a few minor things that needed to be addressed. As I got that house ready, I realized I needed to write a book called *How to Hire Contractors*. After paying one fast-talking guy who quickly left the scene of the crime to find his next victim, I found the kitchen countertop was two inches from the wall, the 220 dryer plug wasn't fastened properly and was curled up in a bedroom closet, and the water heater needed to be re-enclosed because the construction was out of code for not having a large enough access door. The list went on and on. I could detail at least twenty other items I missed before paying him.

So I had to use my trusted handyman to finish the job and resolve the minor issues. The tenants were about to finally move in when I realized I hadn't checked the gas line and that the tenants would eventually want to take a hot shower. I had to pull a permit for the line, which required a pressure test and a licensed plumber to call it in. In keeping with all the other things that went wrong on this deal, the line didn't hold pressure. I needed a whole new gas line more than thirty feet from the main. My plumber told me it was going to cost $2,000 to $2,500 to get it done.

I'd never paid a plumber that much in my life, but my back was against the wall. That house had been sitting for a year. I couldn't beg people to live in the property, and had to go deep into my reserves. Sheepishly I told the plumber, "Do it." I could see my cash flow shrinking as I spoke those words.

It took another week of drama to complete the line, and I just knew that those tenants wouldn't take it any longer and would have loved to move out in the middle of the night. It wouldn't have surprised me at all.

After the gas line was working and everything seemed to be fine, I took a deep breath. And then the phone rang. It was the new tenant the day after the line had been repaired, and she told me every time the washing machine drained it poured into the backyard.

"This can't be happening to me; I'm the Savvy Landlord!" were the only words that came to mind. I fixed the drain issue, and I'm still trying to lick my wounds.

The good news (if there is any) is that the tenants are still renting from me. What I learned is that if you drive down a street and the first eight homes look like government-built housing, you should really consider getting a better deal than $11,000. If not, you'll probably find yourself standing in the middle of a backyard while the washing machine spits waste water on you.

Great Things Come to Those Who Wait

This next deal taught me perseverance and the importance of being genuine when you deal with people.

In 2005, several of my friends wanted to be in real estate and asked if I would show them the ropes by taking them with me as I prospected for deals. "Load up and let's head out," I told them.

We came across a duplex on the east side of town, and one of my friends called the number off the FSBO sign. An older gentleman answered and gave him the details of the property, but my friend thought the owner didn't seem motivated to sell. He thought it was a dead end.

My friend was a little frustrated with the man, and huffed, "That guy is a waste of time. Let's move on." After I dropped off my friends, I looked up the duplex on the county records and realized the owner had several other properties.

I called the man back, chatted with him for a few minutes, and realized he wanted to sell all his properties. He'd been a landlord for over twenty years, knew the game of real estate, and wanted to do owner-carries on all his properties. He wanted the monthly income without the headache of managing property and didn't want to get heavily taxed by selling them.

We met on several occasions and talked about a package deal. He wanted more than I was willing to pay, so we never got the deal done. But we got to know each other and became good friends. He was very laid back and approached real estate as a long-term investment like stocks or income-producing assets, and it was a waiting game for him.

One day he called me out of the blue. "I want to sell two houses,

2201 NE 20th and 1933 NW 29th, for $55,000. Would you be interested?" he asked.

"$55,000 each or for both?" I said.

"Both for $55,000 cash, and I would like to close quickly. There's another house that needs to be rehabbed on the backside of the house at NW 29th. It's 3008 N. Virginia."

I hinted about a lower price, but it didn't do any good. My friend was polite and simply asked, "Do you want these houses?"

I called my bank immediately and pulled appraisals. To my fancy, the two houses appraised for $95,000, and I pulled equity out at closing to rehab the back house. It turned out to be a solid three-bedroom, one-and-a-half bath property. The beauty of the deal was that the first two houses had been rented through Section 8 for over ten years. After closing in March 2011, I was cash-flowing immediately. I've invested about $15,000 additional in rehab money, and I gross $1,700 a month. After debt services and expenses, I cash-flow $800 a month. In two years I'll recoup my rehab money and will cash-flow for life on these properties. I wouldn't own them if I hadn't made one simple call and taken the time to be nice to a person.

Once-in-a-lifetime deals happen all the time. You never know where your next deal will come from, so always be ready for the next opportunity. Be genuine and have the right motives up front, and you'll reap what you sow.

Yes, I Bought a House for $4,000

Two months later things started to get hot. It was the summer of 2011, and I did my normal routine of checking auction houses for any upcoming real estate sales. I found one auction that listed fourteen houses to be auctioned off individually. That's how I got into the game, so I thought I'd go back and see what was going on.

Before the auction I drove by all the houses to make sure they were still standing, and to get an idea of what was being offered. In case no one else showed up there would be deals to be had, and I wanted to be prepared.

There was a small crowd that night, no more than forty people, which seemed odd. I wasn't interested in buying; I just wanted to see what was going on. What was really on my mind was the local REIA (Real Estate Investor Association) meeting that I was going to after the auction. Halfway through the auction, one of the houses I'd looked at (1416 NE 12th) was up for bidding.

There wasn't any action at first, so I bid $500 and the ball slowly started rolling. It stayed slow until the price hit $3,000, when I and another guy went back and forth. After the dust settled, I won the auction for $4,000. I couldn't believe you could buy property for such a low amount. *Even if I have to tear the house down,* I thought, *I could sell the lot for $5,000.* I wrote a check for $440 (my 10 percent earnest money and the fee for the auctioneer) and went to the REIA meeting.

At the meeting I ran into another investor who had been at the auction, and we chatted about how low the bidding was and how many great deals there were that night. It was Gary Armstrong, who did the owner-carry on my first commercial property over ten years ago. Real estate investing is such a small world.

I closed on the house about two weeks later and drove down to see what in the world I'd bought for $4,000. The house wasn't as bad you might think. It had a little foundation issue that was easily corrected by jacking it up and putting some cinder blocks underneath it for support. About ten days after the closing, I received a letter from the city informing me that the property was going to be condemned in seven days, and if I had any questions to call the inspector. I guess the city wasn't too concerned about the $4,000 I'd just spent.

I decided to do a complete rehab on the property because the purchase price was unbelievably low. A memory of the closing day flashed in my head. The owner was overly thankful in the lobby because I bought the property, and this relieved a lot of stress for him. I wasn't sure what to make of it when he pulled away in his Mercedes that day, but I understood when I read the letter from the city.

I picked up the phone, called the inspector, and told him I just purchased the property and was planning on remodeling it. I was instructed to prove the sale of the property and document my plans for the rehab. I had to call the closing company and request a deed, which wasn't a normal thing to do a few days after a closing. They put a rush order on the deed and forwarded it to the city, which meant the inspector was off my back for the moment.

I didn't have much money in the property and didn't have the cash for the rehab at the time, so I let the house sit for several months. It wasn't a priority. After I got some other projects finished, I went to work and had to redo everything in the home. It took six months because I kept pulling my guys off the job to work on other properties that didn't need as much work.

I finally finished the rehab and had my eyes set on renting it out as Section 8 because the income would be consistent. I knew the inspection wouldn't be an issue because everything was brand new. In June 2012, I found a tenant who had been on Section 8's waiting list for over three years, and her voucher was about to expire when we met. I received a letter from Section 8 notifying me of the inspection date, and that day couldn't happen fast enough. I was really proud of this remodel, and my goal was to pass the inspection the first time and start receiving income ASAP.

The day finally arrived. I was ready and had one of my trusted handymen with me just in case we needed to fix anything on the spot. If you want to succeed with Section 8 inspections, it's a good idea to have a handyman on the premises. Some inspectors will cut you some slack and allow you to fix any minor issues they find. Of course, they'll always follow up later to make sure it's done.

My house passed, and I was elated. I couldn't focus on the paperwork I had to fill out proving my property was Section 8 qualified. As the inspector was leaving, I stopped her and asked what the tenant's portion of the rent was. You always want the tenant's portion to be low and for the government's amount to be high. That way, your cash flow is much more reliable.

The instructor opened the file and said, "$652." I was stunned to hear it was such a high amount.

I took a breath. "Section 8 is only paying $48?" I felt like I'd been punched in the stomach.

"It's based on her income," the inspector told me. "There's nothing I can do."

I double-checked the amount and looked the new tenant in the eye. It seemed like she had cheated me, but the truth is, I hadn't asked her the right questions.

As soon as the inspector left I went through the lease process with the tenant and explained what would happen if she didn't pay her rent on or before the first of the month. I also walked her through the eviction process.

The new tenant wanted to move in immediately, and I gave her a prorated amount for the remainder of the month. She promised me she would drop it off later that day, which she did within an hour. She moved in that afternoon.

I learned that time really is money, and delays will always eat your lunch. Be vigilant with your time and money. Owning a property debt-free doesn't give you permission to put a project on the back burner. When renting to a Section 8 tenant, verify the amount Section 8 will pay. Don't base it on the voucher amount. Many variables can come into play, such as the number of children living with the tenant, her income, and her job status.

Fourteen-Eyed Monster

In November of 2011, I was having lunch with my banker. It had been eight months since I'd done a deal with him, and we were catching up. I mentioned I was on my way to look at an apartment complex, but I wasn't really interested because the deal seemed too skinny. I hadn't made a final decision because I always scratch every deal until I know without a shadow of doubt I need to move on.

My banker friend wanted to know more details. I went out to my truck and grabbed a flyer I'd scribbled my numbers on when I was figuring out what the return on my investment would be. As my friend and I enjoyed our lunch and analyzed the deal, he said he would loan on that property. I hadn't filled out one application or given him any information beyond that flyer and a few hand-scribbled notes. I still had doubts because the asking price was $250,000, but when I called the number on the sign, the Realtor (Peter Levinson with Keller Williams) said the price had dropped to $200,000 that day. The timing seemed a little fishy.

After lunch I drove over to the apartment at 200 NE 14th Street, which is near the University of Oklahoma College of Medicine (Go Sooners!).

I got out of my truck and gazed at this brick, three-story, fourteen-unit, soon-to-be cash-flowing monster. I did my inspection and determined this behemoth needed to be completely rehabbed because the previous owners let the structure deteriorate. When a unit had a problem, they shut the door and never returned to fix the issue, even if it was a major issue that could damage another unit, like a busted pipe in the wall or an overflowing sink.

My impression was that when people moved out, the owners simply shut the door behind them until all the units were vacant. By the time I set foot on the property, there were only two vagabonds who drifted in and out at will and didn't have a set address in the building. *No worries,* I thought. *We've rehabbed a lot of homes. This shouldn't be that different, except they're all in one location.*

I brought one of my closest friends to look at the property. He's also my go-to guy in the business. He's my rock, and I wouldn't have been able to grow my business without him. We chatted for a few moments and threw a few figures around. I blurted out that each unit would need only $2,000 in rehab, and he countered that they would need at least $5,000. (We were both way off. By the time it was done, the rehab cost nearly $10,000 per unit.)

My friend and I went back to the office to discuss what we should offer for the property, and whether we could handle the rehab. We chatted about the worst thing that could happen. I always try to be positive, and that attitude helps get me into deals. But during the process, or after they're done, my positivity can wear thin, and I have a habit of asking myself, *What in the world was I thinking?*

Before I made a decision about the apartment complex, I picked up the phone and called my friend Scott Smith. He has owned and rehabbed many multiunit properties, and he always shoots straight with me. When I told him I was considering a property in the Lincoln Terrace area just south of the state capitol, he knew the area and even knew the apartments I was talking about. He gave me some valuable insight about development the city is doing in the area, the pitfalls of owning an apartment building that was built in 1923, and the headaches of rehabbing it.

I gave him my numbers, told him the asking price was $200,000, and explained that the property was in a trust. The previous owner had died recently, and the trustee just wanted the headache to disappear. Scott told me, "You should offer $125,000."

At first I was a little hesitant and wondered if he wanted the property himself. But I reminded myself the worst thing that could happen was that they would say no. I called Peter, the listing agent, and offered $125,000 cash and told him I could close in a week. He said he would get back with me.

He called me back the next day with an offer of $150,000, I

countered with $135,000, and a day later, he said we could get it done for $140,000.

I was excited and called my bank to arrange the financing. They pulled an appraisal that came back two days later with a value of $290,000. Boom! The bank agreed to lend me up to $200,000. I borrowed the full $200,000, but took out only $160,000 to get the ball rolling on the rehab. I planned to draw the remainder as needed.

There are several reasons why I didn't pull the whole amount at once. It didn't make sense to pay interest on money that would be sitting in my bank account. It showed the bank I wouldn't pull money out just because I could. Also, whenever I need to make a draw, I like to keep the bank informed on the project status. I believe this leaves an impression that the rehab is a team effort.

I closed on the property in six days (a record for me), and it was the largest amount I've ever borrowed.

Rehabbing an apartment complex has turned into a more complex undertaking than I imagined. The first issue was the main drain line that we discovered wasn't connected properly to the city main. Then we learned the roof the sellers recently purchased was worthless.

This is by far the biggest real estate project I've been involved in. Many times I've been overwhelmed and felt out of my league, but to grow and go to the next level, you have to do things that are outside of your comfort zone. Jim Rohn says, "To be successful you have to do the things unsuccessful people don't want to do." I've been doing the things I don't want to do, and there have been times I wanted to give up. A few days I felt like David seeing Goliath when I looked at that apartment. But I didn't quit.

When we bought the apartments, we knew we had to make some improvements, and that meant spending money. We started with the roof. I called the trustee and asked the name of the roofing company they used. He gave me the guy's number, and I called him and told him the roof was leaking in several places. I needed him to come repair the leaks, and he seemed agreeable and jovial about doing it.

Before he arrived, I went on the roof and checked the workmanship. I couldn't believe how sloppy the work was. I knew the roof would constantly be an issue, and I thought the previous owner had been taken for a ride. I didn't want to do any business with the roofer who had done this unacceptable work.

I was at a crossroads and called several investor friends to get their opinions on what to do. The responses were all over the map. Some told me to just repair it; others said to replace it. I was even told the best thing to do was to leave the roof as is and wait for an insurance claim. I knew this property was going to be in my portfolio for a long time, and I didn't want to make the same mistakes I made on the Beast, so I decided to put a new roof (including decking and insulation) on the complex.

I sought out the best roofing company I could find and made sure they covered their work with a warranty on labor and parts. I found Don Lighty Construction, who used Dura-Last Roofing and offered a twenty-year warranty. It cost $20,000, but it was worth every penny. Don Lighty did a superb job, and I felt I won my first battle on the road to victory.

Other decisions I had to make included replacing the showers in every unit, choosing the type of flooring to use, and building a fence around the parking lot that gave the impression my tenants lived in a gated community.

Issues and delays have eaten at me like maggots snacking on a buffet line. As I write this book, I'm near the end of the rehab. I have about 15 percent left, and that's mainly cosmetic. I've spent over $75,000 in labor and supplies, and I still have at least $10,000 to go. I've refinanced several properties to finish the Monster, and progress has slowed, as there are only one or two guys on the job site doing touch-up painting and cleaning.

One of the savviest things I ever did was to contact a stager by the name of Mary Hatch, the owner of This Staged Space! Mary helps people make their properties look their best before a showing and helps investors professionally market their available units. She took care of me and designed and purchased all the accessories and handled renting furniture for a photo shoot. We took some incredible pictures I'm able to use in marketing the complex. Mary did such a great job that several people filled out applications online without looking at the property in person.

In June 2012, I called my Realtor Dutch to help me rent out the units as fast as we could. We were ready to get this place cash-flowing. When your project is finished or close to being done, you need to start thinking about who your renters are going to be. I had a specific demographic in mind when I bought that complex. I wanted to rent to the medical and college students who lived in the area, as well as young professionals who were just starting to live on their own.

Even after owning other properties, I learned a phenomenal amount when I bought an apartment complex. I'm in the process of joining the

Oklahoma Apartment Association to connect with other apartment owners and to continue my education. You can never learn too much when you're a real estate investor.

What I learned the most during this project is to be on the job site daily to ensure things are running correctly and to make sure there's enough material on hand to get the job done. Also, many of the materials we work with can be salvaged and reused. Too many times to mention, countertops were torn out and destroyed when I needed them to be saved, and doors were removed and trashed when we could have salvaged them. Not taking care of these things increased the cost of the project. Hiring several different contractors caused issues with material and tool loss, which some people might call theft.

Cash flow is king. Period. There's no way around it. But there are times when you'll have to dip into your reserves. I popped a solid deal after I bought the apartment complex, and I closed with my own cash. It tore into my nest egg and left me with nothing in the bank, which caused a pit in my stomach. I needed money to finish the apartment project, and I worried I wouldn't be able to do a refinance, which caused major stress.

I've learned not to have more than a few projects going at the same time. We aren't supermen, and we have to accept our limits. It wasn't the smartest thing I've ever done, but while I was rehabbing our fourteen-unit apartment complex, I purchased two other properties and rehabbed a third. I also had three other properties that needed flooring and a bunch of other repairs, and I had to evict two tenants. One I got rid of by going to court, and the other one skipped out in the night. Those issues are over with.

I can honestly tell you to never give up on your goals and dreams. It can be a challenge, but you can make it happen.

Options

Fourteen days after I closed on the Monster, I got a call from a Realtor who knows I like properties in a specific area. He told me 4241 NE 32nd was available—a brick home with three bedrooms, one and a half baths, and a two-car garage on a huge lot in desirable area. The same people have owned many of the properties in that neighborhood for more than twenty years, and many owners have passed the homes down to their grandchildren.

What made the deal surreal was that the house sat next to 3301 Maloney, the first house I flipped. I tried buying this property two years earlier, but couldn't get it done because the asking price was $65,000 and someone already had it under contract.

When I got the call, I knew exactly the house the Realtor was describing, and I asked him the selling price. He said it was a HUD REO, and the price had dropped to $35,000. The asset manager was asking for highest and final offers. This Realtor (who had experience with REOs) suggested I offer slightly more than the asking price because there was a lot of action on the property.

"Let's write up an offer for $37,500 and see what happens," I said. I really wanted this property and knew it was going to be a horse of a deal. I didn't want to lose it just because I wasn't willing to offer an extra $500.

Sure enough, I had the winning offer and ordered the appraisal, but it came up short because the surrounding area didn't have enough sales for an accurate comparison of values. I could borrow only $30,000 on the house, but I knew the true value of the property because several years earlier I sold the house next door for close to $90,000. I wasn't worried about getting my money out.

After I closed, I jumped all over the property because I knew I could rent it without delays, and I could demand a higher rent than the market because it was in an excellent location. I put $10,000 toward rehabbing the property and used ten piers to level the house and fix the foundation. I completely expanded the bathroom and replumbed for a new bath tub. I updated the kitchen, adding a dishwasher and a built-in microwave. I added an air condenser, because the house had central heat but only window units for cooling. I also did the normal cosmetics, like paint and light fixtures.

The remodel took nearly sixty days, and I now have it leased at $800 a month. The breakdown goes like this: I have close to $50,000 in the deal, including loans and money from my own pocket. After debt service, insurance, and taxes, I cash-flow a wonderful $400 because my loan payment is only $300 a month. That leaves actual cash in the deal of around $20,000. If you divide that by $400 a month, my return will take just over four years, and then I'll cash-flow like a wild man forever.

I could do a lot of different things with that property. I could refinance, pull all my equity out, and have no cash in the deal, meaning I would cash-flow roughly about $200 a month. Or I could leave it on my financial statement and build more wealth, because it increases my net worth just like any other income-producing asset I own. Isn't it great to have options? Where, other than in real estate, do you have so many choices?

This deal taught me that not all appraisals are 100 percent accurate and in your favor. Sometimes you have to trust your gut and experience. If I hadn't known the area, the deal wouldn't have made sense. I learned that if you spend a little extra on the things your potential tenants want, such as new appliances, you'll almost always get your money back, but there's no hard and fast rule. Each property is unique, and a lot of factors come into play, such as the location.

Look and listen to what's out there and put your own spin on it. I heard about a landlord who offers a new 32" LCD TV as a move-in incentive for new tenants. That idea spurred my buddy into offering an LCD TV if you book his music production company. Marketing is very important. Listen to what other people are doing and incorporate it into your marketing campaigns.

Hit the Road, Jack

Ramping up my real estate business has been my plan since I left my day job. I'm a full-time investor, and nothing's going to keep me from building the best portfolio I can.

A month after the HUD REO, I purchased a brick three-bedroom, one-bath home at 108 W. Marshall. It looked like a sweet deal, and I thought the property was in near rent-ready condition and that only a few minor cosmetic issues needed to be addressed. I know the neighborhood well enough, and the demand for housing in that school district is strong. People with kids line up to rent houses there like they're trying to get tickets to a sold-out rock concert.

I closed quickly, and it was one of those rare closings where the owner/investor came to the closing with cash in the deal. At that time I couldn't figure out why. I thought he might have pulled out too much equity or he bought it wrong. I've learned you can't assume anything, and you have to trust your own numbers and plans to create a cash-flowing asset.

After closing, I did the basic repairs and painting and put the property on the market for $600 a month. I had several showings, and within fourteen days I had a deposit and was ready to roll. Shortly after the tenant moved in, he called and said there was a plumbing problem. I asked him to describe it and he said, "When I take a shower the water sprays through the wall into the bedroom."

"What? You've got to be kidding me." I sent my handyman over to take a look and figure out was going on. He called me back and told me none of the plumbing under the house was connected properly. My handyman had to spend three days in the dirt fixing everything he encountered. It was a complete mess, and I could have avoided it if I'd done my due diligence. I assumed it was fine and thought the owner before me would have taken care of the property. I now realized all he'd done was pass a broken baton to me.

After we cleaned up that mess, I gave the tenant a $50 credit for his troubles and for being patient during the repair. That was as close as he ever got to being current on his rent. His first month's rent was late, and when he did pay (after the fifteenth of the month), the check bounced. I knew we had a big problem on our hands.

The following month he paid his rent late again, so I started a file and documented everything. I knew we were beginning the eviction process. I was frustrated because when I rented to him I'd been in a big hurry. The tenant's job at the city checked out, but I hadn't looked at everything I should have. I was in the middle of several rehabs and had the Monster to contend with. I'd cut a few corners and wound up with a deadbeat on my hands.

The true drama began when the tenant paid only $200 of his rent the second month. He'd been in the property for only forty-five days but had already worn out his welcome. When the third month rolled around, I was all over this guy. I was sick and tired of his 101 creative excuses. He was costing me money, and I wasn't going to jack around with him. He was going to pay or leave. It turned out he was hiding the fact that he'd lost his job. He was in his late thirties or early forties with two teenage children. He told me he ran into a roadblock when his mother couldn't help him after he lost his job.

I suggested he seek assistance from one of the agencies that help people who are having tough times, such as a church. I pointed out the many organizations that had the resources to help him get back on his feet. He told me he would try, but his lack of urgency was evident. It was obvious he thought we would just let him live in our property for free. He had no regard for the expenses we were incurring and had no intention of paying his rent. I would have been happy to work with him, but this guy was looking for a free ride.

I was very disappointed, but did what I had to do. I filed the proper paperwork to evict him and let the system run its course. We had a hearing ten days later, and the deadbeat had the nerve to show up in court and lie to the judge. The tenant said he paid his rent and had left money orders in the mailbox at our office.

At first the judge seemed sympathetic and was going along with this guy's story. Then the judge caught him in a lie and it was over. The judge asked the tenant if he'd reported the money orders missing so he could get them reissued.

The tenant responded, "I've been trying to reach the money order company, but the phone just keeps ringing. I can't get through."

The judge asked the tenant to call the money order company while he watched. The tenant pulled out his phone, dialed a number, and put it on speakerphone. The phone kept ringing and ringing.

I had a great idea. I stepped in, asked to see the money order stub, and dialed the phone number myself. On the second ring my call was answered and we were talking to a representative from the company. By the time I hung up, the judge's gavel hit his bench, and it was like a hammer driving the final nail into the tenant's coffin. He knew the guy was lying, and that was the end of the case.

Getting the judge's order wasn't enough. I had to file the judgment and pay for the sheriff to escort the tenant off the property. For several weeks I pleaded with the guy. I didn't want to put him or his kids through all the drama of having him forcibly removed. "We are going to prosecute," I told him. "Please save us all the anguish. Please vacate the property and take your belongings with you." I did everything I could to give him the chance to leave with whatever pride he had left. He kept telling me he was going to pay, but of course he never did. Even if he had the money, I wouldn't have taken it because I was tired of dealing with his false promises, and I didn't want to endure the same scenario every month.

This deal taught me I must never cut corners when leasing to a tenant, even if I have a good feeling about the individual. When I sign a lease with someone, I must be up-front (if not over the top) when I explain the eviction process during our lease signing meeting. I also learned it's a good idea to turn on a faucet or two to make sure the plumbing does what it's supposed to.

As I've been writing this book, I've bought properties I haven't mentioned here. My goal is to help you learn from the mistakes I've made. I'm not putting my experiences on paper to toot my own horn. It's important to hear about successes, but I believe you can learn much more by studying the failures and challenges that people have overcome. I hope that when you see what I've been able to achieve, you'll be motivated to jump out there and invest in real estate.

OKC's Finest

I have one more deal to share with you, and I hope this will keep you inspired. I thought I found a deal when my Realtor set up a showing for a five-unit property in the southwest part of town. As I approached the property, I was pulled over at a four-way stop by a police officer who wanted to check my ID. The property was in an area of Oklahoma City called Capitol City which is known for its Hispanic residents.

After the police officer allowed me to leave, I went to the property and immediately had a negative feeling. It looked like the textbook definition of housing owned by a slumlord. It would have been a major headache to own the property even if it had been given to me, because it needed at least $30,000 to get it rent-ready. Thoughts of the Monster started running through my head, reminding me that I had no income and none of the units were rented at the time.

I couldn't see the potential in this property, and started getting frustrated that I wasted time driving to see it, not to mention enduring a chat with one of Oklahoma City's finest. Out of respect for the Realtor who took the time to show it, I looked at every unit as quickly as possible, all the time wondering why a Realtor would even list this property. It was way overpriced at $80,000 and needed a lot of rehabbing. I later found out that a California investor owned it.

The listing Realtor was a great guy and realized I wasn't interested. But after some small talk with my Realtor and me, he knew we were serious buyers of income-producing properties. He went to his car and came back with a book of listings. "I have a duplex on the north side that was $49,000, but I just lowered it today to $45,000. Would you be interested?" he asked as he flipped through the pages.

"Where is it?" I asked. I'd invested so much time that I didn't want to miss the chance of seeing any potential properties. I had to make something good happen that afternoon.

The Realtor looked up from his listing. "2304 NW 38th, just off of N. Youngs. It's a great duplex with one bed and one bath on each side, and it comes with a lot next door. We get more calls on the lot than we do for the property itself."

I knew the exact location because I own a great property one street north. I understood the market and demand for rentals and ran the numbers in my head. I figured I could get close to $450 a side and that it would qualify for Section 8.

When I saw the property, I knew the Realtor was correct. It was a great duplex but needed at least $10,000 of rehab. After a quick conversation with my Realtor, I made an offer for $30,000 and expected them to make a counter-offer. I had it under contract for $35,000 the next day.

We closed on the property the following week, and I started marketing the property on Craigslist to see what kind of response I would receive. I was overwhelmed by the need for housing under $500 a month. I've already rented out the duplex for $485 a side and have received two $300 deposits to hold the properties for the new tenants.

I was irritated because I thought I'd wasted my time when the five-unit property didn't work out. But I kept my options open, and something good came out of it. A week later I owned a new property that was completely leased before I closed. I'll cash-flow about $400 total after move-in day, and the deal didn't cost me any of my own money.

It was far from a waste of time.

PART TWO

It's Not a Mistake;
It's the Beginning of a Lesson

*The successful man will profit from his mistakes
and try again in a different way.*

Dale Carnegie

In the first part of the book you learned about how I built my multi-million dollar real estate empire. Now I'll give more details about the mistakes I committed over the years.

People underestimate mistakes and how important they are. When things don't go as planned, it's easy to be hard on ourselves and think we've failed. But part of success is making mistakes. If you keep stepping up to the plate and swinging, you'll strike out a few times.

It's okay. It doesn't mean there's anything wrong with you or that you should give up your dreams. But you have to learn from each and every mistake and understand why things didn't go as planned, and this will turn you into a better person and a better businessman.

I'm not suggesting you should make a bunch of mistakes on purpose so you can grow. The mistakes will come without any help from you. What I am saying is that mistakes aren't the end of the world. They can be stepping stones to new and greater things.

But it's always best to learn from other people's mistakes. Learning what other investors did wrong is better than graduating from the best business school in the country. There's no better way to build a successful business than to watch other people drive into potholes so you can avoid them.

And that's why it's so important to share your mistakes. You'll become great only if you also want others to become great. Learn from my actions and save yourself the trouble. And when you make a mistake, own up to it and share it with those around you.

One of the biggest mistakes I made while doing real estate was to pay a mortgage directly to the owner. In the beginning of my real estate career I purchased several "For Sale by Owner" properties (FSBOs) where the owner was financing the deal. One particular property opportunity came from a real estate investor I knew. In fact, he was one of my mentors. I'd grown to like him and had learned a lot from him. Looking back, I feel like a total fool because he took advantage of me.

I bought a two-bedroom, one-bath property from him for $35,000, put $5,000 down, and he carried the note. Because I thought he was a close friend, I paid the remaining balance with cash three years later after we closed the deal.

Several months went by and I hadn't received a release of mortgage from him. I later learned it was a "wraparound mortgage" deal. He had the loan in his name, I was paying him, and he was supposed to be paying the bank. But he hadn't. He'd taken the money I paid him and put it in his own pocket. When I tried to talk to him, I discovered he'd moved to another state. I almost had a panic attack when I found out he didn't pay the house off. I eventually found him, and he told me he used my money for another deal that went sour, so he couldn't repay me or give the money to the bank. I was totally betrayed by him, but didn't know how to proceed. I couldn't stop thinking about how I just lost $35,000 plus the cost of repairs.

I did what I had to do to get my money back. I called this investor as often as possible even when he changed his telephone number and moved to two different states. After finding him for the third time, I figured he would stay in that state for a while. I hired an attorney to take care of business and sent the seller every letter humanly possible to make this deadbeat pay up.

I eventually received the release of mortgage from the lien holder. I was out $900 and my attorney fees, had lost a friend, and had a stress-induced bout of diarrhea.

The last I heard about my former friend was that he had a fire sale, sold off all his portfolio at a loss or break-even amount, and is no longer in real estate. He now searches for business opportunities that don't require loans or the need for cash up front.

Learn from my mistakes. Always use a closing company to handle transactions for you. Don't be cheap and try to save a few bucks. This will cost you money in the long run.

The Beast

My real estate career was taking off in 2006 when I came across a fourplex in Mesta Park. It's one of the prestigious older neighborhoods in Oklahoma City. It's full of desirable houses with lots of great charm and details. It's close to downtown and a medical center, and the streets are lined with old trees. A lot of professionals want to live there, and good properties sell quickly.

I came across a house (which I now refer to as "The Beast"), and discussed it with my mentor. He'd just walked the property and considered buying it for $110,000, gutting it and converting it to single-family, which would have cost about $50,000. He knew he could flip it for $300,000, which is a normal purchase price for single-family homes in that neighborhood.

My mentor saw I was interested and told me to make an offer of $110,000. I told him, "If they take my offer for $110,000, I'll give you $1,000 for giving me the balls to offer such a low amount." The property was listed for $168,000, and I was running my numbers for the seller to accept an offer of $150,000. The house had originally been listed at $200,000, but it was going through probate when the buyers dropped out. I thought the sellers wanted to unload the house, but I couldn't see any way they would go as low as $110,000.

That was the first mistake I made on the deal. I shot myself in the foot by thinking I understood the market when I didn't. I was overly confident because I thought I was a big-time, multiunit landlord and knew what I was doing. But my career was taking off, and I was finding out how short the runway is.

My second mistake was that I became emotional because I wanted to grow my portfolio. I'd recently connected with an investor bank that would finance the deal. I had nothing to lose, so I offered the seller $110,000, thinking they would reject it. They took my offer on the spot. In fact, they took it so quickly it should have made me ask questions.

I thought, *I know what I'm doing; I'm a real estate investor, I've done this before*. And I started calculating the cash flow in my head. At the time, my bank loaned me 80 percent of the property's appraised value, so I received some fix-up money to make this mammoth sing. I closed on the deal, drove right over, and was super excited until I looked at the garage apartment in the back. All the brick on the side of the garage had fallen off, leaving a big pile of rubble. *No worries,* I thought. *I've got a deal on the place. I can get it rebricked and have enough money left over to finish the rehab.*

I formalized a plan to get this project on its way, but got sidetracked by an aggressive tenant at one of my other properties. I eventually had to evict him.

While I was cleaning up after this deadbeat tenant who left the home in shambles (I vividly remember sweating while I was carrying out over ten bags of trash), I received a call from one of the new tenants at the fourplex.

"We don't have any hot water."

I paused for a moment and told him, "Pay your bill."

"No. *You* pay the gas here," he retorted.

Then it hit me. I had to sit down and take it all in. Gas utilities in Oklahoma are outrageous, and I bought a fourplex that didn't have the gas meter separated. I was on the hook for every tenant's gas bill. My next call was to the utility company to find out how much the average monthly gas bill was. When they told me $500 a month, my heart sank, and my mind went into panic mode. *There's no way I can make money on this place!* My pride welled up, and I grimaced. "I'll just raise the rents."

I started riding a roller coaster of emotions trying to figure out how I could make this deal work. I crunched the new numbers, and it dawned on me I would need 100 percent occupancy to make money. If one tenant moved out before I found another to fill his place, the property would have negative cash flow.

I was dejected and embarrassed. I tried to find some way to make the deal work, but I'd made too many mistakes and couldn't justify the amount of work the Beast would need.

I opted to dump it as quickly as I could. I called my mentor and asked his advice. He gave me the number of a Realtor who had sold a duplex in the same neighborhood. The Realtor found a buyer in California. After $138,000 and three months of rehab, holding costs, and commissions, I barely broke even. But I did learn some valuable lessons. First, do your due diligence. Second, you always need more education in investing. Finally, emotions will kill you in business.

Zeros Can Add Up to Serious Cash

A tenant walked into my office one day and announced he was only going to pay the amount of rent that was listed in his lease. He'd been living in the house several months, and it struck me as an odd comment.

I thought, *What does that mean?* I pulled out his file and looked at the lease. I was stunned. His rent was listed at $5 per month. I couldn't believe it.

After a few moments, I realized the office girl working for me at the time had made a mistake and deleted two zeros in the rent amount. Because of that, the lease read $5 instead of $500.

At first I was a little worried because a lease is a binding contract. As I looked at the lease, all I could think about was this man saying he had a legal right to live in my property for about fifteen cents a day.

I caught my breath and explained to the tenant that it was a clerical error. I also reminded him that he'd already been paying $500 for the last few months. He complained for a minute or two, but I remained firm, and he eventually paid the full amount. The problem was resolved the next month when he broke the lease because he couldn't afford to pay the rent.

The lesson is to double-check everything and write everything down when possible. The typo in the lease was a simple mistake that could have been easily avoided. It could have been costly. At the least, he could have dragged me into court to try and enforce the lease, which would have cost me time, attorney fees, and court costs. Create a habit of double-checking everything. Measure twice and cut once, as the carpenters say.

100 Yards from the Perfect Tenant

One day I thought I found an awesome tenant. This gentleman had everything a landlord wanted. He worked construction and really enjoyed being a handyman. He was willing to do some work around the home for no compensation, if I bought the materials for him. He wanted to install ceiling fans in the bedrooms, and he wanted to paint the kitchen. He had the most likable demeanor, and he was willing to do the work. I couldn't believe how fortunate I was that he was living in one of my houses.

I rushed to the closest home improvement store and bought him everything he would need. I dropped the supplies off at the house and didn't think anything of it until he called a few days later.

I could tell something was wrong when he said my name. "Steven, I have a problem. I didn't know it at the time I signed the lease, but this house is within a hundred yards of a school, and I'm a registered sex offender. It's illegal for me to live here. I have to move out immediately."

I closed my eyes and clenched my jaw as I thought of a few choice words. "Okay," I finally muttered.

Then he had the nerve to ask, "This isn't really my fault, so can I get my deposit back?"

I was still stunned from learning about the kind of man my tenant really was. I don't know what I was thinking when I said, "Yes." Looking back, it was one of the worst decisions I ever made. I can't explain why I gave him his money back.

There are two lessons to be learned here. First, consult with your attorney about the laws regarding renting to sex offenders in your area. You want to be armed with knowledge if you have to deal with a situation like this.

The second lesson is to not give a deposit back when you're not the one who breaks a lease. This man had caught me completely off guard, and I agreed to give him money when I shouldn't have. I wasn't the one who violated the law and entered into an agreement I couldn't honor. I'd acted in good faith and had even purchased materials he was going to use to improve his life. His deposit should never have left my bank account.

Drive-by Loss

I was on the phone one day going over a deal with my friend when he was abruptly interrupted by a loud knock on his door. He told me to wait a minute while he went to check it out. He opened the door and was greeted by a process server who served a summons on him.

When my friend got back on the phone he shared a life-altering story that should strike a chord in your heart, as it did mine. My friend has been an investor longer than I have, and he has shared a great deal of wisdom with me. We've exchanged ideas for years, and I've been blessed by being able to lean on him when I need to.

My heart went out to him as he told me what was happening. About eighteen months earlier, his wife was driving, got in an accident, and seriously injured the driver of another car. My friend expected his insurance to be adequate, but the damages where much greater than his coverage. The woman's medical bills where outrageous, and she'd hired a lawyer to get them paid. My friend and his wife were being sued for the uncovered medical bills, to the tune of $30,000.

The attorney was a real ambulance chaser, and he discovered that one of my friend's rental houses was owned not by an LLC but by the man individually. The attorney had discovered this when he searched for assets in my friend's name.

My friend was upset with himself and felt that he'd been lazy for not making sure all his properties were owned by his LLC. He was stuck between a rock and a hard place. If he went to court he could lose his investment, and even if he won (which seemed unlikely), he would be on the hook for attorney fees.

He and his wife eventually settled out of court for just over $20,000.

I hope this lesson reminds you to protect your assets, and to realize that even when you aren't directly involved in a situation, you may be held accountable. Don't take any chances. Make sure all your properties are owned by the proper entity.

Tried the Triplex

You never know where your next deal will come from. I was renting a small space in an office complex where several different industries and companies were doing business. One of those companies was an insurance office.

The agent seemed friendly, and he told me he was in the process of moving out of state and was trying to sell a property he owned. I informed him I was an investor looking to purchase property and wanted more information.

He owned a duplex on a corner lot, and behind that was a detached garage conversion that needed some work to get it rent-ready. The duplex was good to go and had long-term tenants (it turns out they were underrented), and he was looking for a quick sale so he didn't have to deal with it when he moved to Colorado.

I became excited and asked where the property was and if he had time to look at it. He gave me the address, and he agreed to give me a tour after work.

I got the address, did a little research, and before we set foot on the property I was running numbers in my head. I knew what the value of the property would be. The duplex seemed to be in great shape. It just needed some light maintenance, but the garage apartment really excited me. I knew this was going to be an income producer, and I wanted to get my hands on it. We chatted for about thirty minutes before I asked what he wanted for the property. With almost no effort we agreed on $75,000. I broke that down to $25,000 a unit and knew I could get an average of $500 each, which meant a gross rent potential of $1,500. My total debt service would be about $800 a month, and I didn't think I couldn't go wrong.

"Let's do it."

He told me that he'd just been issued his real estate license, and he would draw up the contract in the morning at his office.

I drove off jazzed and couldn't stop thinking about my latest deal and how I was going to finish out the garage apartment and get the maximum rent possible out of this property.

The next morning couldn't come fast enough. I sat in my office waiting for the phone to ring. I started to wonder what the delay was. When I hadn't heard from him by 11:00 a.m., I gave the guy a call. He seemed a little frazzled and started giving me excuses, saying he was talking to his broker. He said he was a new Realtor, needed help creating the contract, and he would get back with me shortly.

I waited some more and wondered what was taking so long. When I hadn't heard from him by 3:00 p.m., I decided to pop up to his office to find out what was going on. He said that the price we agreed on was too low. His broker told him he could get more money for the property and said he wasn't going to sell it now. I pressed a little harder, and he explained that his broker bought the property under the table for $80,000 and was going to flip it to an out of state investor.

I couldn't believe what I was hearing. What a complete and total lack of integrity from the Realtor and the broker who underhandedly cheated me out of a great property! I really want to mention the broker's name. However, my goal here isn't to put people down but to help honest, hardworking people who want to get ahead.

That story is like a tattoo. It's permanently etched in my memory. I see the broker's signs around town and shake my head in despair. I'm amazed at how unethical and selfish people can be when they stand to make a few bucks, even people who hold themselves out as professional Realtors.

The crazy thing is, the guy asked only $75,000, and we didn't negotiate. It's not like I beat him up and gave him only half his asking price. I learned to keep purchasing contracts in my vehicle at all times. If I'd had a contract with me, we could have signed it that day, and I would be enjoying the income from a great triplex.

I also learned that Realtors are human and may succumb to greed. Be professional and insist that all your agreements are written down. That's why we have contracts. I also learned that there are many levels to the real estate game and that many transactions get done or fall apart because of office politics. There's another game going on between real estate agents and brokers, between banks and investors, and between probate attorneys and friends. When you know it's a great deal, get it inked as fast as you can. Nothing happens until it closes, and don't assume anything.

Buck the Bronco

I got into the car wash business for six painful months in 2008. I thought I was buying property that had the benefit of an attached, established business. It was a terrible experience. I ran into a Realtor who specialized in car washes, and he turned me on to the Bronco Carwash in Mustang.

This Realtor explained how awesome it was to own a car wash because it was a cash-based business with little or no maintenance. And if we put a snack shack on the property, we could bring in even more money than the seller documented in the pro forma he provided. The owner was selling on terms, and the Realtor made it sound like a deal I had to take.

As I was driving to see this cash cow, I daydreamed of quarters pouring in as people washed their cars and stopped to enjoy a snow cone. And I had plenty of time to dream, because the car wash was twenty-five miles from our office and sat on a corner lot in the middle of a residential area not far from Mustang High School. As I saw the property for the first time, my optimistic nature took over, and all I saw was potential. I thought all it needed to get the car wash humming again was a face-lift of paint and a new sign.

I called one of my friends, a real estate investor and entrepreneur with a background in running service-based businesses. "Hey," I asked him, "do you want to own a car wash together?"

"What's the return on the investment?" He cut to the chase and wanted to know what the numbers would be.

I enthusiastically explained, "We can't go wrong with this cash machine. It makes money every month, and we don't have to put that much down, basically only the money for the cosmetics. And it comes with the property, too."

I took my friend to the car wash, and we walked the property while I pointed out all the ways we would make money. I showed him the soda machine (which must have been at least fifty years old) and the vending machines, and told him about the snack shack. We could make a snow cone for 15¢ and sell it for $2—a $1.85 return on each drink. "We're going to be rich," I insisted.

We looked at the numbers and felt we could put $5,000 into the car wash and get our money back in a year, and after that we would cash-flow for life, which was what I wanted. We were serious about the deal and decided to do our due diligence by paying a friend of mine $10 an hour to sit in his car and count all the cars that were washed in a day. We figured a Saturday would be the best day, so we commissioned my friend to give us the lowdown on the type of cars and the activity throughout the day.

When my friend reported back, it was a little nerve-racking. Only four cars drove into the parking lot, and only two people actually paid to get their cars washed. *No worries,* I thought. *It's a bad Saturday, and the place looks run down. After we slap on some new paint and put up a new flashy sign, we'll be on our way.*

My partner and I didn't have any mechanical skills, and we needed someone to check out the water pumps, hot water tank, and the soap dispensing machines. I didn't know anyone in the business, and the only person who came to mind was a handyman who'd recently installed a dishwasher in my home. The handyman drove out to the property, looked at the machinery, and gave us the A-okay. He knew someone who had owned a car wash, or who was involved with the business at one time or another, and in our eyes that made him an expert.

You can see that I didn't know squat about car washes and was severely uneducated in the whole process of running that type of business. But I was wooed by this opportunity. For some reason, it was really sexy to me. After some negotiation, we got the Bronco under contract for $92,500.

When I called my bank to get the financing I was shot down because the financials the seller gave us didn't jibe with my banker. He immediately picked up on some problems. A few days later the Realtor called and told us the financials we received from the seller (which included profit and loss, taxes, and balance sheet) were not accurate because the mother of the seller was withholding information. Apparently, she'd been funding this sinking ship for a long time without documenting her infusion of cash into the business. *What? Are you kidding me?* raced through my mind.

The deal should have stopped right there and then, but I was emotional about wanting to own the business, and that blinded me from seeing clear evidence of a con. I thought I was a slick investor and that there had to be a way to make this deal work. My banker turned me down and warned me that the business's numbers were faulty and that the son was motivated to dump it. It doesn't make any sense now, but at the time I figured the son was in a weak position and that I had leverage over him. I thought he needed to sell the car wash. I smelled blood in the water and felt I could pounce on a deal.

My partner and I pushed to get the deal done on terms, and we negotiated for a lease option so we could get the Bronco healthy again. After we signed a contract for $550 a month, we poured money into a snow cone machine and a four-by-eight-foot sign with a new logo, and we completely repainted the snack shack and eight wash bays. We were ready to cash in the coins.

It was only after a month of rehab and another month of operating a business without making a dime that we realized how deep our hole was. There was no way of getting out. I'm ashamed to tell you how much money we wasted on that place, but I hope my mistake teaches you to run from such a situation ten times faster than we did. The only thing we managed to escape with was our bumped and bruised pride.

Our expenses—water bill, maintenance, natural gas, trash, labor costs to run the snack shack, supplies, and lease payment—totaled over $2,000 a month. With 50¢ vacuums, $1 car washes, and $1 dries, we needed to average $3 per car and to have a total of 666 cars each and every month to break even.

We held on for a few months before I understood that we'd been cheated. I called the Realtor to express how we were betrayed. We'd poured over $10,000 into this hustle, and I demanded to be released from the contract. The Realtor was reluctant to work with us, and I had a feeling he realized he had been scammed as well. He was stuck with a lousy listing and didn't want to refund his commission. After a few nasty letters from our attorney threatening a lawsuit, we were released. We didn't have a party to celebrate, and the wounds we received took years to heal.

The defining moment of the entire experience came when I was standing in line at the bank waiting to change my quarters into dollars. I handed the teller my big bag of quarters, and she counted them out and gave me $65. What a complete waste of my life. I left the bank thinking there was no way to make money in that business.

I learned that partnerships can unnecessarily strain any relationship. Distance is always a factor in running your numbers. What's your time worth? Has the price of gasoline climbed so high that driving to a location is counterproductive?

Numbers on a financial statement are the window into a business. Make sure you have the true financial statement, and always scrutinize it.

Deals may be too good to be true. If the asset is making money, why is the owner selling? Do your homework and research. The reason they give you for selling could be a bluff. Make sure it's legitimate and that they're not selling to dump a headache. Be educated about the industry you're entering. Make sure the people running your enterprise are competent and professional.

Owner-finance can be enticing. Keep your emotions in check, and don't rationalize why you're getting a deal. A good friend of mine, Marc McIntosh, gave me a great thought once when I had a money-making idea. He told me, "I don't leave my sandbox." What he meant was, if it's not directly related to his business, he didn't want anything to do with it. That's something to remember.

Pay Me My Fee

My mom worked at a call center for a while. Like any other mother, she was proud of her son and started bragging about me to a coworker. My mom told her how my real estate business was growing and that I was looking for properties to buy. My mom's coworker was going through a divorce and owned a Victorian duplex in an area called Gatewood she wanted to sell. The property was a reminder of her botched marriage, and she wanted to get rid of it.

My mom passed on to me this woman's phone number. I called her and got the address and the details of the property. The very next day I went over and did a walk-through. The duplex needed a complete rehab, and it seemed too daunting for me. I knew there had to be a way for me to profit in this deal, and I recalled something I'd heard at the previous month's meeting of OKCREIA (Oklahoma City Real Estate Investors Association). An investor was pushing people to send deals his way. He would pay a bird dog fee for any properties he bought. I knew referral fees were common and had read about them in books, but I'd never earned one.

I needed money at the time and was just getting my feet wet in real estate. Even if I wanted to buy the house, I didn't have the finances to rehab it. The investor offering referral fees seemed to be doing it big, or at least he talked the game. He even let me look at one of his deals and told me he wanted to show me the ropes.

I looked at the house and knew I couldn't afford to rehab it, but I knew I could at least earn the referral fee. I called the investor and told him, "I found you a steal of deal on a duplex. If you take the deal, I want the $1,000 finder's fee."

"If I buy it, I'll take care of you," he said with no hesitation. I gave him the address, and we set a time to meet at the property. He loved the house as soon as he saw it.

I gave him the seller's contact information and went down the road, thinking I'd just made the easiest $1,000 of my life. I trusted the guy, and it never occurred to me he wouldn't pay me.

I hadn't heard from him about three weeks later, so I called him to touch base. "I'm still working on the deal," he told me. "I'll call you when it's done." I wasn't worried, and I believed he would write me a check as soon as he closed on the deal.

Another four weeks rolled by, and he hadn't called me. I started to see the red flags and got the feeling he wasn't going to live up to his word. When I finally got in touch with him, he told me he still hadn't closed.

I did some research and found the closing company where the title work was being done and called them. They told me the property had already closed. I investigated a little more, and I found that the investor had flipped the contract to someone else. I still didn't want to believe he was lying to me and thought, *No big deal. He'll pay me now since he just got paid.*

I called the guy again, and he totally blew me off. I was pissed because I trusted him and believed he was an honest man who was helping people.

I turned my frustration into a quest. He was going to make things right and honor his word. Period. It wasn't going to end any other way.

I wouldn't have a pot to piss in if I took him to court, because I hadn't documented our agreement. I was a sucker for trusting him, but that didn't stop me from calling every time I thought about it—which was a lot, because I was really hacked off. I pestered him for about a month or so, and he finally agreed to meet me and pay my fee. I was delighted for my little victory and was proud that I hadn't given up.

I arrived at our meeting and he tried being my friend. When I saw him, I looked at him in a totally different light. I couldn't believe how sleazy he really was. After he greeted me, he said he needed to grab his checkbook out of the trunk of his Toyota Camry. He wrote me a check on the spot, but it was for only $500, half of what he agreed to pay me.

You're a jerk and have no integrity kept running through my mind. I had to bite my tongue to keep from cussing the guy out. How could he live with himself knowing he was taking people for a ride?

I got in my truck and raced to the bank. I wanted to cash the check as soon as I could because I doubted it would clear. Fortunately, the bank honored it, and I took the money and chalked up the other $500 to experience.

I see him occasionally at random investor meetings, and I wonder how his life is. How many other people has he cheated? The crown jewel doesn't even remember who I am when I introduce myself at the meetings.

The $500 lesson is to not take anything by chance. Make sure you have a written agreement, even if it's scribbled in pencil on a napkin. Also, your ignorance is no justification to be a weak business person. Learn the business and take a stand for what's right. But take a stand within reason. Many times I could have (or should have) sued people, but I realized it just wasn't worth the time or the money.

I also learned that not everyone is what that say they are or what they're perceived to be. Do your homework and protect yourself, even in tight-knit circles such as your local investors' club.

Emotions Trump Common Sense

This next mistake may seem obvious to you. I thought about leaving it out of the book, but I want to be real and honest. No matter who you are or where you come from, at some point your emotions will trump your common sense.

When I bought 4006 Dogwood, I thought I was a big-time investor, but I was really just a dumb sucker. The investor who sold me the property was getting his leads from an advertising campaign his company was running on TV. They were getting tons of leads, but his boss wasn't a good person. The investor wanted to farm leads on his own and suggested we work together on some of them.

I thought I was some big investor and saw an opportunity to be an insider. I looked through the leads this guy had. There were more than fifty pages of them. They kept pouring in, and he couldn't keep up with them. If I could convert even a small percentage of them, I would be rolling in cash.

One lead caught my eye. It was a property in Del City (a suburb on the east side of Oklahoma City), and it was a frame house with three bedrooms, one bathroom, and a sweet price of $20,000. Everything looked legit when I walked the property with the investor who had access to the house. I thought he knew what he was doing because I had closed on a property with him not long before this deal.

"I want to buy it. Let's put it under contract and get it done," I told him.

He looked me in the eye and said, "I need earnest money."

"No problem. How much, and who do I make it out to?"

"$500, and make it out to me."

I had second thoughts when he told me to make the check to him. But I'd done business with him before and had even met his family when I went to a cookout at his house. I wasn't worried that he would rip me off. I wrote the check and signed the contract. After ten days or so I called the guy and asked when we were closing.

"I'm having some troubles with the contract, and the guy doesn't want to sell anymore," he told me. "And the guy who was giving me all my leads started jamming me up, and then he quit that job."

"Is the deal going to go through?" I couldn't believe this simple deal was starting to fall apart.

"It's under contract with someone else, and you can't buy it," he finally admitted.

"Sorry to hear about your troubles, but when can I get my earnest money back?" I wasn't about to take another $500 loss when I hadn't done anything wrong.

He was a little withdrawn when he told me, "I'll get it to you when I can." I pushed him a little bit, and he finally informed me he'd spent the money on himself, and I was SOL. So that was the end of the deal. I trusted this guy, bought into the hype of him being a big-shot investor, and now I was screwed.

I tried to stay in touch with him so I could get my money, but he disappeared without a trace. I sent him e-mails but got no response, and I never heard from him again. I called his mobile number, but it was disconnected. I considered showing up at his door, but the truth is I was a fool and got taken for a ride.

I learned a valuable lesson. Always write your earnest money check to the title company or to a reputable real estate broker.

Are We Friends? My Mistake

Friends are important and necessary for survival in our dog-eat-dog world. But in the game of real estate, the words "I know this guy" can come back to haunt you.

After my wife and I had our second child and our first child turned three years old, we were searching for a home in a specific school district. I play in a weekly basketball league, and one of the guys I've played with for two years was constantly approaching me and asking about real estate. He was a retail Realtor and knew I was an investor.

"How's the market, and what's going on in the retail market of buying and selling?" was my usual question when I saw him.

"It's okay. It's at the bottom of the cycle, and there are tons of deals and foreclosures out there."

After two months of hearing about the retail market, I gave in and asked if he would send me an e-mail about homes in the school district my wife and I were looking at. Every week at our basketball games my friend would ask if there were any homes we wanted to see.

We found two houses that were close to our budget, and to show my friend we were serious, we made appointments for viewings. But we didn't have any luck because the homes either had unusual layouts or the pricing didn't line up with our budget.

My friend lived in the very neighborhood we wanted to move to, and one day he called us and excitedly explained that the HOA had posted a message on its website about a house for sale. "Are you still interested in the neighborhood?"

"Absolutely." I was excited because this tiny neighborhood has only eighty-eight homes, and they don't often come up for sale. And if a house does go on the market, it sells quickly because it's in a very desirable place to live. I got even more excited because most of these homes were out of my price range, but we were in a buyer's market, and I thought I could pick up a deal. My wife and I had decided we wanted to live for ten years in the next home we bought.

My friend went over to the sellers' house and got the scoop on why they were selling. It turns out they were moving out of state. The home was in decent condition, but it had a shake cedar roof that was twenty years old, and it needed some updating. I used that in my negotiations and was willing to purchase the house in "as is" condition. After viewing the home twice, I asked my friend to make an offer. The sellers weren't willing to budge, and my friend wasn't used to selling retail homes that weren't move-in ready.

I thought, *I'm going to lose this deal if I don't write a long e-mail explaining the reason for the low offer and what needs to be done to the home.* I planned to write the e-mail and send it to my friend, the Realtor, who would pass it on to the sellers. The home was never listed, so my friend didn't have to share in any commissions. He asked for a $7,000 fee to handle the transaction, which we were happy to give him. In fact, the seller paid him the fee at closing.

I was excited because I knew the sellers were motivated to take my best and final offer. When I submitted my offer to my friend, I said, "If we get this deal, I'll give you my current home as an exclusive listing." I can't believe I told him that. I opened my mouth so wide that a cruise ship could have sailed through. I was struck by his salesmanship. He was very smooth and well versed in retail buying and selling, while I'm a blue-collar type straight to the core.

The sellers took our deal, and at the closing table my Realtor friend said he had a housewarming gift and would bring it by our house. I was a little touched and realized the retail buying world is night and day compared to the investor world, where we have to create lemonade out of lemons.

True to my word, I gave my friend an exclusive listing on our old house. Unfortunately, after closing on the new house, I've seen my friend only three times. And none of those has been at the new house. I saw him once when he had me sign a listing agreement at the gym where we play basketball, once when he took pictures of the interior of the house, and once more when he had the only showing.

My friend, an "expert retail Realtor," gave me the complete sales plan of getting my home sold with his creative ideas and tricks, including pricing it high at first and then dropping it to create the illusion of a motivated seller. The first thirty days he would text and call me, letting me know how hard he was working on selling it. After sixty days, I got a little worried that my friend was just sitting on the listing because I hadn't heard from him in several weeks. Ninety days into the agreement I asked him to give me an account of what marketing he'd done.

I got no response and started retracing my correspondence with him. I discovered all the things he promised but never delivered. To save a tree I'll just list some of the false promises. He said he would drop the price of the listing to create a buzz. It didn't happen. He said he was going to make flyers. It didn't happen. He said he would do marketing. It didn't happen, though he did pay $150 to an online listing service to come and take pictures. He said he would have an online presence. That didn't happen; he didn't even post it on Craigslist. He just listed it in the MLS and automatic listing web sites. He said he would do a mail-out to 500 homes within the area. That didn't happen. He said he would do comps. I never saw any or received any research on the value of the home, but he assured me his friend had sold a house one block north of ours for $72 a square foot. He told me our house would fetch that amount easily because it had been completely updated.

When I signed the listing agreement, he said he would scan the docs and send me a copy. That didn't happen until I requested a release of the listing agreement. Three months later, I finally received them. At the ninety-day mark, I asked him to release us from the listing agreement. He said no (it was much closer to "Hell no!"), because he'd done so much for the listing.

"Can you please show me or give me a detailed list of what you've done on my behalf?" I retorted.

He sent an e-mail saying, "I won't be sending an accounting of costs, time, or efforts over to you in e-mail." So I picked up the phone and called my friend and restated my request and demanded to be released from the agreement because he was unwilling to produce any proof of the service he said he rendered. He refused to release me from the contract.

This is crazy, I thought. I was a fool and believed this guy was my friend. What a mistake I made. As soon as I hung up, I called several Realtor friends and asked what I should do. Should I sue this guy? One of my true friends who's a Realtor (I should have given the listing to him) told me I should save my money and just wait until the listing agreement runs out.

You may know by now that I don't take no for an answer. I pressed harder and called this guy's broker. He was as smooth as glass and said he would oversee the listing, and ensured me that I would be taken care of. Nothing was ever done.

The lesson is, I got myself in a bind because I used a friend, and that made it difficult when things didn't go as promised. I made another mistake that limited my options when I signed an exclusive agreement.

What's Your Net?

I told you a little about this deal earlier. I was a part-time rookie investor doing my first real flip, and I was going through the pains of on-the-job training while attending school and running a business. My Realtor at the time boasted that he was a big-time investor who held seminars and boot camps for which he would charge a large lump sum. He also brought to my attention that he had a crew that did all his rehabs and flips and took care of his out-of-state investors as well. Another investor made a comment about my Realtor that struck me as peculiar: "It's a little odd for him to boast that he's an investor when he doesn't own any investment properties of his own."

I blew off that remark, thinking the Realtor was an active investor at one time and the person making the comment was surely mistaken. I found a great property on my own and handled everything through trial and error. But I got tired of failing and guessing what to do next, so I turned to the Realtor who had all the right things to say. I confided in him and explained I needed to sell the property because it was eating me up and I was in way over my head.

He was smooth and bragged about the house around the corner he sold to an investor. The Realtor told me the investor flipped it and that he handled that listing as well. My emotions started running wild, and I wanted to flip my house and hit a home run like the other investor had. I got reeled in without checking the accuracy of his story.

One thing that frustrates me about Realtors is that when you ask how much you should list a property for, they answer with the same question. "What do you want?" When the Realtor asked me what I wanted for my house, I should have said, "I want the most money possible." That should be a common theme when you're flipping a property for profit. But I didn't know what the house was worth, so I said, "I don't know. Can you pull some comps and let me know what to list it for, since you'll be handling the listing?"

A few days later he told me I should list it for $110,000, and that sounded like a nice round number to me. I was confident I was going to have a big payday from my first flip.

After there was no action for ninety days, he didn't know why it hadn't sold, and of course I didn't know either because I had no experience. We decided to drop the price to $98,000 to attract more buyers. Only one buyer came along, and my Realtor asked what I needed to net on the property.

"$87,000 is what I'll have in it after I pay you." A week later we had it under contract for $87,000. That must have been a magical number. I wonder how the buyer came up with that specific amount.

I learned to add my profit into my net amount. Your Realtor may be chummy, but don't forget his motive is to get paid. Everyone wants to get paid well, especially in his field of expertise.

My Stuff Is in Storage

I was puffed up like a hot air balloon after I bought my first package deal and was ready to take on the vacant house that came with one of the properties. (This deal is also one I've mentioned earlier.) The house had been vacant for more than five years, and it needed extensive rehab to make it livable. Every window was boarded up, there was graffiti throughout the first floor, and the kitchen was missing so much flooring you could see the ground underneath. The project was basically a shell that needed everything inside and out.

I had two guys working on the rehab. One of them was a lovable, overstuffed teddy bear who could move a mountain with his bare hands. The other was my trusted handyman who led the assault and made sure everything got done, or so I hoped.

Like we do for every project, we had a plan and tried to stick to it, but plans tend to fall apart along the way. My goal for the project was to be completely hands-off and let my handyman lead and make all the decisions, including purchasing the material we needed as the project progressed. I focused my entrepreneurial skills on finding more deals.

The guys started off strong but lost steam during the process. This was caused by many factors, but the main one was that I kept pulling one of the guys off the job to attend to issues on other properties. After owning the property for several months without collecting a penny of rent and watching my holding costs rise, I figured out that having both guys on the job would keep the ball rolling much faster than trying to keep costs down by letting only one person work on it. To motivate the guys to finish the job as quickly as possible, I decided to advertise the property as rent-ready.

Within a week a tenant fell in love with our two-story masterpiece and I had her deposit in hand. Before I accepted her money, I asked my handyman when the property would be ready. He assured me they had only three weeks left on the inside and they could address the outside and the siding shortly thereafter. I told the new tenant it would be ready in four weeks (giving my crew a week of grace), and she told me her stuff was in storage. She wasn't excited about having to pay the extra fees while she waited for us to get her house ready.

"I'm sorry, but that's the earliest I can let you move in," I told her. I took her deposit and went back to my little world. Three weeks passed, and I checked in on the guys. I was dumbfounded at how slow the process was going.

I jumped all over the handyman and started firing questions like an automatic weapon at a gun range. "What's going on here? What's taking so long? Do you have any idea what's going to happen with the new tenant?" I was livid and didn't know what to tell the woman who was counting on us to provide her a place to live in a week.

After my blood pressure went back to normal, I thought about what my next move should be. I came up with two options. First, I would apologize and refund her deposit plus pay a month of her storage bill and send her on her way. The second option was for us to pay her storage bill while she gave us another month to finish the property to her expectations. Ms. Storage chose the second option.

Another three weeks flew by, and I checked on the progress of the house. It was livable, but there had been many more delays with the heating and cooling contractor and these set the project back another two weeks. Pulling an electrical permit took a week, and a long list of other issues slowed the project to a crawl and burned time and money.

Ms. Storage actually had moved some stuff into the home without my knowledge, and when I found out, I asked my handyman about it. He explained he felt bad about the situation and didn't think it was big deal. She was storing some boxes in one of the rooms that had been completed, and she was going to be moving in anyway, so he didn't see a problem with it.

I was at a loss for words and didn't know what to do. I had to put on my big boy panties and handle the stress I felt when confronted by an aggressive woman who was on a mission to move in *immediately*. My handyman and I had a powwow, and we decided to let her move in, but made it clear we needed to finish while she was living there. She was thankful and was more than hospitable. She understood the construction world because her boyfriend worked in the field a time or two.

I took her much-needed rent money and agreed to give her a discount to cover her storage bill. I was stunned to find out it was over $100. I pulled my handyman aside (he'd been handling most of the interaction with the new tenant) and told him $50 was the limit we were going to spend. I looked him in the eyes and told him, "I just got stung paying for an agreement I wasn't privy to. It's not going to happen again."

That was the tipping point, and I quickly found myself stuck between two people who were complaining that they'd both been cheated. I had to stop this train wreck before there was any more damage. I drilled the handyman and wanted to know what he'd promised Ms. Storage. He came unglued and blurted that Ms. Storage had hustled him.

"You mean she hustled *me,* because I'm the one paying for all these mistakes," I rudely interrupted. "You're still collecting a paycheck, and you're making decisions that leave me holding the bag."

He said he would make it right with Ms. Storage and offered her a rent reduction for any further delay. He said he would cover it out of his pay.

Now we're talking, I thought. I respected the gesture and the act of restitution, but the amount covered only 10 percent of what I'd lost. The handyman came up with the idea to offer Ms. Storage a rent reduction of $50 for each month the rehab wasn't complete to her satisfaction.

I was free to go on with my other projects. "Do it and keep me in the loop," I told him.

As you've probably guessed, another four weeks flew by and the house wasn't done. By that point, the guys had even helped the tenant move all her stuff out of storage. And they did it while they were on the clock for me.

This rehab was getting out of control, and the only benefactors were the new tenant and my handyman. For six months, the new tenant got a rent reduction of $50 a month, and the amount had become cumulative. By the time the rehab was done she was paying only $300 a month for rent and the handyman had to pay $400.

Anthony Robbins once wrote, "We are motivated by pain or pleasure." The handyman had been motivated not by the pleasure of finishing the job, but by pain. It was too painful for him to deal with Ms. Storage, so he paid for it out of his pocket instead of taking care of minor issues, such as putting up door trim.

I could write a book on this rehab and what I learned and what I should never do again. Here's the short list: Never, I mean *never*, let a tenant move before the rehab on a property is complete. The liability and backlash aren't worth any amount of money. Timing is a major factor in many projects. The right project at the wrong time can burn up a lot of cash and time. Don't overlap rehabs if you don't have adequate staff in place to get all the jobs done. Get serious about your business, and visit the job site daily even if you don't think you need to. Your presence on the property keeps your guys motivated.

When a future tenant is in a hurry, it's never a good sign. Don't feel like you have to accommodate them if it doesn't work for you. You're the landlord. You, and no one else, are in control of your property. Taking orders from a tenant is ludicrous, and complying is even more foolhardy. Communication is the mother of all success. It's imperative for you and your partners to be on the same page in all aspects of your life, whether it's real estate, marriage, or making sure the trim is painted on time.

* * *

So that's my story. There's nothing special about me. I don't have a lot of fancy degrees, and I don't have a family that wrote checks, opened doors, or called the "right" people. I started with zero, but I didn't let that define me. I used it as motivation to build a better future for myself and my family.

For better or worse, now you know where I came from and how I built my portfolio. Of course, there were many successes I chose not to include in this book, mostly because I knew my failures would teach you more. Review the road map I've given you, and you won't drive off the same cliffs I did.

Now it's time to fast-track your investment career by learning more about the practical side of real estate. The next part of the book gives you detailed tips and advice on how to succeed as an investor.

Part Three

100 Tips for the Savvy Landlord

*Even if you fall on your face,
you're still moving forward.*

Victor Kiam

Hundreds of tenants have lived in my properties, and I've spoken to dozens of other investors who have had hundreds or even thousands of tenants. If you ask us about being a landlord, you'll hear a recurring theme: *Because you're dealing with people, you're going to have problems.* None of the people you deal with will be perfect, and you shouldn't expect to run a business without having problems from time to time.

With a little planning, however, you can reduce the number of problems you encounter and minimize the amount of trouble you face.

The following list is about dealing with the problems common to all landlords, problems you're certain to face at one time or another. The vast majority of people you'll deal with are honest people who do their best to pay their rent on time and be good tenants, and the items on this list were not created with them in mind. This list is to protect you from the small percentage of people who lie, cheat, and steal every chance they can. Use this list to protect yourself, your family, and your good tenants.

1. Treat your properties like a business. You're investing in real estate to make money. You're not in it to make friends, become popular, or to have people think you're important. If you treat it like a hobby, your bank account will never grow like it should. Treat your investments as a business, or you'll soon have to find another way to make money.

That being said, you should always be polite and professional with your tenants. They're human beings and deserve respect. But remember that your relationship with them is a professional one. If you treat your tenants as if their only purpose is to pay rent each month, you'll come off as greedy and uncaring. It won't take long before this reputation starts costing you business. You have to avoid being a doormat, but don't treat tenants like ATMs.

2. Before you consider buying your first property, find an attorney and an accountant who are experienced with landlord-tenant issues. Don't do anything until they advise you on what type of business structure you should create.

The business structure you need will vary depending on your situation and your state's laws. Some people will benefit by using an LLC; others will need to set up a corporation. But never operate your rental business without some type of legal entity that will protect you from liability. The stakes are too high.

3. Take your time and find reputable accountants and lawyers. Steer clear of the national chains that offer tax preparation services at a discount. Places like that serve a purpose, but in my experience they don't have the expertise you need to build a multimillion-dollar real estate business.

And don't try to do your taxes or create your business entity yourself. A good attorney and accountant will pay for themselves several times over. Plus, they have the advantage of keeping up on the latest changes to laws and regulations. Do you know if there were any changes to the allowable deductions or depreciation schedules that will impact your business this year? Probably not, but your accountant will. Hire experienced experts in these areas, and you'll sleep easier at night.

4. Due diligence always pays off. Regardless of whether you're selecting an attorney, buying a property, or qualifying a tenant, you'll never go wrong by being thorough. If things go wrong and you didn't take the time to make a call that could have uncovered a problem, you'll always be left with the feeling you could have done more. Take the extra step, and you'll be surprised how many problems you can avoid.

5. Before you buy your first property, select online software to manage your properties. There are several of these, such as Buildium, Propertyware, and RentTracker. It may sound premature to start using management software when you have only one or two properties, but if you start using this early in your business, it will help your company grow. And you'll build good habits that will make life much easier when you have forty, fifty, or three hundred properties.

6. Have a goal and a plan. This may sound simple, but if you don't start off with an idea of where you want to go, you'll never arrive at the place you want to be. I've talked to a lot of people who invest in real estate, and I'm amazed at how many of them seem to be floating through the process with no plan.

Take time to sit down and list your goals. What do you hope to achieve by investing in real estate? Do you want to buy houses and flip them (quickly reselling them for a profit)? Are you hoping to build residual income by owning multiple rental properties? Whatever your situation, have a clear understanding of what you want and how you're going to achieve it. If you want to go to Florida, you wouldn't drive off in the middle of the night without a map while wearing a blindfold.

Remember to be flexible, even when you have a plan. You may encounter a great opportunity you hadn't considered when you started investing, and you want to take advantage of it when you have the chance. And you'll learn lessons along the way that will help you do things better. Don't lock yourself in so tightly that you have no flexibility.

7. Join your local real estate investment association (REIA). You'll have the chance to network with other real estate investors. REIAs are great places to get information regarding investments and trends, and hopefully you can find a mentor for advice and support.

8. Before you buy your first property, select a business insurance agent. Again, you want to find a professional who's experienced with insuring investment properties. You may have a great agent who gets you a good deal on your car or home insurance, but that doesn't mean he should help you with your business policies. It may take you a while to find the right agent, but your effort will be worth it in the long run.

9. Shop your insurance every three years and compare quotes. You'll be surprised how much you can save by periodically reviewing your coverage and what it's costing you. We use Shelter, Allstate, and American Modern for our insurance. I routinely check to make sure I'm not paying more than I have to, and so should you.

10. Don't get married to any property. Good deals will come and go. Let the skinny deals slide. If you get stuck on the idea of "having" to own a particular piece of real estate, you'll lose sight of the big picture, and you may end up making a deal you'll regret in the morning.

11. Have your attorney review or draft your lease agreement. Make sure it's legal and binding. If your lease isn't binding, you may not be able to legally collect rent, and that's a problem you don't want to have.

12. Focus on niche markets. For example, you can build your investments around blue collar rentals, Section 8 properties, or rent-to-own. By placing all your energy on one type of property, you'll become an expert. This will make your life much easier than spending your time and resources trying to understand the rules and regulations that cover different types of properties.

13. Set up an emergency fund. A good rule of thumb is to set aside six months of mortgage payments for each property. Even with the best planning, you'll encounter challenges. Your life will never be problem-free. But if you plan ahead, you can reduce your stress by knowing your mortgage payments are covered for the next six months, even if you aren't able to rent your property.

There are many things that happen beyond our control. As you know, economies across the world have slowed in the last few years, with many people losing their jobs and unable to afford their homes. Many landlords suddenly found themselves with empty properties through no fault of their own.

Plan ahead and protect yourself by having enough cash on hand to cover any unforeseen problems.

14. Understand the true value of your property. Make sure you know the monthly rental rates of properties similar to yours. Keep your rental price $10 cheaper than your competition. It may not seem like much, but to some people $10 a month is the difference between renting your property or someone else's. Would you be willing to give up $120 a year to make sure one of your houses is rented?

There's another important reason to know what your competition is charging. You may not be charging enough. You need to know if similar properties are charging hundreds of dollars more a month. That's serious money, and you don't want to leave that on the table.

15. Make sure you understand laws prohibiting discrimination. You'll be dealing with people from all walks of life as a property owner, and if you have trouble working with any of them, you should probably look for another way to make money. We live in a very diverse culture, and you don't want to do something that's misinterpreted or that inadvertently offends someone because of cultural differences. Again, this is an area where a good attorney is worth his weight in gold.

16. Round your monthly rates down to the nearest five dollars. If your property is worth $800 per month, round it down to $795. There's something magical about those $5. To some people, there's a huge difference between $795 and $800. And $995 sounds much less expensive than $1,000. The point is to get qualified, reliable, honest people in your properties, and that's worth much more than $60 a year.

17. Don't rent to someone who knows more about landlord-tenant law than you do. If you're talking to a prospective renter and she casually mentions a specific part of the law governing landlords and tenants, run (don't walk) to the nearest exit. It's a giant red flag when someone knows that much about landlord-tenant law. That person will be a problem, and the headaches she causes will not be worth any amount of money she pays you. Be patient, and a better tenant will come along.

18. Be careful about renting to people who bad-mouth their previous landlord. Bad landlords are out there, but there are two sides to every story. How a potential renter speaks about his current or pervious landlord is a statement of how he'll talk about you. Do you want to do business with someone who talks negatively or gossips about you? Again, this is a red flag. Listen to your gut, and rent to someone else.

19. Make sure a new tenant has the utilities turned on in his name before you hand him the keys. And make sure he gives you proof. If someone's not able to have the utilities turned on in his name, that's a sign of a bigger problem. Utility companies have deep pockets and access to lots of credit information. Let them work for you, and don't let anyone in your property until he has been approved by the local utility companies. The last thing you want is to have your pipes burst in the dead of winter because a tenant couldn't have the electricity turned on.

20. Take a picture of every new tenant when he signs his lease. This may seem silly if you have only one or two properties, but as your business grows, it will be harder and harder to remember faces. If you have a picture attached to each lease, you know who's entitled to be on your property and who isn't. If there's ever a dispute, having that picture can save you a lot of headaches.

21. Before you buy a property, ask the postal carrier what she thinks about the neighborhood. Mail carriers are a great resource. They become familiar with who lives in a neighborhood and what goes on there. They know if someone doesn't care for his property or if he lets his dogs run wild. Carriers know if they would want to live in the neighborhood. And they're very friendly and helpful. You can learn a lot by investing a few moments of your time to talk to one of them.

22. Before you agree to lease one of your properties to someone, drive by his current home to see how he lives. Is the lawn mowed? Are rusted-out cars sitting on blocks in the middle of the front yard?

Are the porches covered by piles of trash? You can learn a lot about a person by driving by the address he lists on his application. And it takes only a few minutes.

23. Always photocopy a prospect's identification when you accept his application. If you get in that habit, you can prove who you talked to if you ever have to take legal action against him.

24. Always run a credit check on prospective tenants. Do this even if he has explained he has credit problems (due to a divorce or health issues) and you have a good feeling about him. Sometimes, his credit won't be as bad as he thinks, which will be a comfort to both of you. And if it's worse than either one of you thought, it's better to know that up front than later on.

25. Request recent paycheck stubs from a current employer as part of your application process. Make sure your prospects are telling you the truth about where they work, and verify that they can afford to pay their rent.

26. Use Landlord Locks (landlordlocks.com) for all your keys and locks. When you become a landlord, you'll use more locks than you could have imagined. When you buy a property or lease it to a new tenant, you'll need to change the locks. Landlord Locks is a great company that will make your life much easier. They're easy to deal with and have great prices.

27. Always have a written agreement with contractors who work on your properties. The agreement doesn't have to be complicated. A one-page agreement will do if it covers the details of what you're paying for. Always outline when payment will be made; you don't want a contractor coming around every Friday asking you for money when you agreed to pay him when he completed the project. You can solve this problem by putting your agreement in writing.

28. Some deals are too good to be true. Every once in a while, a prospective tenant will call you about a property and tell you he needs to move in immediately. He'll have cash in hand (literally) and wave the bills in front of you. It will be very tempting, but don't rent to these people. It's always a red flag when someone has to find a place to live on such short notice. If you rent to him, you may get a quick payday, but it will never be worth the trouble he causes you in the long run. Trust me, I know.

29. Protect yourself from crime. When you rent to people, you're bound to come across a few bad apples. Most of your tenants will be honest, hard-working people who'll pay their rent on time and won't cause problems. But a few will lie, cheat, and steal at every turn and take advantage of anyone they can. Protect yourself by taking small steps, such as bolting down the refrigerator and stove, to make sure a few bad tenants don't destroy your business.

30. Create a welcome pack to give to new residents. It doesn't have to be fancy, but if you give your new tenants a professional-looking packet that includes information such as addresses and phone numbers for the local utility and telephone companies, it will create a lot of goodwill. You might even include information such as when the trash is picked up, or who to call when something goes wrong. They'll appreciate anything you can do to make their lives simpler. Moving is always stressful, and even the smallest gesture will leave a lasting impression on your tenants.

31. Put lock boxes on your available homes. This is a great way to leverage your time and allows Realtors and contractors to have access. You can even let prospective tenants see the property themselves while you're working on other projects. You won't have to run across town every time someone wants to look at one of your properties.

32. Avoid showing a property until it's ready to be rented. You may have the perfect property for a prospective tenant, but if you show it before it's painted or the carpet is replaced, you'll lose the chance to make a great first impression. And you might not get a second chance.

33. When you enter a home to make a repair, always leave a note explaining what you did if the tenant isn't there. This is a great way to document what you did, and it also lets the tenant know you were in the house and why. People can tell when someone has entered their space, and you don't want them to think there's anything strange going on. You'll never regret going the extra mile and documenting every time you need to enter one of your properties. It's also a good practice to give tenants twenty-four hours' notice before you enter their property.

34. Videotape your move-in inspections. This allows you to make sure your property is in perfect shape and protects you from any allegations that things were not as they should have been. Video cameras and memory cards have become so inexpensive that there's no reason to not record your inspections. Take advantage of this technology and record your tenants inspecting your property.

35. When you have your prelease meeting, be sure to cover the subject of eviction and how it affects your tenants. You don't want to dwell on the negative, but you do want your tenants to understand what happens if they don't pay their rent. Leasing a place to live is an important commitment, and you want to be sure everyone's on the same page.

36. Document everything when you talk to a tenant, and follow up with a confirmation letter. This is especially important when you find yourself dealing with a situation where a tenant isn't living up to his end of the contract, such as when he fails to pay rent or cut the grass.

37. Know the difference between "repairing" property and "rehabbing" property. It may not seem like much to you, but from a tax standpoint, the difference can save you thousands of dollars. Repairs (also called "maintenance") are treated as expenses, but rehabbing is treated as a capital improvement. Generally, you can deduct expenses immediately, but a capital improvement will have to be depreciated over the life of the asset. If you've hired an attorney and accountant who are experienced in real estate investing, they should be able to steer you clear of any problems in this area.

38. If you need to inspect a property, tell the tenant it's for insurance purposes. There are many reasons you need to document the condition of your property, such as when you're having it appraised. Of course, you shouldn't just show up one day. You'll need to give the tenant notice and at least a few hours warning, but it's a good way to get in the house and make sure your property is being treated the way it should be.

39. If you allow pets, always charge a nonrefundable pet deposit of at least $200 per animal. Not everyone likes animals, and you don't want to lose a potential tenant because your property smells like the previous tenant's dog. It will take some effort to clean up after pets move out, and you need to make sure you charge a deposit that's high enough to cover your expenses.

40. If you do allow pets, never allow dogs larger than fifty pounds. Large animals inflict more wear and tear on your property, and there's no deposit high enough to make it worth your while.

41. Be creative when it comes to offering specials to attract new tenants. If you offer a free month's rent when a tenant signs a two-year lease, it comes out to about a 4 percent discount. Prices on flat-screen TVs have plummeted, and it doesn't cost more than one month's rent to give one to a new tenant. You have many options, and the only limit is your creativity.

42. If you have any doubts about a tenant, don't hesitate to ask for a cosigner. You would rather ask questions at the start of a lease and risk losing a tenant than have the deal fall apart three months into a two-year lease. It's easier to find a different tenant than it is to dig out from a bad deal you could have easily prevented.

43. Rent appliances to your tenants to make extra income. You'll probably wind up with an extra refrigerator or two as you increase the number of properties you own. Put them to use by renting them to tenants who would be renting them from somebody else anyway.

44. When buying multifamily units, make sure the utilities are separated. Each unit needs to have individual meters. If not, you may be responsible for all the utilities. You don't want to have to pay for something if you can easily avoid it by making sure each unit has its own utilities.

45. You can't go wrong renting homes in a good school district. People will flock to houses where their children can get a good education. Take this into account when you start buying properties.

46. Prequalify tenants with two simple questions. Before you get in your car to meet a new prospect, ask, "When do you need to move in?" and, "Have you driven by the home?" You'll learn a lot by listening to the answers. If they don't know when they want to move in or they need to do it immediately, this can signal a problem. And if they haven't seen the property yet, you may be better off waiting until they've inspected the property by themselves.

47. Paint the interiors of your properties neutral colors. We paint interior walls brown or a light coffee, and we paint the trim white. It's much easier to rent property that matches most people's furniture than a house with purple walls and black trim.

48. Contact the people who live around your property to see if they know someone who would like to live there. How many people would like to live near their best friend? You could send out a flier saying, "Do you want to live next to your friend? 1215 NW 15th is available, so call your friends and let them know."

49. Be proactive in pursuing properties you're interested in owning. If you see a rental property you would like to buy, don't hesitate to call the number listed on the rent sign and ask the owner if the property is for sale. The worst they can say is no. If they say yes, you may wind up with a great new property.

50. Use vivid and colorful words to describe your properties. Instead of saying, "three-bed, two-bath house for rent," say, "Great brick home in Edmond Schools is available." Use every opportunity to create a picture that makes prospects jump at the chance to rent the home you're offering. Of course, you always want to be accurate in your descriptions.

51. Laminate floors can be cheaper than carpet. When I rehabbed one of my houses, I wasn't sure if it was better to put in laminate floors or carpet, so I did a little research. What I discovered surprised me. It turns out that laminate floors are cheaper to install, last longer, and don't cost as much to maintain as carpets. It's a no-brainer. Whenever we buy a new house, we never put in carpets. We use only laminate floors, and every time I look at one I see money jumping into my bank account.

52. Carry a carbonless notebook in your vehicle. When you're dealing with contractors in the field, you can write your own bid and will have a written record of your offer.

53. Carry a purchase contract in your vehicle. You never know when you can make an offer. I lost at least one sweet property because I didn't have a purchase contract with me. The seller went home and consulted with a broker. By the time I met with the seller the next day, the broker had purchased the property from under me. That will never happen again.

54. Carry a digital camera with you. Take pictures of houses you're looking at, any ideas that inspire you, and any work that's being done on your properties. Pictures really are worth a thousand words.

55. Use Craigslist to find quick day labor. You'll be amazed at how many people want to work.

56. Hand-deliver your financial statement to your banker before he asks for it. Whenever you ask for a loan, you know you'll have to give your banker professional, complete, and accurate financial documents. Have those done when you start the process. It makes a great impression on your bank.

57. Keep your bank involved with the status of your projects. Send them pictures and e-mails detailing your progress. And invite your banker to a showing when the property is ready to be rented.

58. Go to lunch once a quarter with your banker. Nothing beats having face-to-face contact with your bank. It's easy to assume that bankers care only about numbers. But bankers are people, and they'll appreciate getting to know you as a person.

59. Surprise your handyman by bringing him a cold drink or a cup of coffee. Being a handyman must be a hard job. We usually don't need them unless something's broken and needs to be fixed immediately. If they don't get the job done quickly and properly the first time, tenants are sure to let them know. And they often have to work outside in unpleasant temperatures. Show the people who work for you how much you appreciate their effort by giving them a refreshing beverage.

60. Pay your contractors as soon as the job is done, even if it's inconvenient for you. Admit it: you like it when people pay you quickly. It makes you feel valued and important. When people slow-pay you, you never want to do business with them again. Your contractors feel the same way. If you pay them as soon as they complete their jobs, they feel appreciated and will answer the phone when you call them. If you don't pay people on time, you can bet they'll find other people to work for. Plus, if a contractor does a lousy job for you, paying him quickly means you get him out of your life sooner.

61. Use a car wash to clean out a dirty fridge. You'll see a lot of dirty refrigerators, some of which will be filthy. It can take hours to scrub them clean. A great tip is to load up dirty refrigerators in the back of a pickup and use a car wash to get rid of the grime. It doesn't take much time, and you'll be shocked at how clean they'll be when you're done.

62. Use the same paint for the ceilings, walls, and trim in every house you own. Make sure you save the UPC codes and buy it from the same supplier. Using neutral colors will appeal to most people, and if you use the same paint in every house you won't need multiple cans. If you have to do touch-up or repaint, you know which cans to grab. It will make your life much easier.

63. View property you want to purchase at night to gain a different perspective. The neighborhood will look much different when the neighbors come home. It's a great way to gain insight about the people who are going to live next to your investment.

64. Go with your gut. If you're apprehensive about a tenant, there's usually a reason. If you have any concerns, call the utility company and see if the tenant is current on his bill. Also make sure the utilities are in your tenant's name. A new trend is for people to not pay their utilities, move to another place, and put all the bills in someone else's name.

65. Use Google Voice as your main phone number. Google Voice is a great service that gives you control over your phone number. And never, ever give out your personal number. You'll never stop answering calls.

66. Buy a professionally made "For Lease" sign and flyer box. You want to make a great first impression. Don't risk losing a good tenant because your sign looks like a child scribbled it with crayons. Have some flyers made and keep them in a box next to the sign. Your job is to make it as easy as possible for people to rent from you. Don't give them any reason to look for another property.

67. Stage your homes (or hire a staging company) to attract the right clientele. Again, you want to create the best possibility for success. I've used a professional staging company, and it was worth every penny.

68. Encourage tenants to purchase renter's insurance, or buy it for them. Renter's insurance is fairly cheap (some policies are only $12 a month), and it can save you and your tenants a lot of headaches. Most people will probably never need it, but when you do it's worth its weight in gold.

69. Keep a few flyers from lawn care companies in your car. If your tenant isn't maintaining the yard in accordance to his lease, this can be a gentle reminder. You don't want any of your neighbors to get upset at the appearance of your properties, and you don't want to get any notices from the city threatening to make you pay a "weed tax."

70. Drive by your investments on a regular basis to inspect them. I take a shortcut to my office that takes me by several of our properties. This is a great way to stop small problems from becoming big ones.

71. Allow your tenants to make deposits and pay rent via automatic drafts. This makes it easier for both of you. Your tenants won't have to write a check and send it to you, and you won't have to collect checks and deposit them. It removes one more step from your ladder to success.

72. Use a furniture rental store to stage your properties. You want to make a great first impression when you get ready to lease a property. Give yourself the best chance for success by renting new, clean furniture when you have a showing.

73. Get a contractor lien waiver when you pay a contractor. Your contractors shouldn't receive a check until they sign a lien waiver, which will protect you if things go sideways in the future. You don't want an unethical contractor slapping an unwarranted lien on your property after you've paid him.

74. When you begin your career, always run your deals by an experienced investor. I ran almost every one of my deals through an experienced investor for the first eight years I was in the business, and I still take my mentors out to lunch when I do a big deal.

75. Don't exchange handyman services for rent. Eventually, one of your tenants will ask to do some maintenance (such as painting or tile work) in exchange for a reduction in rent. When someone asks me that, I say, "Yes, and Merry Christmas." They look at me like I'm crazy, and I tell them the rent reduction will apply only to the December rent. This almost always stops the conversation. I've never had anyone take me up on my offer. It can put you in a bad position if they don't do the work or if the work is shoddy. Don't barter services for rent. You'll regret it. Trust me.

76. Get your pest control license. It doesn't take much to do this, and when you're licensed you can buy and use the same chemicals as a professional exterminator. This is an easy way to save a ton of cash.

77. Order supplies from suppliers that offer pick-and-pull services. This is a great time-saver. I place an order online (usually at Lowes.com), and when I drive over my order is on the cart and ready for loading. I don't want to waste time strolling the aisles looking for things when the store's employees will do this for me.

78. Take advantage of free online services, such as Craigslist. These are great places to find tenants, workers, used appliances, and staging furniture. You'll be amazed at what you can find on these sites.

79. Offer deadbeat tenants $100 to move out. Cash can be a great motivator, and this can save you in the long run. If you have to evict them, it's going to cost you more than $100, so don't be afraid to solve the problem early by paying them to leave.

80. Include a mold addendum in your lease. This should include a statement that you have no notice or knowledge of any mold on the premises and that you've never occupied the property.

81. Be tough and matter-of-fact when you review the lease with your tenants. Be clear and tell them what will happen if they don't pay the rent on time. Make it personal. Tell them you're not going to lose your job because they didn't live up to their end of the bargain.

82. Include a self-addressed envelope with your invoices. We include one with every month's rent statement, and about 50 percent of our tenants use them to mail the rent or to drop it off at our office. It's another way to make it easier for your tenants to pay.

83. Make copies of rent checks. I make copies of the rent checks I receive from my tenants and keep them in the tenant's file. I make note of any changes to telephone numbers or names. If I ever have to collect a judgment, having the banking information can be very useful.

84. If you have to evict a tenant, use a collection agency to recoup any money he owes you. Collection agencies have an unbelievable amount of resources at their disposal. Take advantage of that by hiring them to collect on your behalf. Don't waste any more of your time trying to get money out of a deadbeat. Turn it over to a collection agency, and move on to bigger and better things.

85. Use Shoeboxed.com to keep track of your receipts and to prepare your taxes. With programs like Shoeboxed, you can scan in your receipts, and the software puts them in a spreadsheet. When it's time to meet with your accountant, all your information is organized and ready to go. If you ever need to find something, it's as easy as typing a few letters into a search bar.

86. Don't be lazy when you inspect property. Make sure you look in the attic and underneath the house to see if anything's out of place, or if there are any holes, questionable wiring, or missing or broken pipes. You should also make sure there haven't been any funky or shady repairs.

87. Always negotiate with contractors and suppliers. Save money wherever you can. And remember these seven magic words: "Is that the best you can do?" Every penny matters.

88. Remember the Rule of 20 Percent. Calculate your financial statements with a 20 percent vacancy rate. It can be tempting to project your income at full occupancy, but be realistic. You won't always have every one of your properties rented. Apply this principle to construction projects and rehabs, and assume you're going to pay 20 percent more than your budget. You should also use this rule when you hire laborers or purchase paint and lightbulbs. When you become seasoned, you can lower this to 10 percent, but always factor in a cushion.

89. When it's time to evict someone, get it over with. Don't delay the process. Evicting someone is like taking off a bandage. Just yank it off and be done with it. Evictions are controlled by a tight timeline, and if you wait to evict someone, you're only delaying getting a new tenant in your property. And that means delaying cash flow, which is never good.

90. Enforce all lease terms from day one. Whether it's a small point, such as cutting the grass, or a major point like having additional people live in your property, let your tenants know you won't put up with them violating the lease. If you let one tenant get away with violating one term, it won't be long before other tenants are seeing what they can get away with. Save yourself time and trouble by stopping this before it starts.

91. Start a paper trail. It's essential that you keep written documentation of your interactions with tenants in the event you ever need to take them to court. Make notes of your conversations, and keep copies of e-mails, voice mails, and text messages to support your allegations.

92. Shop at your local Habitat for Humanity store. You can find great deals on painting supplies, tile, and used appliances. Plus, you support a great organization that helps deserving families buy homes.

93. Work with a good investor Realtor to find prospective tenants and to show properties. Make sure the Realtor understands what investors need, and that he or she has worked with investors before.

94. Don't invest in a property just because it seems cheap or you think it's a steal. Only buy property when it fits your investment strategy and meets your long-term goals. Buying property based on price alone is a guaranteed way to make a mistake.

95. Focus on cash flow, not equity appreciation. Equity appreciation can be an important part of your investment strategy, but you can't feed your family with what a property will be worth in the future. You need cash flow today, and that's how you should structure each and every deal.

96. If you have to evict someone, don't prepay the process server. Don't deliver the check until the paperwork has been served. You want the server to be motivated to get his job done, and the best way to do that is to pay after the papers have been delivered.

97. Convert your IRA to a self-directed IRA and purchase property in your account. This is a great way to prepare for retirement and to build your portfolio. Check with your accountant before you make this change, but many people are able to use this technique to build their empire.

98. Have a plan in place for when a tenant gives you a thirty-day notice. Eventually someone will move out of your property, and you need to know what to do when this happens. At the very least, you should mail him a letter explaining when you'll return his deposit. Two weeks before the tenant moves out, you should send a flyer detailing any repairs that will have to be made and how much they'll cost. The week before he moves out, call and remind the tenant of his move-out date and encourage him to have the property in tip-top shape.

99. Charge a lock-out fee. If a tenant calls you and tells you he's locked out of his house, remind him you charge $25 dollars to let him back in (and make sure this is in your lease). If you offer it as a free service, you'll be amazed at how many times you'll have to crawl out of bed to unlock doors.

100. Make sure each property you purchase has at least $10,000 equity. You make (or lose) money on every deal the day you buy it.

If you don't run the numbers, or if you pay too much, you may never recoup your investment. Take your time, do it right, and build your empire.

PART FOUR

The Nuts and Bolts of Being an Investor— 52 Guidelines

Buy land; they've stopped making it.

Mark Twain

As we continue exploring the practical side of real estate investment, let's zero in on some nuts-and-bolts issues.

1. Real Reasons to Own Real Estate

You may still be deciding whether real estate is the right arena for you. Based on my experience, I don't think there's a better way to provide for your financial freedom and the security of your family than investing in real estate. It offers more long-term stability and more potential to make money than virtually any other investment—for several reasons:

Everyone has to have shelter, and there aren't many other products that qualify as necessities. According to recent census data, there are over 110 million households in the United States. That means you have 110 million potential customers who put your product at or near the top of their "must have" list. Not many industries can claim that. Owning rental property puts you in a unique position to tap into this enormous market.

Real estate value almost always appreciates, and it almost always does so at a rate higher than inflation. When you're invested in real estate, you can be confident that the odds of losing money are fairly low. Of course there's some risk, but not as much as there is in the stock market or other businesses you might be tempted to create.

Real estate is a tangible asset you can see and touch. When you invest in stocks or bonds, you really don't own anything; what you're actually buying is the reputation of the company and the hope that the business will continue to operate as it has in the past. But if you try to walk down to the corporate headquarters with your stock certificates and declare, "I own this building!" you'll probably get chased out. When you own rental property, you can reach out and touch your asset. It's not some abstract idea in a faraway place.

Real estate is a traditional asset, and banks are used to dealing with it. This means there are a broad variety of ways you can finance it. With other investments, if you don't have cash, you may not be able to get financing. Of course, even with stocks you can "buy on the margin," but if there's a margin call, you risk losing everything and could even wind up owing money. Traditional financing prevents this instability and allows you to build your portfolio easily.

Real estate provides income. If you've done your homework and invested wisely, your properties will create a stream of income you and your family can count on for years to come. As we've all seen in the last few years, the stock market can fluctuate wildly. One day your portfolio and its returns can be fat, and a few days later your circumstances can completely reverse. Real estate is a much more stable way to create a stream of income you can depend on.

2. Going Up? Reasons Property Values Increase

Economists and others have spent years trying to determine why property values increase. As you know, I don't have a college degree, and I don't read a lot of books on economic theory. But I can suggest a few reasons why you can almost always count on real property increasing in value—and they aren't as complicated as some might think.

The most important and powerful reason is supply and demand. No one has produced any new land for a long time, and, as far as I know, there won't be any more created in the near future. It's not like cars or hockey sticks where a manufacturer can increase output and guarantee more products will arrive at dealerships or stores. If you own property, you own something that can't be duplicated or replicated.

Another factor that impacts supply and demand is the location of your property. For example, in recent years, there has been a decline in the number of manufacturing jobs in the United States. Most of these jobs were traditionally in northern states. As these jobs dried up, the workers who held them had to relocate to other places to find work. There was a lower demand in those manufacturing towns, and home prices there dropped.

Inflation will impact investment property just like everything else. Over time, the price of rental property will slowly creep up, just like the price of oil, bread, and other staples. You've heard stories of people who reminisce about the good old days when a nickel would buy a loaf of bread or a movie ticket. You can barely buy anything for a nickel today; you have to get a lot of nickels together to do anything. A large part of the difference in the buying power of a nickel is due to the inflation that naturally happens in growing economies.

Some neighborhoods will become more popular, and this will also drive up the price of homes. This really has to do with supply and demand, but when you start investing in real estate, you'll notice that certain areas go through stages when it seems everyone wants to live there. These locations might be within well-respected school districts, and parents flock there for their children's sake. Some areas of town may just become trendier. In Oklahoma City, the trend for decades was to build homes on the outskirts of town so families could have larger lots and live in quiet areas; meanwhile he downtown area was largely ignored. But recently, the downtown area has received increasing attention, as numerous apartments and condos have been built there. By understanding your market, you can tap into developing trends.

Your state or local government has a great deal of power over the price of investment properties. Governments can change zoning regulations that allow certain areas to be developed, or they can change them so residential dwellings are no longer allowed. They may push for capital improvements or developments (such as adding sewer or water service to an area previously without such service, or by widening roads) that make areas or neighborhoods more desirable.

Again, it's important to understand what's happening in your markets so you can take advantage of these changes.

3. Open Your Eyes

A lot of new investors ask me about hiring an inspector to examine a property before they buy it. When you begin your investing career, it may be worth a few hundred dollars to have someone else look over the property. But as you become more experienced, you can train yourself to be your own inspector. Ask your mentor what to look for in houses. And if you do hire an inspector, take careful notes about what he does.

I rarely use an inspector. I feel comfortable that I can spot most problems. Plus, the price of many investment properties I purchase doesn't justify the cost of an inspection.

If you use an inspector, avoid the temptation to trust everything he says. Make sure he has a written list of all the things he's going to inspect, and verify that the list is complete.

You need to educate yourself on how to inspect property so you can do it yourself. It's easy to rely on an inspector and tell yourself, "This guy knows what he's doing. I don't have to worry about it. After all, every other property I own passed inspection, and I haven't had any problems." Don't become complacent. Just because you haven't had any problems yet doesn't mean you won't have them in the future. If you know what to look for, you can spot potential problems and avoid buying the wrong property, or you can use that information to negotiate a better price.

If you're allowed to inspect the inside of the property, look at the ceilings for water stains. Water damage can ruin properties quickly, and if you see any signs that water is coming in from the outside, make sure the roof has been fixed or that the price has been reduced to account for the expense of repairing this problem. If the property has an attic, be sure to get inside it and look at the inside of the roof. You can spot many water leaks by looking at the wood panels or the insulation.

Plumbing problems can also allow water in or near the house. If you see a puddle on the side of the house and it hasn't rained in days, this may be a sign that the water main is broken. Check inside to make sure there's no water or water stains in the bathrooms or kitchen. Plumbing problems and water damage can be very expensive to resolve, and you want to make sure you catch these before the damage gets out of control. Thoroughly inspect any area where water could be causing you problems. Roof vents leak a lot. Be sure to inspect around them.

Look for discoloration in the concrete or new paths of water where water has run off. There may not be a puddle, but the ground may be soft.

Look for insect damage, especially termites. They may be small, but they're mighty, and over time termites can devour your bottom line and leave your financial future crumbling. If you know where to look (such as where wood comes into contact with soil), you can easily see the tubes that termites left behind in their wake. If you catch the problem early, a good exterminator can rid the property of termites quickly. But if they've been dining on the wood for a long time, it can be expensive to resolve. And you should have this information to know which properties to avoid or to use it to your advantage during negotiations.

Inspect the foundation and structure of the property to make sure they're sound. Check for cracks in the exterior walls, and look for cracks in the drywall. Is it difficult to open or close doors? These are all signs there may be issues with the foundation. It's not unusual to see slight settling in older homes, but excessive settling or cracks in newer homes may point to larger problems.

Make sure the property has a clear title. When you take ownership of any property, you want to be sure you can show a clear chain of ownership. This is something that will probably be covered as part of any financing package, but it will be worth your time to sort out any obvious problems early. You might be interested in a house that belongs to an estate that hasn't been probated yet. In some areas it will take months, if not years, to get clear title on that property. Don't waste time looking at property if you won't be able to own it with a clear chain of title. I swear by title insurance and won't purchase a property without it. It costs a few hundred dollars, but the peace of mind is worth it.

Keep in mind you can negotiate the cost of title insurance with the title company. Be sure to review the HUD information carefully because some companies will try to charge you for everything.

Make sure there are no issues with the property lines. You don't want to get in the middle of a dispute where a neighbor alleges that part of a property encroaches onto his land. And you don't want to have to correct a situation where a neighbor's property encroaches onto yours. Hiring an attorney for a "quiet title" suit can cost you a lot of time and money and is very stressful. Avoid this problem by making sure this issue is resolved before you purchase a property. If there's any doubt about where the property lines are, hire a surveyor and deduct the cost from your offer.

You can avoid other traps by being familiar with the area. You wouldn't want to buy a house if you knew a landfill would be developed only half a mile away in two years. Most people wouldn't want to live that close to one, and it would be difficult, if not impossible, to rent. There also might also be some type of assessment or taxation scheduled to take place in the future. Make sure you know all the costs of ownership, present and future, before you buy. Check with the local planning commission to find out about any roads to be developed or constructed near the area anytime soon. If people have a hard time driving to your property, they won't want to rent from you.

4. Be Smarter Than the Average Joe

There's risk in any business deal. There's no way you can ever buy a property and not face the reality that something could go wrong in the future. The goal is to have as much information as possible so you can minimize your risks. You want to have the odds stacked in your favor—so as few things as possible go wrong, and those that do are minor and won't break your bank.

Here are a few things to look out for when you're buying property:

Watch out for properties that have been repainted but are in need of major updates such as plumbing or electricity. A property that needs a paint job but has everything else updated may be a better deal than one that looks prettier on the outside. Looks can be deceiving. Be sure to scratch beyond the surface.

If you're buying property that has existing tenants, read their leases thoroughly and be sure to review the tenants' payment histories. Some leases may contain terms that you wouldn't have negotiated, such as a five-day grace period on late rent. I used a lease like that, and it didn't take long before most of the tenants were paying their rent on the fifth because they knew there was no penalty. My loans were due on the first, and having so many people pay me on the fifth really jammed me up. I got rid of that lease as soon as I could.

You can have each tenant sign a document verifying you have a true and complete copy of his lease. Reviewing the payment history of each tenant is important because you need to know which ones have a history of late payments. If the seller of a property has allowed the tenants to pay late, you'll have to put an end to this as soon as you take over the property, and this is going to add to the time, expense, and frustration of buying the property. Be sure to factor this into your offer.

Verify the financial information the seller provides to you regarding his income and expenses. Sometimes this can be difficult because people can be reluctant to talk about how much money they make. And the few dishonest sellers you deal with may try to inflate the income they earn from a property so that you'll overpay. Always ask for bank deposits, cancelled checks, and tax reports. Any responsible owners will have those available and won't have a problem sharing them with a prospective buyer. And if they can't or won't let you look at those things, they probably aren't the kind of people you want to do business with, and you should consider passing on the deal. Trust your gut.

If you buy a property with a tenant in place, verify that you have the tenant's information before you purchase the property. I bought one commercial property and didn't realize the seller didn't have a social security number for the tenant. They tenant had been in the property for a while and didn't want to move his business. Fortunately, everything went as smoothly as it could have, but if I'd been forced to collect back rent, I would have had a very difficult time because the seller hadn't done his job. When you close on a deal, you're stuck with the tenants you have, and you need to make sure you have the information you need to collect your money.

Most responsible landlords will be able to give you a "rent roll," which is a list of the tenants and their contact information. If you need to go to the bank to borrow money, they may require you to provide one.

There will be a few things that are hard to put on paper or that some people will avoid. One of them is being able to document that all the scheduled maintenance has been performed and paid for. Just because the property has a new coat of paint doesn't mean the owner has cleaned the carpets, serviced the air conditioner, or paid the roofing company. Make sure the seller can prove he has done those things, and compare the checks and invoices. Make sure that all work performed on the property has been paid for and that no material or workmen's liens have been filed for unpaid bills. Ask for receipts for foundation or roof work that has been done recently, so you have a copy for warranties, for resale value, and for insurance.

Make sure you understand how much time it will take to manage the property and how you'll pay for it. Income and expense statements also don't generally outline who's managing the property or how much time it takes. If you're buying the property from a large company, they may have hired a management company, and you should see that expense listed on the statements.

Pay attention to the words the seller uses and how he describes his dealings with others. If a seller tells you that he pays cash "under the table" to all his contractors, that he offers discounts to tenants who pay in cash so he can hide the income, or how he cheated the insurance company on the roof he replaced last year, be wary. He's telling you he has no regard for the truth. If he lies to others to save a few dollars, he'll also lie to you to do the same. People will tell you everything you need to know about them if you'll listen. Be careful about the people you choose to do business with, and you'll avoid headaches down the road.

5. It's Not Just a Building

People will tell you a lot of reasons for buying real estate. I've purchased millions of dollars worth of properties and have spoken to hundreds of other real estate investors. When I asked them why they invested in real estate, there were a few ideas that every one of them brought up.

In my experience, here are the most important reasons you should invest in real estate:

Being a real estate investor allows you to be your own boss. You own the company, and you don't have to worry about a supervisor who's more concerned about her future with the company than yours. Your hard work is putting money into your pockets and not your boss's. You set your own hours, and you aren't tied to the clock on the company's wall. If you want to take a vacation or need time off to see your daughter at school, you don't have to ask for permission. You just go. I value this freedom more than anything about owning income-producing properties.

You can make a lot of money as a real estate investor. In fact, you can make as much money as you want. There are no limits, and you don't have to wait for your boss to sign off on your next raise. Of course, money doesn't grow on trees, and you have to be willing to work to get it. But if you educate yourself and put in the effort, you can reap greater financial rewards in real estate than in most other jobs.

You don't have to have a formal education to be successful in real estate. I don't have a college degree, and I've managed to build a large portfolio of properties, a portfolio that will continue to grow. Real estate investing is something most adults can do immediately. They don't have to wait for some date in the future after they've spent years and thousands of dollars pursuing a degree.

Owning investment property allows you to invest in assets that will appreciate in the long term. When you decide to retire, you'll own property that will continue to create income for you and your family, or you can sell it for a profit. There aren't many investments that virtually guarantee you can sell them in the future for a profit, but holding onto real estate long enough is almost always certain to make you money.

I bought a house at the height of the market. The Realtor assured me it was a turnkey deal and the property was ready to be rented. Once I took possession, I found out the property was in terrible shape, and the plumbing wasn't even hooked up. Now that I've done the repairs and rented it, my cash flow is only $25 a month. Even though I did a terrible job purchasing the property, I know I'll make money eventually.

Investing in real estate allows you to take advantage of our tax laws. Many of the legal deductions your accountant will tell you about are available only if you own property. If you plan ahead and put your money in real estate, you can legally lower the amount of taxes you pay.

Owning real estate is a great way for families to work together. When you start building your real estate empire, you can work with your spouse, your children, or your parents. Many successful companies have been built around family ties. It's your company, and you can hire anyone you want to. It's a great way to spend time with your family and strengthen your bond. Few other opportunities offer this type of flexibility.

6. How to Successfully Manage Your Properties

In order to succeed as a real estate investor, you'll have to manage your properties well. You can buy the best house in the most desirable neighborhood, but if you don't manage things properly it won't matter.

Begin with these thoughts in mind and watch your business grow:

Have a clear idea of your goals. I know this sounds simple, but you have to begin with your destination in mind. How many properties do you want to own? What are your financial goals? Do you want to work full-time or part-time? If you don't know where you *want* to go, you'll probably never get there.

Understand your market. You have to know how much your property is really worth in order to make the most money. Are you trying to rent a house for $750 a month when every other similar property in the area is renting for $500? Or, even worse, are you renting a house for $500 a month when it's really worth $800? You have to know your market to understand if you're making good or bad decisions.

Before you sign a lease with a tenant, do a thorough background check. It's much easier and cheaper to not rent to someone than it is to evict him. You can avoid a lot of problems by understanding who you're dealing with. If a potential tenant has been evicted twice in the last three years for failing to pay rent, do you think you might have problems with him? Would you like to know that he has lived in the same property for twelve years, and the only reason he's moving is that he wants his daughter to go to a better school? Do your homework and your life will be easier. There are many online resources for landlords, and they're only a mouse click away.

Take care of your tenants. Make sure you live up to your end of the agreement, and treat them with the respect they deserve. If you need to repair something, do it as quickly as you can, and make sure it's done right. Your professional attitude will create a positive atmosphere and allow you to have the expectation your tenants will pay their rent on time. If you're slow in taking care of problems, it won't be long before your tenants feel they have good reason to be slow in paying their rent. You can avoid that problem by being professional and treating your tenants' concerns with urgency.

Have fair rules and enforce them. Make sure your tenants know what their rights and responsibilities are. When you need to, don't hesitate to penalize a tenant who doesn't follow the rules. If you start making exceptions or fail to follow through on threats to punish tenants, it won't be long before other tenants also stop following the rules. Don't put yourself in a position where you've allowed tenants to do as they please because you haven't been following the terms of your leases.

Know what's going on at your properties. Inspect your units on a regular basis. Your tenants should expect to see you or one of your staff regularly. I even have my mother drive by my properties when she's near them. She'll call me to let me know if she sees any problems. If you keep your eyes open, you'll spot problems when they're small and resolve them before they turn into big ones.

Document everything and keep those records where you can find them. If one of your tenants has been blasting his stereo in the middle of the night and you talked to him about it, follow up with a certified letter. Make copies of the letter and the certified receipt. You can even go online and print the tracking record that shows when the letter was delivered. Protect yourself and the majority of your tenants who follow the rules by keeping records of everything you do.

7. Elvis Is About to Leave the Building

If you're in the real estate business very long, it will inevitably happen to you: One of your tenants will owe you rent, and you can't reach him by phone. You drive over to the property only to discover the house is empty. You talked to him last week and he assured you he would be in first thing in the morning to pay you, but he has suddenly vanished into thin air. He has pulled a "midnight move," left you high and dry, and bolted to greener pastures.

Looking back, you start to connect the dots and can see warning flags that should have let you know something was going on. If only you had put two and two together, you could have protected yourself.

Here are a few of the red flags that someone's about to abandon your property:

The tenant starts slow-paying his rent. When he first moved in, he hand-delivered his rent check two days before it was due. Then he "forgot" to sign one of the checks and couldn't come in until after the due date. Last month he didn't even try to pay on time, and this month he didn't pay at all. When you see a change in someone's payment history, it may mean he's about to head for the hills.

The tenant won't answer or return your calls. When he's late with his rent, you call to find out if there's a problem. It goes to voicemail and you leave a message, but you never hear from him. There may be many good reasons why a tenant doesn't return your call, but it should always concern you. You call his job and send him a fax at work, but you still get no response. You put another message on his voicemail using Slydial, but he never calls back.

You drive by the house and notice that things have changed. Maybe the plants that sat on the porch since the day he moved in are gone. Perhaps the grill he used every weekend is no longer in sight, or the old car that hadn't been moved in months has suddenly disappeared. Maybe all the curtains have been taken down or the windows have been covered completely. If he was meticulous about mowing the yard but it hasn't been mowed in weeks, it's never a good sign. When you start seeing sudden, drastic changes, it may mean your tenant is about to fly out of his nest.

The mail is piling up or the utilities have been turned off. If you drive by the house and see a notice taped to the front door from the electric company, or you trip over letters spilling out of the mailbox, it's probably too late to say good-bye to your tenant. He has already left and taken your rent money with him.

When a tenant bolts, get into the property as soon as you can. Hopefully, you won't have too much work to do before you can rent the property to a new tenant and minimize your losses.

8. It Happens to All of Us
Some tenants will not pay rent or will occasionally bounce a check.

If you've screened your tenants carefully, you can minimize this. But it will eventually happen to anyone who rents property. Even the best tenants occasionally have financial issues.

Before you rent to your first tenant, visit with your lawyer and make sure you understand what the legal process is for dealing with tenants who are behind on their rent. Have a game plan before it happens so you know what you're going to do.

Make sure your tenants understand what will happen if they don't pay according to the terms of the lease. And enforce the rules when a tenant doesn't pay on time. If you start making exceptions, it won't be long before a few other people think they can get away without paying. Stop this problem before it starts.

Pets will cause problems. Again, it's important to have a game plan before the situation starts. Even with the best tenant, dogs and cats will make a house or apartment smell. Occasionally this will get out of hand and other tenants will complain, or you may wind up with a property that has to be cleaned extensively before it can be rented. Have rules in place before the tenant signs the lease, and make sure he understands the rules and what the consequences will be if he doesn't prevent the smell of his animals from causing problems.

Other issues you'll face from pets are fleas, aggression, and barking. Again, have policies and procedures in place so you'll know how to handle these situations before they happen.

Some tenants will violate the terms of the lease or cause damage to the property. It's not unusual to see tenants allow people who aren't listed on the lease to live with them, or they might use a residential space for commercial purposes. You might drive by one of your properties and see broken windows or stained carpets, or you could discover holes in the walls. Maybe a car has been leaking oil and the driveway needs to be repaired or cleaned, or there's damage to the property that no one has told you about.

Some tenants will use the property for illegal purposes. It's not unheard of for tenants to sell drugs out of a rental unit. If other tenants complain about a high volume of traffic at one of your properties at all hours of the day, it may be a sign something illegal is going on.

Tenants may complain about offensive behavior, such as another tenant peeking into windows. Again, these are situations you need to discuss with your attorney before you begin leasing.

9. Going Once, Going Twice…

I'll always have a soft spot for buying property through auctions. After all, I bought my first property at an auction. Auctions can be a great way to find properties that help you meet your goals. But if you fail to take the time to prepare, they can also cause you a lot of problems.

I succeeded at my first auction mostly because of luck. I hadn't done any research on the property, and I was a total newbie. Looking back, it was a miracle I didn't lose every penny I had.

Here are some ways to prepare to succeed at auctions:

Make sure the property you're bidding on fits into your overall strategy. You don't want to buy property just because you like the neighborhood or because it sits at the end of a cul-de-sac. Don't even attend an auction if you don't have an idea of how the property for sale will fit into your portfolio.

Attend an auction or two before you bid on property. If you go and see how they're held, you'll have a much better idea of what to expect. You don't want to walk into an auction for the first time when you're going to spend tens of thousands of dollars on a property. You'll be nervous before your first bid. Don't make it worse by being unfamiliar with the process.

Prepare financially for the auction. Most auctions will require you to put a deposit (usually 5 to 10 percent) on the property if you have the winning bid. You'll be required to pay the balance within a short period of time, usually thirty days. Make sure you can afford to meet these deadlines before you start bidding at auctions.

Have a limit on the amount you'll pay for any property at auction. Bidding on property can be a very emotional experience. Once the bidding starts, it's not uncommon for adrenaline to take over and for people (especially newbies or the unprepared) to overbid. After you've made a bid or two and the price of a property rises, you can feel emotionally invested, wanting to get the property at any cost. Avoid this by knowing what you'll pay before you walk in. Of course, this requires understanding the market and what the property is really worth.

Don't be afraid to walk away. If you get into a situation where the bidding gets out of control or you start to feel uncomfortable, quit bidding. There will be other properties and other auctions. No one property is worth making a deal you'll regret as soon as you sign the check. Some of the best deals in your life will be the ones you *don't* make. It can take you months or even years to recover from a single bad deal. I'm not saying you shouldn't take risks, but they should always be managed, calculated risks. And auctions can take on a life of their own, so be prepared and be disciplined when you decide to bid on property at an auction.

10. All About the Benjamins

Owning investment property is all about money. You've purchased real estate and you're reading this book because you're interested in improving your financial situation. And nothing's more important than financing your properties using OPM, "other people's money." It's not always possible to get bank financing, so sometimes you have to find creative ways to get your deals done. If there's a will, there's a way.

Here are the terms identifying the "Quick 6" ways to find the cash to build your portfolio (some of these are covered in more detail in other sections):

Owner carry. The seller agrees to finance the property. But there are two caveats with this. First, the interest rates can be high. Second, the balance may have to be paid off in a relatively short period, such as five to seven years.

Subject to. The buyer purchases the property *subject to* existing financing, which means the existing financing stays in place. The buyer makes the payments to the seller, and title stays in the seller's name. This isn't a long-term solution, and most investors who purchase property this way will refinance it and have title transferred to their names after a few months. Both parties face high risks with this method.

Seller second. Sometimes the buyer won't have enough cash to cover the down payment required by a mortgage. The seller can offer a second mortgage on the property equal to the down payment to get the deal done. Don't use this method until you verify that the first mortgage allows it.

Lease option. This method allows the tenant to get in the house as quickly as possible with little or no money down. After a few years, the tenant has the right to buy the property.

Nothing down. This is the Holy Grail of investing. My bank loans at 70 percent of appraised value. It used to loan at 80 percent, but those days are gone. Sometimes, I can get a property under contract for 70 percent or less of the appraised value, and I can borrow the entire amount. I buy the property with none of my money. I get excited just reading about these deals.

Some banks will even loan up to 103 percent of your home's value. The extra 3 percent is to be used for closing costs.

If you don't have the cash for a down payment, or you want to maximize your leverage, buying a property with no money down is a great way to go.

Wraparound mortgage. A seller can sell a property with their loan in place. For example, assume the property is worth $50,000, while the seller owes a balance of $25,000 and is paying the bank $300 a month. If the buyer offers $40,000 at 10 percent interest for eighteen years, his payment would be $400 a month. The seller would collect the $400, pay the bank $300, and pocket $100 every month.

With each of these methods, there are risks. Make sure you do your due diligence before you buy any property. One of the great things about real estate is that you can be as creative as you want.

Do you have a story about how you thought outside the box to get a deal financed? I'd love to hear it. E-mail me at info@ thesavvylandlordbook.com.

11. Cut to the Chase

Eventually you'll find a piece of property that fits into your investment plan. You've researched the area and understand the market. You've been able to walk around the property and it passes the eye test. You want to buy the property and know exactly what you'll pay for it.

Your time is valuable, and so is the time of the property owner. How can you begin negotiations with the owner without having to spend a lot of time in case you won't be able to reach an agreement? One of the best ways to cut to the chase is to send a letter of intent.

A letter of intent is a simple letter that allows you to make a non-binding offer to an owner to find out if he would be interested in selling the property on your terms. In the letter, you outline all the important issues, such as the price and financing terms, including down payment, how much existing debt would be assumed, how much would be paid at the closing, and how many months the payments would last.

The main advantage to a letter of intent is that it's easy to draft. It's not a formal, complicated legal document, and you don't necessarily need to have your attorney review it. There's no commitment, so if the offer is rejected, you haven't lost anything except your time.

A letter of intent should not be used if you're trying to "lowball" the owner; send one only if you have a reasonable offer. Most owners know what their properties are worth, and if you send an offer that's far below the actual value, you won't be taken seriously. Even if the owner isn't ready to sell when you send a letter of intent, if you make a fair offer he may contact you at some point in the future when he's ready to sell. If your offer isn't reasonable, your letter will wind up in the trash and you'll never hear from the owner. It may look to you like good business sense to send in a really low offer, but it can cost you opportunities and lost profits in the future.

If you send a letter of intent, be willing to listen to counterproposals. If you've done your homework, your offer should be a fairly reasonable one, and the owner may have few objections to your offer. He may just want to change the amount of the down payment or the number of months the balance will be financed. If you're serious about buying a property, these issues can probably be negotiated without much difficulty. Even if you're not able to reach a deal, you've hopefully created a relationship and can connect on future projects.

12. CYA

One of the most important decisions you'll have to make as a real estate investor is the type and amount of insurance you'll carry, or if you need insurance at all. I can't imagine owning a real estate company without having insurance. I have too much to lose if something goes wrong. Plus, when you become successful (or at least look like you're successful), some people will see you as a giant bull's-eye. These people look at business owners and all they can see is a giant payday. They start sizing you up from the moment they see you and start plotting how they can get a slice of your pie, regardless of whether they've earned it.

The sad reality is that all businesses will be sued, and you need to take this into account when you're building your company. Insurance is a way to make sure your business is protected, and it can keep you from losing all you've built. Insurance is one of the best ways you can legally protect yourself.

If you finance your property, you may not have any choice about insurance. The lender may make it a condition of the loan. But you still need to understand the types and amounts of insurance you need.

Dwelling and casualty insurance is one of the most important policies you should consider purchasing. It protects you against damage from your property from events such as flood, fire, wind, and hail. In Oklahoma, every spring we have months of very unpredictable weather. One moment we can have clear blue skies, and the next we can be running for cover from a tornado or hailstorm. Any Oklahoma property owner who didn't have adequate insurance to protect her property from these events would risk losing her investments. And it's the same in other parts of the country where people face hurricanes, floods, fire, and devastating snowstorms. There's too much risk from things out of our control, and insurance is safe and easy protection. This is an area many people neglect, and you need to pay careful attention to it.

The amount of casualty insurance you carry should be tied to the value of your property. The policy limits should be high enough to repair or replace your property to the condition it was in before the accident. And you should also consider getting a policy that will protect you from loss of income while the property is being worked on. I don't have this type of insurance because it doesn't make financial sense for me. But it's an issue you need to discuss with your insurance agent.

Another important policy each and every investor should consider is general liability insurance. This protects you in the event someone's injured on your property. Suppose one of your tenants claims he slipped and fell because one of the stairs was broken. Liability insurance will cover the expenses of any lawsuits and will pay most, if not all, of any judgment against you. It's disappointing, but today, when so many people are prone to sue, you have to protect your business.

The amount of liability insurance you carry will not be tied to the value of the property. You and your insurance agent should talk about the policy you need. But you should always ask, "How much can I afford to lose?" Your policy should protect you from losing more than you can afford.

Insurance costs less than you might expect. In fact, it's super cheap. I pay a monthly average of $20 per month per house for $1,000,000 in coverage.

You should also consider buying a life insurance policy to protect your family in case something happens to you. My wife isn't involved in my business, but I have loans on many of my properties. I have a policy that will pay off that debt so she won't have to worry about those loans if something happens to me. I pay $55 per month, and the peace of mind is worth every penny of it.

If you decide to get insurance, educate yourself about your rights and responsibilities. Learn as much as you can.

Here are a few insurance terms you need to understand. Once you learn them, review them from time to time because insurance is a living organism that keeps changing. Nothing's written in stone, and what's true today may not be true tomorrow. This list isn't meant to be exhaustive. (See also the thorough glossary of terms at the back of this book; use these lists to become a savvier investor.)

Actual Cash Value/ACV: The cost to replace insured property with property of similar quality and kind minus depreciation.

Adjuster: Someone who investigates insurance claims and recommends an appropriate settlement amount.

Agent: A professional who sells insurance policies.

All perils deductible: A dollar amount beyond which an insurance company begins to pay for a loss.

Appraisal: A valuation of property by an authorized person.

Bodily injury: Physical damage to a person.

Deductible: The amount an insured must pay before an insurance company will begin to cover a loss.

Hail and wind deductible: A 1 to 2 percent deductible you pay in addition to your regular deductible to be covered for hail and wind damage. This is a new term I saw on one of my recent statements and is an excellent example of why you need to keep up on insurance definitions that impact your business.

Liability limits: The maximum amount payable as a benefit under an insurance policy.

Loss: Injury or damage that occurs to a person covered by an insurance policy.

Market value: The price a property would sell for in a competitive market between a buyer and seller who are both prudent and informed.

Personal property: Any property which is not affixed to or associated with land.

Premium: The periodic payment made to an insurer to provide insurance for a specified period of time.

Property damage: Physical damage to property caused by the negligence, recklessness, or intention of a person.

Renter's insurance: A policy that covers an individual's personal belongings while he resides in rental property.

Replacement cost: The cost to replace insured property with property of similar quality and kind. Unlike actual cash value, depreciation is not a factor in replacement cost.

13. Making the Numbers Work

When you buy a piece of property, make sure you understand the market and what your expenses and income will be so you can calculate the yield or return on your investment.

Always begin with the end in mind. You need to know how much rent to charge in order to make a profit and wind up with positive cash flow. After all, making money is the name of the game, and if you don't crunch the numbers before you start, you'll never make as much money as you should.

The easy way to calculate return is to subtract expenses from income and add your expected profit. For example:

Monthly operating expenses: $200
Monthly mortgage and taxes: $200
Total monthly expenses: $400

Your goal is to make at least $100 per month, so the monthly rent needs to be $500.

Most savvy investors look at these numbers on an annual basis. But when I started investing, I couldn't grasp numbers that large, so I've always done it on a monthly basis. Here's a breakdown of the numbers on an annual basis:

Annual operating expenses: $2,400
Annual mortgage and taxes: $2,400
Total annual expenses: $4,800

Your goal is to make at least $1,200 per year. So the monthly rent needs to be $500, which is $4,800 (annual expenses) plus $1,200 (annual profit) divided by twelve.

Will your property rent for $500 per month? Is it in an area that will support this? Or should it rent for $750 per month? You'll know the answers to these questions only when you research the market for each piece of property you buy. Don't ever buy property without understanding what you can reasonably charge for rent. If the numbers don't work, pass on the deal.

Of course, there may be situations where you expect to take negative cash flow from a certain piece of property for a year or two. You may have factored that loss into your tax planning. But any such loss should be the result of planning with your accountant. It should never be the result of a failure to plan.

Whenever you look at a property, begin by understanding the numbers involved. Start by asking yourself, "How much will the mortgage cost me? What about taxes and insurance? How much money will I have to spend to rehab the house? How much rent do I need to charge to maximize my cash flow?" If you buy property without having these numbers, you may never have positive cash flow.

14. Smooth Talker

When you show a property to prospective tenants, you'll inevitably face some objections. You'll hear a laundry list of why your property isn't good enough for them. Some people will have valid concerns, but others will just be trying to negotiate. Other people will just complain because it's their nature.

Regardless of why people raise concerns, if you're prepared, you can counter these objections and turn those prospects into paying tenants.

You might hear prospective tenants say the property is dirty, it needs repair, or that the carpet needs to be cleaned or replaced. None of these should ever be a real concern because you should never show anyone a property that's not in "move-in" condition. Never allow anyone inside one of your properties if it desperately needs to be repainted or the carpet is soiled or outdated. You have only one chance to make a first impression, so you always want to put your best foot forward. If you show a prospect a property that's not ready to be lived in, you may have just lost all the time and energy you spent on getting him to the property. Even if you tell them, "This will all be fixed before you move in," you've put yourself in a bad situation. Avoid that by taking care of any needed cleaning or repairs before a tenant sees a property.

Some tenants will complain about the kitchen or appliances. They may tell you the kitchen is too small, or say that the appliances are old or the wrong color, or they don't like them because they're electric and not gas. Obviously, it would be prohibitive to replace the appliances every time you rent to a new tenant, and I wouldn't recommend replacing a stove as long as it works. You might tell the prospect that many people prefer smaller kitchens because they're easier to navigate and they don't take floor space away from a dining room. Or mention that electricity is safer and cleaner than gas, and that's an added benefit to the property.

You might hear someone say the closets or rooms are too small. Small rooms are more efficient and cheaper to heat and cool. Smaller closets mean that the rooms are larger. You can also solve any issues about closet size by going to your local hardware store and investing a few dollars in an efficient shelving system that will maximize the space you have.

Once again, if you've done your homework, you can counter virtually any objection a prospective tenant throws your way. And after you've gained enough experience renting to people, you'll know when someone has a real objection and when he's trying to negotiate. The key is to have information at your fingertips.

Interestingly, I rarely hear someone complain about the rent. However, this is one area where other investors receive a lot of questions. I've always been insecure about raising the rent, and I may undercharge for many of my properties. However, high rent is such a common issue that a man recently created a political party called "The Rent Is Too Damn High Party." I don't know how serious he was about running for office, but the issue was important enough that the party was featured on nearly every national news channel.

If you've done your homework (including reading this book) and understand your property's market, you'll be able to explain your rent charges. If you know that there are four similar houses in the area and you charge the same amount as the owners of the other properties, you can explain this. Or if your property has more square footage or more bedrooms than other houses in the area, you can use that to overcome a concern about the rent. The key is to have that information available to you before you start renting the property. If you don't do your homework before you purchase property, you won't be able to give the information you need to overcome objections about the rent.

15. Cleaning Checklist

Part of your job as a real estate investor will be to maintain property and to clean it when a tenant moves out. When you first start, you may do much of this work yourself. It may not be cost effective to hire someone to do these things for you if you have only one or two properties. But as your business grows, you'll need to hire people to do these for you.

You can find good cleaning people by talking to other investors. You'll go through them more quickly than you expect. I try to have a list "three deep" for cleaners, electricians, plumbers, and other handymen. The first one I call is the most reasonably priced; if he can't solve the problem, I move onto the next one. Outsource as much as possible so you can focus on building your business. If you don't, your business growth will be stunted.

If you don't hire people when your business grows, you're stepping over dollars to get to dimes. But most investors will clean properties themselves when they start.

Here are a few items you should have on hand to make sure your property is always at its best:

Cleaning supplies—

- vacuum cleaner
- mop, wringer, and bucket
- brooms and dustpans
- paper towels
- sponges
- plastic trash bags
- scrub brushes
- soap/cleanser

- window cleaner
- toilet-bowl cleaner and brush
- oven cleaner

Basic tools—

- stepladder
- razor blade scraper
- hammer
- screwdrivers (Phillips head and flat head)
- pliers (channel lock, needle-nose, and locking)
- electrical tape
- painting supplies (brushes, rollers, and pans)
- wire cutters and strippers
- flashlights
- saws (wood and hacksaw)
- wrenches (crescent and adjustable)
- tape measures
- electric tools (drills and saws)

I keep a tool bag filled with some simple tools and supplies in my truck. I carry wall patch, a screwdriver, masking tape, zip ties, and other items I need to do simple repairs. But I farm the big jobs out. My time is too valuable. And so is yours.

16. Watch Out for These Traps

Investing in real estate can be one of the most profitable and enjoyable ways to build financial freedom. For many people, it can be the fastest way to build real wealth. But you have to build your empire the right way.

Here are several ways investors who start out with good intentions shoot themselves in the foot:

The property depreciates faster than they considered because it's neglected, or the investors didn't understand the market. For example, an investor didn't do his due diligence, and didn't realize a sprawling retail complex was being planned for the property adjacent to his house. Some investors don't realize the time and energy it takes to care for property and aren't able or willing to make the effort to care for it. Once that happens, it's only a matter of time before the property begins to lose its value.

Some investors run before they can walk. One of the things I enjoy about real estate investing is that there are no limits on how far I can go. I don't have to go to school for four years to start making money. The only thing that matters is that I have the knowledge and experience to make sound business decisions. But with that freedom comes responsibility. I can't buy every property I see. I have to take the time to make wise decisions, and I can't take chances without understanding what I need to do to make the deal work. Some investors will buy one property, make a little profit, and start buying like crazy. Before they know it, they're in way over their heads and can't possibly manage all the properties they own.

Take it slow, learn from each deal, and don't push things along. Once you have the experience and wisdom that comes from doing several deals, you can put the pedal to the metal and get on the fast track. But don't go there before you're ready, or you may get run over.

Some investors don't understand the amount of time it takes to maintain property, and this impacts their personal lives. If you own multiple properties, at some point you may feel like you're on a treadmill headed nowhere. There's always something that needs to be fixed at one of them, whether it's a stove that needs replacing or walls that need repainting. After a while, some investors feel like they can't take any time off.

Remember that you don't have to do everything by yourself, and you can hire contractors to take care of most repairs. If you don't take time off occasionally to take care of yourself, you'll wind up being burned out and won't be any good for anything.

If your investments start to feel like a noose around your neck instead of a ticket to financial independence, it may be a sign you need to take a vacation. Trust your gut. You (and your family) will be grateful.

17. If Their Lips Are Moving

As I've mentioned, I'm passionate about helping people becoming successful real estate investors. I want my message to reach as many people as possible and for them to create the lifestyle they've always dreamed of.

Part of becoming successful is discerning how to listen to people. Here are a few of the lies I've heard about real estate investing (and if someone tells you one of these, look elsewhere for your advice):

"Real estate investing is a guaranteed way to get rich quick." Real estate investing is a great opportunity; it's a way for most people to build wealth. But there are no guarantees. Your success will be determined by your discipline, commitment, enthusiasm, and the effort you put into it. You'll have to make wise business decisions, learn from your mistakes and from the mistakes of others, and sacrifice. And you'll constantly

have to educate yourself. But the good news is that everyone's capable of doing those things; the real question is whether you're *willing* to do them. If you are, you can live a life most people only dream of.

"I don't need to inspect the property because the seller and his agent seem honest." I'm not a cynical person; I believe most people are honest and will do the right thing most of the time. But I don't play around when it comes to money, and neither should you. A few people will do whatever they can to make money, even if it means being dishonest or cheating you. You should always inspect property before you invest your money. There may be some situations where you're not allowed to go inside, but you should factor that into your offer. Never assume that anyone who's trying to get you to buy something has your best interests at heart. That's a sure way to eventually get burned and wind up (like I did) with a property that gives you only $25 cash flow each month. And the real kicker is that the seller made over $20,000 on that deal. I got duped because I trusted but did not verify.

Of course, if you've built a relationship with a Realtor, seller, or investor, and that person has earned the right to be trusted, you can begin to take him at his word. If you have any doubts about a deal, have another investor look at it. The opinion of someone you trust is priceless.

"I've been doing this for a while and don't need anyone's input anymore." This is one of the big, fat lies investors start telling themselves after they've done a few deals. After you've been investing for a while, you'll become more confident. That's totally normal. But there's a big difference between confidence and arrogance, and you have to make sure it doesn't keep you from making good decisions. You should never

start thinking, *I've done this a million times; I don't need to review the contract or inspect the property. That would just be a waste of time.* Always listen to your gut, and if you have any questions, don't be afraid to ask investors you know and trust. If you rush into a deal without thinking it through, you can put yourself in a bad position. But you'll never regret getting a second opinion.

You can ask questions until you've closed on the property. Make sure you know why you need to have a flood certificate and who pays for the abstract. It's not a done deal until the closing is done, and don't sign the paperwork until all your questions are answered.

In one closing, the seller tried to charge me a courier fee for delivering the check to the bank. My banker pointed that out and told me I could save the fee by driving to the bank (which I passed on my way home). I took the check and dropped it off, and saved the fee as well as the interest that would have been charged if the check hadn't been delivered that day.

"I haven't closed yet, but it's okay for me to start repairing the property." Never repair property until the deal is closed. I once put a new roof on a property before I closed on it. It was a roll of the dice, but I wanted to push the deal along. It was a risk, and I could have gotten burned, but it was a calculated risk.

18. The More the Merrier

Buying a duplex can be a great way to start your investment career. This is especially true if you live in one of the units and let a tenant on the other side pay your mortgage.

But you have to be careful about buying a duplex, especially if it's your first property. You don't want to buy a run-down property and end up living next to a tenant who's constantly knocking on the door telling you that something needs to be fixed.

Find duplexes that don't need a great deal of work. If you're looking at a property and it needs a major rehab, you may want to pass on it, especially if you plan on living in one of the units while you rent the other out. Where will you live if you have to completely renovate the property? Can you afford to pay for a new duplex while you have to live somewhere else?

With a little effort and research, you can probably find a duplex in reasonably good condition in a working-class neighborhood that doesn't need major repairs. This is true especially if the seller has lived in the property and is now ready to sell. Like you, most people won't want to live next to a tenant who has reason to complain that the property is in constant need of maintenance.

The big issue with duplexes is that you need to verify that all the utilities are separated. If a property doesn't have separate meters for the utilities, you'll have to pay for both of them. There are other issues involving common maintenance, such as who cuts the grass. These need to be clarified before you rent the property.

One of the real benefits to buying duplexes or fourplexes is that they qualify as a regular home. You can get conventional financing (like thirty-year notes) and use them to make more money each month.

19. We Tote the Note

One of the best ways to finance a property is through the seller, known as For Sale by Owner (FSBO). Generally, the buyer puts down a percentage of the purchase price and the seller finances the balance. It can be a win-win situation. For the buyer, it can be much easier and take less time than going through a traditional bank, and he can save costs and fees associated with traditional lending.

For the seller, FSBOs are great opportunities to guarantee a steady income in the future. I recently sold one of my businesses and structured the deal so I would receive monthly payments for several years. The business was very successful, and I could have negotiated a lump sum payment, but I wanted the security of knowing I would have passive income for the next few years. I also lowered my tax burden by doing the deal this way. It worked out well for the buyers because they were able to structure the payments the way they wanted. Buying properties from someone who's ready to retire and willing to finance the deal can be a great way to build your portfolio.

I would make FSBOs a priority if possible. It's not easy, but it's worth the effort. It takes a lot of discipline to succeed in this area, but it can be a great way to build your cash flow.

One of my first deals was a FSBO from an investor who wanted to retire and needed the cash flow. But you have to be careful. If you don't understand the market, it can be easy to overpay for FSBOs.

20. Don't Give Your Money Away

One of the major benefits of real estate investing is the number of deductions you get to take when tax season rolls around. Deductions are a great way to legally reduce the amount of money you have to pay the government each year.

Nobody likes to pay taxes. But you can't avoid them; you have to deal with the tax man every year. But you and your accountant can structure your business in a way that allows you to take advantage of every deduction you're legally entitled to.

When you properly set up your real estate investment company, you may be surprised at some of the deductions you're allowed to take. These include all your office equipment (such as computers, printers, and all the toner and paper you use), tools and supplies you use to maintain the property (such as hammers, power tools, and cleaning supplies), the interest on your mortgage payments, the depreciation on your properties, payroll taxes and Social Security payments, any utilities related to your business, repairs to the properties, and any travel that's business related, such as seminars or conventions. Even the cost of this book can be deducted if you bought it for business reasons.

That's only a partial list of the things you're allowed to lawfully deduct. The IRS frequently changes what it does or does not allow, and it would be impossible for me to create a list that would cover all of them. Always discuss your deductions with your accountant, and make sure you're taking advantage of everything the tax code allows.

21. Contract for Deed

One of the easiest ways to buy or sell property is by using a contract for deed. When you've been investing for a while, you'll become familiar with these agreements. A contract for deed is a fairly simple contract between a buyer and a seller.

The parties agree on a price for a property, and the seller leases the property with an option for the tenant to buy it. The buyer gets to move into the property immediately and is able to make any improvements he wants. Unlike traditional financing, title to the property isn't transferred until the buyer has paid off the balance in full. He won't build any equity in the property until he makes his final payment.

The advantage to the buyer is that it can be cheaper (at least up front) because there are no expenses such as closing costs like there are with a traditional mortgage. Plus, it can be an easy way for people who have bad credit to buy a home. Banks are becoming less willing to take chances on people who don't have perfect credit scores, and a contract for deed gives such people a chance to buy property.

Both parties benefit from the fact that the process is much quicker than going through a bank. Once the parties have negotiated their agreement and the buyer makes his down payment, the deal is done—compared to the weeks it can take financing to be approved by a traditional bank.

We used a contract for deed on a house we couldn't sell. A couple agreed to buy it for $170,000, put down $5,000, moved in, and started making monthly payments of around $1,300. We paid the mortgage, but after sixteen months the couple moved out and left the home high and dry. We added it up, and they'd paid us over $20,000. So we started the process over again. Some statistics show that only about 50 percent of contract for deed actually go the distance. So if you're using them, the odds are that you'll be able to sell the same house more than once.

The real beauty of a contract for deed is that you're not responsible for any maintenance. If a pipe bursts, you don't have to rush over and take care of it. It's the buyer's responsibility.

I know one investor who only does contracts for deed. He's a master of it, and has twenty properties but no maintenance. If it works for you, it's a great way to build your business.

22. Keep the Chill Out

If you own property in places where winters get cold, you know how snow, ice, and low temperatures can take their toll on your investments. Do everything you can to help every one of your properties survive the winter.

One of the best investments you can make is installing heat tape around the water pipes. Heat tape is ingenious. It wraps around pipes and plugs into an electrical socket. It has a built-in thermostat, and when the temperature drops below a certain point, the tape turns on, heats the pipes, and keeps them from freezing. If you've ever had to replace a pipe that burst because it froze, you know the tape is worth the investment. It will save you hundreds of dollars by preventing water damage and plumbing bills.

When you know cold weather is approaching, remind your tenants that freezing cold can damage pipes, and that this could harm their belongings. By phrasing it that way, you'll hopefully motivate them to take action. I have a rubber stamp that tells tenants about cold weather. Every month during the cold season, I stamp their rent statements. Every one of my tenants should know when it's time to let the faucets drip to prevent frozen pipes. You could also send out e-mails or call tenants. Some apartment complexes often put a sign in front of the entrance to their property. Whenever the tenants leave or pull in the drive, they see a reminder about taking cold weather precautions.

Hot summers can also hurt your properties. I have another rubber stamp I use during the summer to remind tenants to check their air conditioning filters. You can't remind them too many times about the damage extreme weather can cause.

One of my properties was vacant in the middle of the winter, but I didn't take the time to protect it. For the cost of a small heater and a few dollars in utilities, I could have saved myself hundreds of dollars in repairs when a pipe burst. That also taught me to check on vacant homes as frequently as possible. I didn't find the damage until ten days later, and that was my mistake. I never should have let the damage get to that point. During another winter, I had a well freeze in a garage because I didn't put insulation on the pipes.

Be overzealous when it comes to protecting your property from the elements. You can't be too careful with your investments, and you can't afford to be careless. Do your best to keep Mother Nature from taking money out of your pocket.

23. Good Help Is Hard to Find

When you first start investing in real estate, you'll need to decide how you'll clean and maintain your properties. Doing it yourself may be the easiest and cheapest way to go at first. But as your company grows, you won't have the time to personally take care of every house. Eventually you'll have to hire people to handle these things for you.

Honest and dependable cleaning and maintenance people are worth their weight in gold. When you find them, do everything you can to keep them happy. They can be very hard to replace.

One of the best ways to keep good help is to pay them as quickly as possible. I always pay them as soon as they finish their jobs. If you pay them on the day they finish, they'll remember you when you call. There should never be any delay in paying your help. Contractors call me back because they know I'll pay when the job is done. And trust me, if you're ever late paying your help, they'll remember that, too.

I find good manual laborers (such as when I needed to clean out an apartment building I bought) by going to Craigslist and starting a "cattle call." I'll invite nine or ten people to show up, and hope for the best. Usually only one or two will keep the commitment, but I've connected with some great help that way.

If you have a good relationship with another investor, he may refer cleaning people and contractors to you. But many investors are reluctant to refer their help to other people. It's hard to find good help, and they don't want to risk losing them.

24. Where There's Smoke

You should always be looking for ways to protect your investments. When your income depends on owning property to rent, you'll start to see risks everywhere. But you can take a few simple steps that will help reduce the likelihood a catastrophe will happen to one of your properties.

Two of the simplest things you can do are to install smoke detectors and to make sure there's a fire extinguisher in the kitchen of each property you own. Your insurance company may even give you a discount if you do these two things.

Smoke detectors are valuable safety tools. Not only will they help protect your tenants and give them a chance to escape a fire, they also give them the chance to notify the fire department. Hopefully, they'll arrive in time to put the fire out before it totally destroys your property.

Make sure the batteries in each detector are replaced regularly (you might do it every six months when it's time to set your clocks with daylight savings) and tested frequently. You should include it as part of your annual inspection of every property. New smoke detectors can be hardwired to your electricity. It's worth the cost, and you won't have to buy and install new batteries every year.

An extinguisher in each kitchen can keep a small grease fire from turning into a blaze and burning down your property. Of course, you need to check extinguishers on a regular basis to make sure they're still functioning. Each one will have a date from the manufacturer that states when it needs to be replaced. Some great times to inspect extinguishers are when you rent each property, when you do your annual inspection, or at the start of each year, but always stay within the manufacturer's recommendations. If you provide the extinguisher, you should consider charging a deposit for it. A few people will steal anything that's not bolted down, and you don't want to pay for new extinguishers every time a tenant moves out. I encourage tenants to buy one for their safety, and sometimes I get lucky when they move and leave it behind.

25. Welcome to the Neighborhood

One of the most important things you'll do when you start leasing property is to establish a professional relationship with your tenants. This should start the moment you hang a "For Rent" sign on one of your properties, and it should continue until the tenants move out. There are many positives to starting off on the right foot. Remember this every time you interact with a tenant.

The new tenant interview is one of the most significant moments you'll have. I do this when it's time to sign the lease and hand over the keys. We review the lease and make sure everything's in order before we sign it. I make sure we talk about all the policies we have in place and answer any questions. It's a great time to set expectations and goals, and I think it helps the tenants understand we take the business seriously and that we have their best interests at heart.

I create an atmosphere that's professional when my tenants come in to sign a lease. We sit across from each other at a table, and I look them in the eyes. I want it to look and feel just like a house closing. We go over each and every line in the lease, and I have them initial each and every part of it. I make it a very formal process. In a certain sense, I want them to be scared about the responsibility they're undertaking.

One thing I make sure to emphasize is that the rent is due at the first of the month, and there are no exceptions to this. Period. I explain the consequences that will happen if they don't pay their rent on time.

I don't like evicting tenants. It's not pleasant, and I don't do it lightly. To make sure things don't get to that point, I do everything I can to work with people. But I won't be a doormat, and if someone doesn't live up to his end of the bargain I'll do what I have to do.

I also make clear that they'll owe the entire amount remaining on the lease if they're evicted. To see the potential magnitude of that figure, I'll add up the entire amount of the lease and state that number to them. If they sign a two-year lease, I multiply their rent by twenty-four and mention that figure. I also tell them that an eviction will impact their credit, and that we'll garnish their wages or refer the account to a collection agency if we need to.

My tenants have a clear understanding of the eviction process when they leave the new tenant interview.

Knowing that I've looked my tenants in the eye and explained to them that I'm not afraid to exercise my rights makes it easier for me to do what has to be done. If they choose to not pay their rent when they agreed to, there's nothing else I can do.

Savvy investors will have the tenant sign eviction papers the same day he signs his lease. I've started doing that, and it's a powerful way to stop a potential problem.

26. The Early Bird Gets the Cash

One of the most frustrating parts of being a landlord is making sure you get paid on time every month. You aren't running a charity, and you need to have money in your bank account in time to pay your expenses.

Landlords have tried a lot of different ways over the years to make sure tenants pay on time. The one that has been used the most is to charge a late fee. If a tenant doesn't pay on time, he has to pay his rent plus a small fee. If you choose to use this method, check your state laws first. A few investors have abused this, and some states have outlawed late fees. Any late fees need to be clearly spelled out in your lease. Your tenants need to understand what the consequences will be when they sign on the dotted line.

Some investors use a more positive approach. Instead of charging a late fee, they offer a small discount if the rent is paid on or before the due date. If the rent isn't paid on time, the tenant must pay the full rental amount. For example, if the rent is $650, the tenant may have to pay only $600 if he pays on or before the first of the month. This doesn't violate laws regarding late fees and hopefully encourages tenants to make their payments early or on time.

I used this on a tenant I'd had for about a year. He'd been a solid tenant but often struggled to pay on time. His lease was up, and he let me know he had to pay a lower rent or he would move out. I agreed to reduce his rent by $50 a month if he would pay on the first of the month and sign a new lease. He agreed, and as long as he pays on or before the first of each month he gets the discount. It's been six months now and the tenant has paid early or on time each month.

27. Your New Best Friends

Whenever you buy a new property, there's a group of people who want you to succeed. They want every tenant to be honest, respectful, and responsible. And they want it as much, if not more, than you do.

These people are the neighbors at your new property, the people who live near your investment. Hopefully, you started meeting them before you bought your property. Maybe you stopped to talk to one or two of them when you did your inspection. Getting to know them is a great way to protect your investment. Think of them as extra eyes and ears working for free.

The neighbors can be invaluable. If you've owned a certain property for years, you can develop relationships with the people who live near it. They can tell you which tenants treat your property the way you both want it to be treated. And they can help you weed out any problem tenants. Who knows your tenants better than the people who live next door to them? Take advantage of this great resource and get to know your neighbors, who'll be happy to safeguard your investments for you.

28. Blood from a Turnip

It will happen to you eventually—one of your tenants will move out in the middle of the night, owing you a month of rent. You call the phone numbers he provided when he filled out his lease, but he no longer works at the company he listed, and the other number is disconnected. It's not worth the time and expense to go to court, but you deserve to be paid. How can you collect from this deadbeat?

A technique that some investors are using allows you to use the IRS to put pressure on your tenant. If you forgive a debt (including unpaid rent), it's treated as ordinary income and you can send your tenant a 1099-MISC. They'll have to report that income on their next tax return. Some people (especially those who are receiving assistance based on their income) think they can't afford to make more money. (I don't understand that logic either.)

The idea is that if you send a deadbeat tenant a letter threatening to turn the money owed to you into taxable income, some people will magically find the cash to pay you. Just seeing those three letters *IRS* on a sheet of paper is enough to scare some deadbeats into finding a way to pay.

29. Crunch the Numbers

As you begin to build your empire, eventually you'll be faced with an interesting choice: Should you buy as many properties as possible, or take the same money and buy fewer, more expensive ones? If you have $160,000 to invest, is it better to buy one home or spread that same amount over four properties?

Remember that real estate investing is all about cash flow. You want as much money coming in as possible. It may not make much sense at first, but four inexpensive properties will always give you more cash flow than one expensive property.

A $160,000 property will rent for about $1,200 per month. But you could rent each of the $40,000 properties for at least $500 per month, which nearly doubles your cash flow. Don't get caught up in the appraised value of any one property. Only worry about building your portfolio to maximize your cash flow.

You have other options as well, and can leverage the same amount of money even more. If you had $160,000 to invest, you could put $60,000 of it in savings and use the remaining $100,000 to buy a $500,000 apartment building by putting 20 percent down. Even if you put 30 percent down you could buy something for $400,000.

Whatever you do, be sure to crunch the numbers to make sure your money is working for you as hard as it can. Don't assume that a more expensive house is a more profitable one.

30. Point and Click

No business can grow to its maximum potential if the owners don't take full advantage of the Internet. The World Wide Web has become a major resource in our lives, and if you're not using it to build your empire, you're leaving a lot of money on the table.

E-mail allows you to communicate with contractors and tenants immediately and gives you a written record of your conversations. Don't be afraid to try text messaging. It's a great way to quickly communicate with people.

You should also consider creating a website. A website opens up your business to the entire world. If someone's moving to your area from London or China, they can view properties on your website before they leave. Websites have become fairly cheap to set up and maintain; we use Buildium.com, but there are many good companies that will help you do this. A website lets your business be open twenty-four hours a day. It's like having a storefront open to everyone who has an Internet connection. And the best part is that you don't have to pay any employees to work there.

There are many websites built specifically for real estate investors. There's a mountain of information at your fingertips. All you have to do is point your browser in the right direction and you can find answers to most, if not all, of your questions. Many of them have newsletters you can sign up for, and they send great information to your inbox on a regular basis.

One helpful website is MrLandlord.com. The owner is a real landlord who has been in the trenches for years and understands the challenges we face. If you ever have a question or an issue, I would recommend visiting his site and searching for the answer. Biggerpockets.com is another great resource.

Landlordlocks.com is a great place to order locks and keys. You'll save yourself time and trouble by becoming familiar with this site when you start building your portfolio. You might also check out rhol.com and reitips.com.

There are also many great apps for smart phones. I use my Craigslist app whenever I need a handyman or contractor or buy used appliances.

Don't limit the growth of your company. Learn to use technology to help your business grow and move over to the fast lane.

31. Buy Low, Sell High

Consider diversifying your portfolio. If you have a large number of single dwelling properties in one part of town, it may make sense to start buying properties in a more upscale area or to buy multidwelling units.

Your goal as an investor is simple. You want to bring in more money than you spend, just like any other business. It's a simple theory, and if you know where to look you can find properties for sale at bargain prices.

I would never wish anyone hard times, but the truth of the matter is that people go through challenges. Life isn't always fair and we all have times when things aren't going our way. But those challenges create opportunities for other people, and you need to keep your eyes and ears open so you can build your empire. If you're not willing to purchase property from someone who's forced to have a fire sale, you can bet another investor will snatch it up in a heartbeat. And he won't flinch when he cashes the rent checks every month.

Don't be embarrassed to buy property from someone when you know he's having a hard time. If you hear of an investor who needs to raise some quick cash, remember that this is business. As long as you didn't create the problem, purchase any properties that fit your portfolio.

Divorce is a terrible thing. It tears apart families and creates stress and turmoil. Sometimes it means that people have to sell properties as quickly as they can, even if it means taking a loss. If you know someone who's going through a divorce, it may create a chance to buy property at a discounted price while you help him get out of a difficult position.

Bankruptcy is another event I would never wish on anyone. I'm sure it must be embarrassing to have to file papers announcing to the world that you're not able to pay your bills. Sometimes people file for bankruptcy because they've made bad decisions. Maybe they bought more properties than they could maintain. But people also file bankruptcy because bad things have happened to them, like a divorce or unexpected medical bills. Whatever the reason, when another investor is forced to declare bankruptcy, opportunities are created for buyers. If you time it right, you can acquire property by short sale before someone actually files for bankruptcy.

Many investors get themselves into trouble and are short on cash from time to time. I bought a house from a person who got himself in a bind and was robbing Peter to pay Paul. After he got himself back on his feet, he asked me if I wanted to sell the property back to him.

"No thanks," I told him. "I'm cash-flowing on that property and getting my investment back. Call me in ten years."

You may hear of other great opportunities from your banker. I've developed a good relationship with my banker, and it has paid off more than once. Recently, another real estate investor was in default on his loans and the bank was about to foreclose on him. My banker mentioned this to me, and I was able to pay a few thousand dollars for the equity on the property and assumed the loans. It was one of the easiest deals I've done, and the only reason I was able to make it happen was that the bank trusted me. Many banks will do anything to avoid bad debt on their books, and that can create opportunities for you.

Some investors will eventually get out of the business. They may retire, they get burned out and just want to move on, or (as will happen eventually to all of us) they pass away. These situations create chances to buy property at bargain prices or as packages.

One of the best ways to know about properties available at fire sale prices is to be involved in your local real estate investing group. Once you start connecting with the other members, you'll have an inside track on opportunities.

Regardless of how you find out about potential properties, make sure every one of them fits into your overall strategy. Don't buy a property just because it's inexpensive. You can maintain positive cash flow only when you spend less money than you make each month, and you won't do that if you buy every property that comes your way.

In order to know what bargains are out there, you have to understand your market. Every market is different. What works in New York City may not work in Oklahoma City and vice versa. And there may be several different markets within your city. You have to know the market in order to be able to discern which properties are good values.

32. Finding the Right Agent

Another great way to find value-priced properties is to build relationships with Realtors in your area. They'll know the market as well as you do and can point you to great investment properties you might not otherwise find. A real estate agent will also have access to every listing in your area.

But you have to make sure you choose the right agent to work with. You don't want to pick a name from the phone book at random. You need to make sure the agent has experience working with investors and is motivated to help you build your portfolio. He should understand your goals and how the process of fixing rental properties works, and he should understand how these properties are financed. You'll be building a relationship with your Realtor, and you want to be sure you're on the same page.

The agent needs to be motivated. Regardless of how much experience someone has, if he's not willing to put in the time and effort to stay successful, you don't want to do business with him. Realtors get paid only when they make a sale, and if they aren't hungry to build their business, they'll only keep you from growing yours. You don't want to spend weeks working with a Realtor only to discover he isn't as passionate about building his business as you are about building yours.

Ask other investors you know for names of Realtors they've worked with. If people you know and trust have found agents who thoroughly understand real estate investing, chances are they'll be able to help you.

After you have a few prospects, qualify them with a few questions. Do they have any experience dealing with investors? Do they know and understand investing terms? How familiar are they with technology? Will they be able to respond quickly if you text or e-mail them? Do they represent any other investors?

But the most important factors aren't technology or experience. You want to choose someone you have good chemistry with and who shares your vision.

33. FSBO

We've all seen them. We drive by houses with a sign staked in the front yard that reads "For Sale by Owner." A hand-written phone number is scrawled across the bottom of the sign. I used to pass by these without giving them a second glance. Now I look at FSBOs and I see piles of cash.

FSBOs can be found as you drive around or as you're looking in the classifieds. One advantage to buying these properties is that because the seller is handling the transaction himself and not using an agent, he doesn't have to factor in the agent's commission into his price. And this can mean savings for you.

You have to be disciplined when searching for FSBOs. It's not always easy to call people about their properties, but if you're serious about building wealth through real estate, you have to overcome any anxiety you have. I recommend setting a time every week when you make your calls. You might block out every Monday from 1:00 p.m. to 2:00 p.m. for this. Get the numbers from the Sunday paper, and keep a pen and paper in your car so you can write down the numbers you see on signs posted in yards.

Calling on FSBOs is a numbers game. You won't find a property that fits your investment strategy on each call. In fact, you'll strike out on most of the calls you make. The key is to make a lot of calls on a regular basis. You need to make as many calls as you can. When you come into the office each morning, don't look at your telephone as just a phone anymore. Think of it as the key to a safe, and each time you call on an FSBO, you're closer to cracking the combination and taking hold of the treasure inside it.

Most FSBO sellers won't want to deal with an agent, and only in a few cases will an agent be able to get you a showing more quickly than you can on your own. In my experience, most FSBO sellers are uneducated, naive, or cheap; sometimes they're all three.

When you buy FSBOs, you don't want to alienate your real estate agent by giving the appearance you're going around his back to find deals. Even if you do a lot of the legwork on your FSBOs, you can keep your relationship with your agent solid by sending him referrals.

34. Private Lending

Another great way to finance your properties is through private lending. Many people have accumulated cash during their lives and want to make a safe, reliable return. They look to the real estate market, but instead of buying property, they loan money to investors. It can be a great way for people to profit from the security and stability of real estate without having to worry about tenants or maintenance. Of course, these lenders make their profit by charging interest and fees.

Private lenders can be some of the best ways to secure financing to grow your business. There's almost always less red tape when you borrow from a private lender as opposed to a bank, and private lenders are often willing to overlook a rough credit history. Many banks will not loan on a property if the applicant hasn't owned it for at least a year, but this is generally not a concern for private lenders. However, they generally charge a higher interest rate than banks.

35. The Eye Test

Buying a new property can be a challenge, especially when you're just starting in the real estate game. After you buy a few houses, you'll have the savvy to know what's a great deal and what isn't.

With a little experience, you'll be able to walk the property during your inspection and learn enough to know whether the property is a good value or not. Look at the windows. Are they new? Has the roof been replaced? What about the air conditioning? Has it been upgraded to a central unit, or are there window units?

Look at any repair or remodeling that has been completed on the property. Does it look professionally done, or does it look like an amateur trying to save money did it? Look at the foundation. Can you see any cracks or crumbling?

Inspect the appliances in the kitchen. If they're new, are they high-quality, or are they the cheapest ones available? There's nothing wrong with inexpensive appliances, but if they're used, it tells you the house may be owned by an investor.

Inspect the plumbing and the fixtures. Do you see any water leaks? Is the water heater new or will it have to be replaced?

Look at the neighbors' houses. Are they well maintained? Are their cars in running order? Are any of them parked on your property?

Making sure properties pass the eye test is the lifeblood of being a savvy landlord. Once you master it, your deals will start to fall in place much faster.

36. Handyman or General Contractor?

Whenever you buy a property, you'll need to calculate how much work needs to be done before you can rent it. Will it be tenant-ready with new tile and fresh paint, or will you have to redo the plumbing, replace the roof, and have it rewired? Your answer will have an impact on whether the property will bring you positive cash flow.

Depending on how much work needs to be done, you'll have to decide whether to hire a handyman or a general contractor. Handymen generally take care of smaller tasks. They can inexpensively come out and repair a fence, paint a room, or replace carpet. I pay $15 to $20 an hour for a good handyman.

If the property has to be rehabbed, you'll probably need a general contractor. Contractors will hire all the people needed to come out and repair the property if one person can't do the job in a day. Contractors are usually required to be licensed and bonded. Of course, they'll be more expensive than a handyman, and you don't want to use one if you don't have to. They probably will charge by the project rather than by the hour. But when the job is big enough, a good contractor will save you time and money in the long run.

To save money you can be your own contractor and build a team of great tradesmen. That's how I do it. Before you decide to handle everything yourself, make sure you factor in how much time it will take to organize and interview your new team members. You'll need an HVAC guy, a carpenter, a plumber, an electrician, someone to do flooring, and a roofer, plus painting and drywall people. Get to know your team as intimately as possible. You'll be working together closely, and the better you know them, the smoother things will go.

37. Look Before You Leap

Before you purchase your first property, understand that owning rental property is a "people" business. A big part of your job will be interacting with people. Sometimes the people you deal with won't look like you, talk like you, worship like you, or believe the same things you do. However, you have to treat everyone you meet with respect and dignity.

Not everyone's cut out to deal with people on a regular basis. Some deal with social situations better than others. If you can't deal with different types of people, real estate investing may not be the business for you.

Make sure you understand federal laws regarding housing, as well as any local statutes or ordinances. You can't refuse to rent to people because of his race, religion, gender, disability, age, sexual orientation, or marital status. You need to talk to your lawyer about this before you rent to your first tenant.

Discriminating against someone for any of the above reasons can cost you plenty. You could be fined or sued, and you might have trouble getting any future contracts with the government for Section 8 housing. Don't make a bad decision that could cost you money and ruin your reputation. Treat everyone with the respect and dignity you expect, and you won't find yourself in the crosshairs of an attorney looking to cash in.

You'll never go wrong if you're professional with everyone you come in contact with. But if you utter the wrong words at the wrong time, your empire could quickly start to unravel.

38. Never, Ever, Ever, Ever Change the Locks on a Tenant

There'll be times where a tenant makes you feel like your life would be much better if you'd never heard of him, especially if he hasn't paid his rent. Sometimes you may even be tempted to call a locksmith and have the locks changed. But you should never change the locks while a tenant is still living in your property.

In some states, landlords can be fined if they lock a tenant out of his property. Not only would you have to pay the fine, you'll still have to expend the time and money to hire an attorney and go to court to get rid of the tenant. It's just not worth the potential trouble to change the locks. File whatever paperwork is necessary to evict the tenant, and let the process take its course.

You can draft a clause in your lease that says if the home looks abandoned for more than ten days, the landlord assumes the property has been abandoned and has access to the property. That way, if the tenant has abandoned the property, you can enter without having to wait for a judge to give you permission.

The only time you should ever change the locks (unless your lease gives you permission if the property has been abandoned) would be if you have a court order giving you permission. If you do it any other time, you might be knocking over a hornets' nest. It's not worth getting stung.

39. It's In Your Hands

I know that I'm repeating some of this material. I'm not trying to waste your time, but I want to hammer in how important these ideas are.

Allow me to emphasize again that one of the things I like best about owning real estate is having control over the properties. If I want to make changes (like painting it or landscaping the yard), I just do it. I don't have to ask anybody's permission or deal with a board of directors in a city halfway across the country. If I decide the time is right to sell a property, I put a "For Sale" sign on the property and start negotiating deals.

You generally won't have that level of control if you put your money in stocks or bonds. You may get to vote at a shareholders' meeting, but you won't be able to call the CEO and tell him you don't like a decision he has made. When I invest my hard-earned money, I want to have the ability to control the business. And owning real estate offers me more control than any other way I know of.

Another great reason to invest in real estate is that it allows you to leverage your money. You can buy property by borrowing against it, even when you don't have the cash in the bank. Leveraging property is how people like you and me turn hundreds of dollars into millions of dollars.

Here's an example. Suppose you buy a property for $40,000. You put down 30 percent ($12,000) and take out a loan on (or leverage) the remaining $28,000. You've multiplied the value of your money over three times by borrowing against it. Assuming you've done your homework, when you start renting the property your tenant's monthly rent will cover your mortgage. You get all the benefits of owning the property even though you haven't paid off the mortgage.

I'm not a big believer in debt. I don't think people should have a lot of credit cards, and I don't buy something unless I know how I'm going to pay for it. Debt can be crushing, and life's too short to carry around a mountain of bills.

But leveraging real estate is different. Most of us don't have the cash to write a check for properties, especially when we're starting out, and that's okay. Leveraging property creates opportunities for those of us who don't have family money or who haven't picked the winning lottery number.

Plus, there are so many deductions you get to take on your taxes when you leverage property, including the interest you pay on your mortgage. If you were to pay cash for every property you bought, you would be throwing money away.

The smartest way to stretch your money as far as possible is to leverage your property. Let your tenants make the mortgage payments and take every deduction possible. That's the way savvy landlords build their empires.

40. Be the Kind of Person They Want to Do Business With

Every time you ask a lender for money, you need to act like the godfather and make the bank an offer it can't refuse. I'm not saying you should threaten to show up at your banker's house with a horse's head, but you have to get all your ducks in a row. You don't want the bank to have *any* reason *not* to do business with you. Make sure you have all your income and expense reports in order and that your loan-to-value ratio is no more that 70 percent. Try not to borrow more than 70 percent of the value of any property when possible.

Never take it for granted that a bank is going to loan you money. Even if you have a long-term relationship with a bank, loan officers still need to document how you'll be able to pay back the money you borrowed. So treat every loan application like it's your first, and make sure everything's in order before you apply for another loan.

You should also pull a copy of your credit report and review it occasionally. Reporting bureaus and lenders occasionally make mistakes, and some people have been victims of identity theft. You want to correct those before you ask to borrow money from your bank.

You don't want the hassle or embarrassment of being denied a loan because something was on your credit report that shouldn't have been. There are three major credit reporting agencies, and they're required to give every consumer one free report a year. If you time it right, that means you can get one report every four months. Take advantage of that and keep an eye on your credit.

Your credit will be the lifeline of your business. You won't be able to grow your business to the level you want if you don't have the ability to borrow money.

If you're just starting out or have good credit, you need to understand what banks look at when they determine whether someone is credit-worthy. And if your own credit history has a few bumps in it, you need to know what to do to get things back on track.

You'll sometimes hear about the "Six Cs of Credit." Banks normally look at six separate areas to determine if they'll loan money to an investor:

- character (also known as credit reputation)
- capacity
- capital
- conditions
- collateral
- common sense

A person with good *character* (*credit reputation*) willingly and responsibly lives up to the agreements he makes, and this includes paying bills on time. Your credit report states whether you make payments by the due date, and this information will be a major factor in determining whether you qualify for loans.

Do you have the financial *capacity* to repay the loan? Your bank wants to make sure you can pay your monthly expenses, including the payment for the loan you're seeking.

How much *capital* do you have? Assets that are worth more than your debts are known as capital. The value of the things you own should be more than your debts.

The lender will look at other *conditions* in your life, such as how much debt you have, your work history, and your living arrangements. A person who has held the same job for five years and lived at the same address for seven years will probably be a better credit risk than someone with four jobs and six addresses in the last three years.

How much *collateral* do you own? In many instances, bank will require that some type of property be used as collateral to secure the debt. In real estate, there's almost always a lien placed on the property. If the borrower defaults on the loan, the collateral is sold to pay the debt.

The bank will also try to figure out how much *common sense* you have. They'll look at your history and try to determine whether you make good decisions. This may come down to a gut decision by the lending officer, and it's important that you give good answers to all the questions you're asked. They'll look at your employment history and why you left each job, your credit card debt, and even the people you list as references. Assuming all your "Cs" are good, most banks will be willing to do business with you.

When you meet with your banker, remember that it's a professional relationship. You want to professionally dressed and prepared. Even if you have a great relationship with your banker like I do, you never want to give him any reason to deny your loan or cause any doubt about your credit-worthiness. I consider my banker a friend, and part of the reason we have such a great relationship is that I remember I have to treat him like a professional when I go and ask him for money. I never think our friendship gives me the right to get any freebies or a loan I don't qualify for. In fact, our friendship makes me work harder, because I never want to let a friend down.

Create as much credibility as you can. And don't give your banker any reason to not lend you money when you need it.

41. The Best of Both Worlds

Depreciation is one of the real estate investor's best friends. Your accountant can explain depreciation in more detail, but the short version is that, according to IRS guidelines, property loses its value over time. Every year you're allowed to deduct the depreciation allowed on your property as an expense, and this lowers your tax liability. You don't have to do anything to your property. All you have to do is have your accountant look at the guidelines and calculate how much depreciation you're entitled to. You'll be able to claim the depreciation on your properties for a set number of years (it's normally twenty-seven and one-half years for residential properties), and after that you can't claim it any more. But it's a great ride while it lasts.

While the IRS treats your properties like they're declining in value and granting you a deduction, your property will still be increasing in value. So you get the best of both worlds. You get to reduce your taxes while you build your empire. Depreciation is one of the greatest reasons to become a real estate investor.

42. Time to Sell

There'll be times when you consider selling property. Selling property can be a valuable strategy to help you build wealth, but you should do it only if it makes sense for your long-term plans.

You should sell property if it no longer fits into your goals or investment strategy. As your empire begins to grow, you'll make changes and move in different directions. You may decide to buy more multifamily dwellings such as apartments; that would be a valid time to sell all your single-family units.

You should also consider selling if you believe the market has peaked, or if you have an offer that justifies getting rid of a property. If a buyer contacts you about a property and offers you the chance to make a reasonable profit, you should consider taking the profit and investing it into another property. Good (or great) offers don't come along every day, and when you have that opportunity you should consider grabbing it.

Another reason to consider selling is if you're burned out or you're retiring. Everyone will eventually stop building their empire; the only question is when or why. If you don't have the desire to be a landlord anymore, you should consider selling and getting into another line of work, or hiring a management company. Managing properties can be hard work, and it can overwhelm people. If you plan it right and are disciplined, you'll have a great deal of freedom while you make a lot of money. But if you aren't willing to put the time into to finding new properties or maintaining the ones you own, consider selling and moving on to something else.

43. The Waiting Game

There are also times when you shouldn't sell. Never sell simply because someone makes you an offer. If another investor contacts you about one of your properties and makes you an offer that doesn't fit into your goals or plans, don't sell. If you can't explain why selling the property will help you build your empire, or if you don't know what you would do with the money, hold on to the property.

Don't sell because the market is soft and you're afraid of losing money. If you've done your homework and are willing to wait, the market will turn around, and you'll be in a much better position later on. By not panicking, you'll avoid taking losses you could have avoided with patience and discipline.

If you're in any way uncertain about selling a property, don't sell. Always trust your gut.

Action is important; if you don't take action, you'll never achieve the things you're capable of, and you'll be stuck in the same quicksand that has held you back in the past. But it has to be the *right* action. If you want to drive from New York to Los Angeles, you don't just get in a car and start driving. You have to know which roads to take, or you'll wind up someplace you never intended.

44. Cash Is King

As I've mentioned, owning real estate investment property is all about cash flow. It's about making sure your company brings in more money than it spends. To put it another way, you have to make a profit. If you don't, you won't be able to pay yourself a salary, and you'll be working for your tenants for free. That might work well in some places, but where I live money is pretty important.

I keep a close watch on my cash flow to make sure things are going like they should. It's also important to have an accurate knowledge of your cash flow to show to the bank when you need a loan, or to document the value of your company if you decide to sell to another investor.

Calculating cash flow is easy. You take all your income and subtract your expenses. A simple table outlining cash flow for one property looks like this:

Monthly rental income:	$1,000
Less mortgage:	-$400
Less taxes, insurance, and maintenance:	-$200
Total monthly cash flow:	$400

Of course, you can determine cash flow by the quarter, twice a year, or yearly. You can do it for each property so you know which ones generate the most money, or you can do it as a total for the entire company. The important thing is that you're savvy with your money and you know how your business is doing.

45. Contingencies

In almost every real estate contract you sign, there'll be items listed as contingencies. In other words, the contract is void unless these things happen. For example, many contracts are contingent on the buyer being approved for financing. If the buyer isn't able to secure financing for the loan, there's no contract between the parties.

It's also standard for the seller to have contingencies. He may require the wiring be brought up to code or the roof be repaired.

Always scour every contract you sign so you know your

responsibilities. You don't want to miss out on a good deal because you didn't know the contract was contingent upon you doing something.

46. They Came with the Deal

Sometimes, you'll buy property that comes with tenants who are under a lease. Inherited tenants aren't always a good thing. They may look good on paper because you don't have to worry about finding people to pay rent. But you need to do your homework and make sure they're the right tenants.

You don't want to inherit people who don't pay their rent and who cause problems for you every day. You also need to review their leases and make sure they're being charged a fair amount for rent. The previous owner may not have raised the rent in some time, and the tenants may be paying less than market value.

Make sure to get a copy of each tenant's lease when you close the deal, and schedule a meeting with every tenant so they know what to expect from you and what you expect from them. We also send them a letter notifying them of who we are and where to send the rent.

47. The Pro Forma

One of the best tools I use is called a pro forma. It's a simple sheet that helps me determine whether a property will generate the type of cash flow that justifies me buying it. Some people call it an "Operating Statement." Other people use it only for commercial property, but it can be useful whenever you're about to invest your money.

You can create a simple spreadsheet in Excel and let your computers crunch the numbers, or you can print it out and fill in the numbers by hand when you're on the property. I won't buy a property if I can't make the numbers work, regardless of how much I like the property or how smooth the seller's pitch is.

The pro forma has a place for a description of the property, including the number of rooms and selling price. It also has a table for me calculate the expenses and income. I have a good idea of the cash flow the property will bring long before I make a bid or sign the check.

Using a form like this is a great way to keep your emotions in check and to make sure you don't forget any important details before you buy a property. Savvy investors don't rely on their memories when they're making the decision about whether to purchase a property. They use a pro forma on every deal.

Your pro forma should include a space for revenues, which will include rent, profits from any other businesses on the property (such as laundry or vending machines), and any adjustments you're entitled to. The sum of these items is your total revenue.

The space for expenses will include the total of items like taxes, mortgage payments, repairs and maintenance, fees (if any) for your property management company, and utilities such as electricity, sewer, and water. To determine your cash flow (or operating income), you subtract your expenses from your income.

Keep in mind that the pro forma is meant to be detailed, but you don't have to create a financial document that meets IRS standards or one that you would submit to your bank. It's only meant to give you an accurate, detailed snapshot of whether a property will make you money. If you build it as a spreadsheet on your computer and you need to make a more detailed document later, all you need to do is cut and paste the information.

48. Phone Skills

One of the most important skills to develop as a landlord is the ability to talk to people over the telephone. Most of the business you do, including talking to contractors and interviewing prospective tenants, will be over the phone. If you don't feel comfortable making these calls, your business won't grow as it should. But the good news is that anyone can improve his phone skills.

But talking on the phone isn't enough. You have to learn how to communicate clearly—and more importantly, how to listen. With good telephone skills, you can keep small problems from becoming big ones. You can also learn about people by listening to how they answer your questions and what words they use. If you really listen, you can hear what's going on in the background. Once you improve these skills, you'll know more about the people you do business with than you would by just asking questions.

We use Google Voice as the main number we give out. We use it on our flyers, signs, and website. With Google Voice (which is free), you can forward your calls to any phone number, and there's even a smartphone app for it. With Google Voice, we can program this number to ring to different phones at different times. In the morning, calls are forwarded to our maintenance man; in the afternoon they ring on my phone; and in the evening the calls go to our secretary.

When we first started, we used a system called Novicecall, which charged by the call. Once we got a call, the service would e-mail us.

But since we discovered the convenience of Goggle Voice, it's the only phone system we use. We can e-mail and text through Google Voice, and it's a great way for us to stay in touch.

49. The Name Game

I've used the word *landlord* throughout the book, and it's even part of the title. So what I'm about to say may come across as a little strange, but this one little tip will make your life much easier.

Never refer to yourself as a landlord, especially when you're dealing with tenants.

When people hear the word *landlord*, many of them associate it with something negative. They think of a short, fat troll smoking cheap cigars who refuses to fix anything, and who shows up only at the first of each month demanding rent. You don't want your tenants to see you this way. You can solve this problem and eliminate headaches by calling yourself something else, such as the "manager" or the "property manager." But never refer to yourself as the landlord. You're only asking for trouble. Using a neutral word like *manager* cuts out the negative emotions people attach to the word *landlord*, and they won't think you're soft.

But the name game is a two-way street. Instead of referring to people who live in your properties as "tenants," call them "residents." This creates a much more professional relationship and makes them feel more valuable.

50. Trouble Right Next Door

One of the biggest mistakes I've made was not getting an agreement in writing.

When I was starting out, my goal was to buy three houses. I bought one FSBO from a successful investor I emulated. I was new and didn't pay attention to many of the details like I do now. The house I bought was next to an empty house that I wanted to buy in the future. I started rehabbing the house I bought and the seller assured me he wouldn't sell the house next door. He'd been a mentor to me, and I took him at his word.

One day, a group of rough guys showed up at the house next door. They were yelling and throwing beer bottles. I'm not a small guy, but these guys really intimidated me. It eventually dawned on me that the house had been sold, in spite of what the seller had told me.

I was pretty upset and confronted the seller. I felt betrayed and was really intense when I chewed him out. He eventually agreed to sell me another house in a different part of town, so everything ended up okay. But I could have (and should have) avoided the problem by having our agreement in writing. It should never have been an issue, and I could have saved myself a lot of trouble with a sheet of paper or two.

51. The Art of the Deal

I use a fairly standard process when I consider purchasing a property. I've developed this after buying millions of dollars worth of property and after visiting with dozens of other investors.

The first thing I do is pull up the public records to find clues. I look at the property taxes. What are the taxes for the year? You have to factor taxes into your deal because taxes eat cash flow. Are they paid on time? When are they paid? In Oklahoma, we're allowed to pay property taxes in full in December, or we can pay half in December and the other half the following March with no penalty. If the taxes are paid in full in December, I suspect the owners have a loan on the property and their escrow account is paying the taxes. If the taxes are split, the owner probably handles the taxes on his own or he has no debt on the property. I look at at least three years to see a pattern.

I then look at the sales history and when the title has been transferred. One of the things I'm trying to find is how much the current owner paid for the property. I look at how many transactions have been made. How long has the current owner owned the property? Is the property in his name, or is it held in the name of a corporation, trust, or another person? I need as much information as I can find to understand his motivation for selling. Once I know that, I can use it to get the best deal possible. I also research his name to see if he owns multiple properties, and, if so, if he is selling more than one.

I then find as much information about the house as possible. When was it built? How many square feet are recorded and how many rooms are recorded as living space? Have there been any additions, or has the garage been converted to living space? Knowing this information gives me power. I can ask the seller about the property, and if he gives me correct answers, I know he's an honest person. If he doesn't tell me the truth, I know he's not the kind of person I want to do business with.

I look at pictures of the property to see if I can find any clues about it or the owners. If I get lucky, I can compare photos to see when the roof was replaced. I might be able to see what cars are parked in the driveway, if bushes have been removed, and if the home has been painted and maintained. Hopefully, I can look at the windows to see their age and whether the house has window air conditioning units.

After that, I look at what the county assessor thinks the market value of the property is. Has this value gone up or down recently? How does it compare to other houses in the area?

Then I review comparable properties that have sold, and I use that to determine the average square-foot sales price. Is the asking price above or below this?

Then I move on to the school district. This is one of the most important factors in renting properties. You can take the same house, put it in a different school district, and the rent you can charge could vary by hundreds of dollars per month. Parents will do everything they can to help their children, and this includes moving to a better school district, even if it means paying higher rent.

Once that's done, I look at the size of the lot. Homes with larger lots can be rented for more money.

I view the property in Google Maps using both aerial view and street view. This lets me get a feel for the neighborhood.

Once I have all the information about the house and know what it looks like, I run the numbers. If my calculations demonstrate I'll be able to have a decent cash flow, I set up a time to view the property. If I don't see anything at the viewing that throws my numbers out of whack, I buy the property.

There's an art to pulling the trigger on a deal, and it's important to have as much information as possible about each piece of property before you decide to buy. But it's possible to have too much information. Sometimes investors will overanalyze a deal and catch a severe case of "analysis paralysis." Sometimes you just have to pull the trigger and do a deal so you can grow. You'll miss some deals when you do your due diligence because some moneymakers don't look good on paper.

The longer you're in the business, the more deals you'll conquer, and this experience will guide you when it's time to make a deal.

52. The Short Version

By using the tips in this book, you can race into the fast lane instead of limping along on the sidewalk. You don't have to learn everything the hard way.

Here's a summary of some proven ways you can build your empire and make your life simpler.

Choose your tenants carefully. Nothing will sidetrack your business faster than having a bunch of tenants who don't pay on time and whose only goals in life are to frustrate you. You can solve many of the problems you'll face by doing business with the right people. Screen your tenants thoroughly and carefully, and prequalify them to save you time. And make sure you keep all that information in a file. I now scan every piece of paper into my computer. Everyone in my office can access those documents anytime they want.

Find a mentor and join a local real estate investors' club. Regardless of what problems you'll face, someone has probably gone through them before you. Take advantage of the people around you. And be sure to offer advice and support when someone comes to you. As you become more experienced, new investors will start respecting you and will ask you questions. Give back when you have the chance. I still call investor friends for the most random questions.

Treat your investments as a business, even if it's only part-time. If you put the time in, this will soon turn into a full-time opportunity, and you don't want to spend the time and trouble of reorganizing sloppy records or disorganized files. Even if you have only one property, act like you own a hundred. You'll have enough growing pains as you expand, and you don't want to make these worse by creating problems for yourself. Create a system that helps you grow.

Trust but verify. When it comes to your money, you should never trust the information anyone gives you, especially when you first meet them. When tenants fill out their lease applications, verify as much of the information as possible. Call the work and contact numbers listed. Don't assume that any of the information is correct until you speak to someone, but even then it may be a premeditated fraud. Always trust your gut. If you're buying a property and the seller gives you an income statement, double-check his figures and verify them if you can. When you hire a contractor to do a job, stop by the site and make sure he's doing it. This keeps everyone accountable.

I'm not saying you can never trust anyone again, but until you have a longstanding relationship with someone, you should avoid taking him at his word. Always have a written agreement. Even family members have been known to be confused over the terms of a deal (and sometimes even cheat each other), and it's just common sense to keep a close eye on your wallet regardless of who you're dealing with.

Avoid doing business with family and friends. One of the worst mistakes I made was buying a house from a close friend. I trusted him and didn't think I needed to verify what he was telling me. I made the payments on time, but when the time came for me to get a lien release, I found out he hadn't been applying my payments to the mortgage. I felt completely violated. I eventually had to hire a lawyer to track him down and issue the release. I should have hired a closing company to escrow the deal for me, but I cut corners because I trusted the guy.

Set up an emergency fund. Investing in real estate is traditionally one of the safest ways to create wealth. But we've all watched real estate prices decline over the last few years. Things have started to turn around, but one of the lessons we should learn is to be prepared. Have enough money set aside to cover your expenses in case you have trouble renting properties or there's another glitch in the market. With proper planning, you can weather storms that make other people cringe. A good rule of thumb is to have six months of expenses per property. If your mortgage on a property is $300 per month and your expenses there are $100 per month, you need to have $2,400.

Don't be afraid to think outside of the box. If you find a deal where the numbers work and the property fits within your investment strategy, don't be afraid to take a chance even if you have to be creative to get it done. If you keep doing the same things you've always done, you'll never get different results. Calculated risks will help you build your empire. Being afraid to take chances will keep you on the sidelines forever. Safety nets are great, but don't let them become anchors.

*   *   *

You've read enough about the basics of investing. You know why you should invest in real estate, how to find and purchase properties, and how to manage them. Now it's time to hear from investors in the trenches. This is where you'll really ramp up the learning curve. Welcome to the fast lane.

PART FIVE

Learn from Those
Who've Gone Before You

Experience is simply the name we give our mistakes.

Oscar Wilde

Learning from investors who have gone before you is one of the best ways to build your business. I decided to write this book because I wanted to give my readers a chance to hear the stories of other successful real estate investors. If I'd learned and applied this information before I purchased my first property, my business would be much bigger than it is now, and I would have avoided many of the mistakes I made. My goal is to bring people together so that everyone will have a better chance of being successful.

Below are the questions and answers from my interviews of many successful investors I've had the privilege of knowing. Regardless of whether you're a total newbie or a seasoned veteran, you'll learn from these stories. Apply these lessons, and take your business to the next level faster than you dreamed of.

I want to thank each investor for giving me his or her time. I contacted these people because I know they have valuable insight and reflect a broad set of backgrounds. Some of them are fairly new to investing; others have built huge portfolios. You'll find someone here who has travelled the same road you have.

J. DUTCH REVENBOER

Dutch started doing real estate in 1997 after he lost his job and was wondering how he was going to survive. While he was lying on the couch, he saw an infomercial titled *Nothing Down* presented by Carleton Sheets. Dutch used his last $200 to buy the course. *I've nothing else to lose,* he reasoned. He knew he couldn't change his life without taking action, and Dutch wasn't going to let another opportunity pass him by.

The first thing Dutch did after he studied the course was call the owner of every FSBO property he could find. Dutch didn't have any money, so he tried to purchase those homes with creative financing. He wasn't able to close one deal. But Dutch eventually connected with an investor who was rehabbing homes and flipping them for a profit. He offered to teach Dutch, but Dutch had to agree to stay out of his neighborhood. The man didn't want Dutch working his side of the street.

What are the three most important lessons you've learned?

First, how to rehab. Second, how to use no money down to buy properties. And one of the toughest lessons I ever learned was to never use a partner.

What advice would you give to someone beginning his investing career?

Just do it. Pull the trigger. Stop dreaming and try! If I hadn't been willing to buy that course, I might still be sitting on that couch. You don't know what you can do unless you try, but if you don't try, you can't do anything.

What are the biggest mistakes you've made?

Not doing thorough background checks on tenants when my gut was telling me to do them. If I'd listened to my gut, I would have saved myself a lot of trouble and aggravation. And I learned the hard way to avoid partners whenever possible.

Why do you enjoy being a landlord?

I'm not a big fan of being a landlord. I generally buy properties and sell them. I like doing contracts for deed instead of managing properties. In some circumstances I have to be a landlord, but I prefer not to be one.

What's your most memorable experience?

At my first sheriff's sale, I thought I did all my research and sat through several auctions. I was really confident and felt ready to get in the game. The house I wanted to buy was the second house on the list, and the starting bid was $50,000. I raised my hand but no one else did. I thought that was weird, so I was little uneasy, but I made the commitment and bought the property.

I started working on the house and put about $2,000 worth of time and materials into it. It needed a lot of basic things, like a furnace and tile work. When I was in the middle of ripping out the countertop, a man from across the street stopped by and asked to buy the home. We started negotiating on the spot. Within moments, we settled on $75,000. I'd owned the property for about three weeks and made nearly a $20,000 profit. I couldn't believe it.

When I think of that story, it reminds me that you have to take a step forward and hold on to win—in life and in the game of real estate.

What would you do over if you had the chance?

I would have hired contractors earlier instead of doing all the work myself in the beginning. I think a lot of new investors fall into that trap. They buy property and then think they have to do all the work themselves. Leverage your time by hiring people to do the work for you.

What has been your best deal so far?

It's the house I bought at the sheriff's sale by far. But hopefully, there'll be a few more like that in the future.

What advice would you give to a newbie?

Take it slow. Don't dive into the deep end until you're ready.

Are you happy where you are right now, professionally speaking?

No, I want more. I'm always looking for the next deal. I don't want to become complacent.

What do you like and what do you not like about being a real estate investor?

I like the people. I love the money. The thrill of the deal motivates me. I don't like crooks.

Has there been a book you liked? Or one that helped you along the way?

I really liked Bill Bronchick's course, *Alternative Real Estate Financing*.

Single-family units, multifamily units, or commercial properties—any thoughts?

Single-family is what I prefer.

Any mistakes you've made that stand out in your mind?

Here's one that cost me $30,000. When I was starting out, I thought I needed to do all the work myself to save money. I was working a full-time job and doing real estate on the side. One day I was painting a house with all my gear on. I was wearing a jumpsuit and face mask. My cell phone rang in my pocket, but I was too covered up to grab the phone, so I let the call go to voicemail.

An investor was calling about of one my "We Buy Houses" signs and wanted to buy one of my properties. When I was able to return her call, she told me that after she left the message for me, she called another "We Buy Houses" guy and bought a property from him. I later found out the guy who answered his phone made $30,000 on that one call.

I was taught a valuable lesson. Hire workers to do the work so I can create the deals. I cost myself $30,000 by trying to save a few hundred dollars. That one still stings.

Do you have a mentor, or have you had one in the past?

No, but OKCREIA was a great place that helped me get started. Local real estate investing groups are a great place to connect with people who can help you when you have a question.

How did you learn what you know about real estate?

I'm self-taught. I've read the books and listened to the courses. And I've gone out and learned while I was doing the deals. There's no substitute for experience. It's the greatest teacher of all.

Dutch Revenboer can be reached at 405-590-6563 or
www.DreamHomesOKC.com. He lives in Edmond, Oklahoma.

STEVEN EARP

Rate your experience as an investor—with one being a newbie, and ten being a full-time, seasoned investor.

I would rate myself as a six. Currently, I just invest on the side for long-term investments. I've been full-time in the past.

How and why did you get into real estate?

I grew up with a family of investors. My grandparents were real estate investors. They had rentals, lease options, owner-finance deals, rehabs, and so forth. Periodically I would help them clean out rentals or do minor repairs, so I was exposed to real estate very early.

My first job as an adult was as a carpet layer's helper. I went from that into remodeling. We bought our first house when we were only nineteen years old. When we moved, we rented it out. Really, we got involved in real estate almost by accident. There wasn't much forethought—just keeping the houses we bought rather than selling them when we moved.

From there, we would buy a house here and there, rehab it and sell it.

When I was close to thirty, I transitioned over to working real estate full-time. We would wholesale properties for immediate income, then rehab and hold on to whatever we could afford to keep. I'm thirty-seven now.

I enjoy every part of real estate, from negotiating the deal to getting the houses rehabbed.

What advice would you give to someone just getting into real estate investing?

If you're just starting out, I recommend you buy a cheap house you can rehab. Do as much of the work as you possibly can yourself just so you can learn the ropes; it will be easier for you down the road that way.

What's the biggest mistake you've made as an investor?

There are two major mistakes that have plagued me. First, I bought a house outside my target area. The house was far underpriced, so I just couldn't resist buying it. The deal turned out to be a nightmare that has mostly been vacant for the better part of six years. It's too far away from where I live, so I didn't check on my contractors frequently enough and got bit by poor workmanship and overspending.

Second, I bought into some of the "gurus" that recommend taking overpayments on someone's house subject to the existing financing. After doing many of these deals, I would have to say that I don't recommend buying houses like this. The main reason is that if the seller ever files bankruptcy, you'll lose the house.

Why do you enjoy being a landlord?

The long-term wealth is in owning and leasing properties. That will make you a millionaire. Rehabs and wholesaling are for immediate bundles of small cash.

What's your most memorable experience?

I remember the rush of buying and selling my first wholesale deal on the very same day. This opened a new world of investing to me when I made several thousand dollars with only a few signatures on paper. At that point, I was hooked on doing deals with none of my own money and none of my own credit.

What would you do over if you had the chance?

I would start earlier buying more consistently. Since you generally have to do poorly at something before you can do well at it (whether you're learning a sport, an instrument, or a business skill), I would rather have spent more time at the start of my real estate career to speed up the learning curve so I could have made more money later.

What's the best deal you've been a part of?

There have been many. At one point, we bought a house for $2,000. It was 2,200 square feet. There were three years of taxes owed on it, and then we invested another $50,000 into the house. When it was fully rehabbed, the house was probably worth close to $130,000. That's likely our best deal so far.

What's your worst tenant story and why?

The worst tenants I've had were the ones I didn't do my due diligence on before letting them move in. I allowed the sad story they told me to play on my emotions, and I let them come in without a full deposit or a full month's rent and without checking their references. I had to fight with them each month to get paid, then I had to go all the way through the court system and mediation to get them out of the house.

What are your long-term goals? Did you have goals when you started, and have you achieved any?

For the long term, we just plan to continue buying and holding houses as we're able to. At this time, I'm involved in ministry as a vocation so I'm not in full-time investing any more. By the time we retire, we'd love to have thirty to forty rental units.

At one point, I had a goal of becoming a significant wholesaler in our area. We were able to do this after working at it for about a year. Wholesaling properties put me on a whole new level of investing by exposing me to more great deals than I'd previously seen.

What do you like about being a real estate investor, and what do you not like?

I enjoy every part of real estate, from finding deals to negotiating to the construction work.

Has there been a book you like or that helped you?

The best real estate book I've read is *The Millionaire Real Estate Investor* by Gary Keller. If I could have two different books, then I'd also get *Who Took My Money?* by Robert Kiyosaki.

Do you prefer single-family units, multifamily units, or commercial properties?

Single-family units are the safest investments because the tenants can't "gang up" on you if you have a problem. Also, with single-family units there's more margin because you can sell to other investors or you can sell to homeowners. With multiunit and commercial, you can build your portfolio faster, but it's tougher to find great deals. We invest only in single-family units.

You can contact Steven Earp at steven11@netzero.net.

SCOTT NACHATILO

Rate yourself from one to ten, with one being a newbie and ten being a seasoned professional.

I'm a ten. I make my living from real estate.

Tell me about your background and how and why you got into real estate investing.

I came to Oklahoma City from Madison, Wisconsin. I'd been in school in Wisconsin, but that wasn't working for me, and I needed to make a new start. I threw everything I owned in the back of my Nissan truck and drove to Oklahoma. I didn't know anyone or have any family here except for my girlfriend. I didn't even have a job lined up. I found a minimum-wage job and stayed in a little "pay by the week" hotel until I got kicked out of there. I wound up sleeping on couches for a while. I started knocking on doors and finally managed to get what I thought was a decent job as an environmental consultant. I worked in that for a few years and worked up to what I thought was the ideal job. I really thought I'd arrived.

But I found out that when you work for a big company you may be well paid, but you're pretty much scraping by. You may be able to save a little bit, but it's not a place to build real wealth. I had a choice of 401(k)s, but they were all lousy. I started to see that if I stuck to what I was doing, I would get only a 3 or 5 percent raise each year, and when I retired I wouldn't have enough saved up to live on. And that was including my Social Security, which I didn't want to rely on.

So I knew I had to do something different. I tried day trading and multilevel marketing. I lost money on anything having to do with the stock market, and I sucked at network marketing. I learned that you could make money with real estate just by buying and renting property. It made sense to me that people would always need places to rent and that property would increase in value.

By the time I was thirty, I got a beginner's course and a few books. The first real book I bought was Carleton Sheet's *No Money Down*. That gave me the idea that you could buy real estate without the cash or the ability to borrow money, neither of which I had at that point.

When was the date of your first deal?

I bought a pair of side-by-side duplexes in the summer of 1996.

Only one of those units was rented out at the time. The owner was willing to carry some financing. I wasn't in a position to borrow from the bank, and the few that I visited weren't interested in helping me. The properties were built in the 1930s and needed a lot of updating. I was lucky enough to have a friend who had the knowledge to help me fix up those properties. I didn't know anything about real estate except for what I learned from *No Money Down*.

What advice would you give to someone who's just starting out?

People don't realize how powerful it is being a landlord. You can make money in a lot of different ways. For example, on my first property, even though I probably paid too much for it, I was able to make money from my tenants' rent. The principle is that the tenants pay the property off.

My mortgage was for fifteen years, which is what you should do. After you get a few properties, you really start paying off the principle pretty quickly.

Never take out a thirty year mortgage. It takes too long to pay off.

Also, property increases in value every year. We can count on 3 percent per year in Oklahoma.

What's the biggest mistake you've made in real estate?

When I first started, there were two mistakes I made. First, I didn't understand that you make your profit when you buy a property. If you pay too much for a property, it's hard to recover from that. With those duplexes, at least I had the advantage of using financing. If I'd paid in cash, I wouldn't have been able to pay for the improvements.

The second thing I learned the hard way is that poor management equals poor cash flow. If you don't have the systems in place to manage your properties, you'll never get the kind of cash flow you need to sustain and grow your company.

The goal of any landlord should be to have as many properties as possible. You need to have enough to generate decent cash flow.

Why did you become a landlord? What's the most memorable experience?

Probably the experience of doing the first deal. When you're starting out and you look at people who have hundreds of properties, they look superhuman. You think it would be impossible to do that. As you get your feet wet, it can be a lot of fun, and then you start to see that the opportunities are limitless.

When you get your first check and it comes from a tenant and not from punching a time clock somewhere, it's a pretty cool feeling.

Is there anything you would do differently?

I wish I'd bought more properties when I first started and held on to them. But I started thinking that always paying a mortgage ties up your cash flow. I would have figured out ways to buy more aggressively.

What's your best deal?

My favorite deals are when the seller loans the money with no interest. I get one or two of those a year. They're really nice because they pay off really quickly, usually within ten years. The sooner they get free and clear, the sooner the money goes into my pocket and not the bank's.

What's your worst tenant story?

I had a tenant leave a dead, eight-foot boa constrictor in a property once. I had tenants who poured concrete down sewer pipes. It was nasty but fixable. Every landlord has stories about bad tenants.

What's your long-term goal?

I think a good plan is to have some type of growth in the number of properties. Adding ten or so every year is pretty good. Having that kind of growth is exciting to me. If I can add ten or twenty a year, and if one or two are paid off each year, that's great.

Where do you want to be in the future?

Everybody wants to make more money. I'm no different. I'd like to achieve more.

Is there a book that inspired you?

I love to read. In the last year I've started reading three books at the same time. If you do that, you can get a variety of information you can put to use.

Dan Kennedy has a series of books called No B.S. If there was one book I would recommend, his book on time management would be it.

Any thoughts on single, multi, or commercial?

Single-family. I think when you first start you need to focus on one thing. Single-family is a good place to start. Commercial property is scary because it can go unrented for a long time.

How many units do you own?

The last time I counted I owned ninety units.

Scott can be reached at OKC Metro Houses, 1516 N. Classen, Oklahoma City, OK 73106, sanachatilo@swbell.net, 405-232-5800.

JARED BOND

Rate yourself as an investor, with one being a newbie and ten being full-time.

There are many areas of investing. In some areas I'm a two, and in others I'm a seven. Overall I would give myself a five. I work full-time, wholesale part-time, and I manage my rentals and owner-finance deals in between.

Tell me about your background.

I got into real estate because I love money. I wanted to be rich even when I was a kid. I used to collect the change that fell out of my dad's pocket when he sat on the couch. I took that money and bought coins at the coin shop. I was obsessed with the idea of buying coins that were worth more than their face value.

When I was nine, my dad paid me five dollars to mow the yard every two weeks. It took me a month and a half, but I saved up enough money to open my first bank account.

What are you going to do with your money?

I want to become financially free so I can focus on the important things in life—health, family, spirituality, and self-actualization. I want to have time to raise a family, to travel, and to continue to grow as a person. I want to start a charity for underprivileged kids. When I was a kid, I knew I would never go to college, and I want to help others in the same situation.

Would you consider yourself thrifty?

I'm very thrifty. I've always been that way. Even as a kid I worried about spending too much.

What advice would you give somebody getting into real estate?

Networking is very important. Get involved with your local investment groups. One of my favorite quotes says, "Every dollar you ever make will come from someone else." It's important to know as many people as possible. That's where your buyers and sellers come from.

What's your biggest mistake in real estate?

When I finally thought I made money on a deal, the contract was unclear as to who paid for what closing costs. When we got to the closing table, the buyer and the seller each thought the other was going to pay certain costs. One of them threatened to sue the other, and I felt so bad I paid the costs out of my own pocket. I made only $50 on that deal.

What do you like about being a landlord?

My favorite part about being a landlord is getting all the cash flow and not doing any of the work. I use lease options and owner-finance deals because the buyers do their own maintenance and repairs. Actually, owning rentals is important too. They serve as a hedge against inflation and add security to your portfolio. I like to use property managers.

What's your most memorable experience so far?

It was when I finally made decent money on a deal and realized I had a business that worked.

What would you do differently?

I would do the same thing, but a lot sooner. I was treading water for a long time until I walked into the doors of the OKCREIA. If I could have done that five years sooner, it would have made a huge difference.

What's your best deal?

I had a deal in my first year when I made $10,000.

What are your long-term goals?

I want financial freedom, but I don't want to limit myself. For now, I'm concentrating on my portfolio. I want $3,000 a month in cash flow. Then I'll decide where I'll go. I might get into commercial property.

Are you content with where you are?

Yes. I've done everything I wanted to do.

Is there anything you like or don't like about real estate?

I like the fact I'm in control of my destiny. I spend my time and energy making me rich, not someone else.

I don't like that it can be uncertain and there's some risk. But that's true with anything. And even though you can set your own schedule, you're always working.

Is there a book that helped you?

Rich Dad, Poor Dad and *The Maxwell Daily Reader*.

Single-family, multiunit, or commercial?

I'm sticking with single-family. There all good, but it's my strength, and I'm going to exploit that.

Jared can be reached at (405) 586-0289
or at jaredbond007@gmail.com.

GARY LIEBER

Gary is a twelve-year veteran real estate investor and seven-year veteran real estate broker. He has closed hundreds of real estate transactions. He owns two investment companies, a construction company, and a realty company. He has focused on foreclosures and helped his clients buy incredible deals over the years. His company motto is, "We help people make money in real estate."

Rate your level as investor, with one being a newbie and ten being full-time.

I'm a ten. I'm a full-time investor.

Tell us a little about your background. How and why did you get into real estate? How long have you been doing it, and how old are you?

I've owned many businesses but was looking for a better business model. Real estate made sense to me. I've been in real estate for twelve years and am forty-three years old.

What advice would you give to someone just starting real estate investing?

Learn as much as you can at first, but don't spend thousands of dollars on "guru" courses. You can learn most things on your own for free on the Internet. I do recommend buying books like *Rich Dad, Poor Dad* or anything about real estate by Donald Trump.

What's the biggest mistake you've made as an investor?

I purchased a property via lease option and the owner stopped making payments to his lender. The property was going into foreclosure and I had to take over the property and sue the owners for my losses. I learned the hard way that it's much safer, if you're buying lease options or subject to conditions, to put the property in a trust and have the owner sign over their beneficial interest to you as the trustee.

What do you like about being a landlord?

Rental property takes time and effort, but it will build long-term financial wealth.

What's your most memorable experience?

There are a lot of them. I've been involved in hundreds of deals.

What would you do differently if you could?

I would concentrate more on building rental properties for the long term.

What's the best deal you've done?

I purchased a three-bedroom, one-bath house for $13,000. It was in fairly good condition. I sold it for nearly $20,000 in less than two weeks. That was a great deal.

Do you have any bad tenant stories?

Not really. I had one tenant move in and stay only thirty-two days, but he kept the property clean and gave up his deposit, so I really have no complaints about that. I rented the property again seven days later. I guess I've been really lucky in that regard.

What are your long-term goals? Did you have goals when you started, and have you achieved those?

I'm not sure I had any real goals when I started, other than to make money in real estate. And yes, I've made a lot of money in this business. I would like to be further ahead than I am. But everything takes longer than you think, so I really don't have any complaints.

What do you like and what do you dislike about doing real estate?

I love almost everything about this business. I really like being an investor and a real estate broker. It's the best of both worlds, but like with all businesses, it does take a lot of time and effort.

Has there been a book you liked or that helped you?

Rich Dad, Poor Dad is one of my favorites.

What does the future hold for you?

Financial freedom.

Do you prefer single-family, multifamily, or commercial properties?

There are great ways to invest in each category. I primarily do single-family homes. They're the bread and butter of this business. If you can learn to do those, you can always make money.

Gary Lieber of Vision Realty & Investment Services, Inc., in Edmond, Oklahoma, can be reached at (405) 844-6800 or at glieber@cox.net. You can also visit his website at www.okcinvestors.com.

REGINA A. BEENE

Please rate your level as an investor, with one being a newbie and ten being a full-time investor.

I'm a three.

Could you please tell us about your background? How and why did you get into real estate? How long have you been doing it and how old are you?

I've always loved houses. When I was a child, our family would go look at open houses on Sundays just for something fun to do. My parents bought a very small house for my sister when she started pharmacy school so she would have a place to live close to school. Once she was out of college, my brother started audiology school and he lived there. But he was the stereotypical bachelor and pretty much destroyed the house. I asked my parents if they would sell it to me. They just wanted to get rid of it, and sold it to me at a really good price. I fixed it up, sold it, and made about $30,000 on that one deal. I was hooked.

I was thirty when I bought that house. I took that money and bought a house at a sheriff's sale that my husband and I fixed up and sold. We made about $90,000 when the deal closed.

With that profit we paid cash for a rental property that someone moved into right away, and since then have bought and sold one more and have bought another one that someone's currently renting. I'm now forty-one and plan to buy another eight properties within the next fifteen years.

What advice would you give to someone who's new to real estate investing?

Don't be in a hurry. Deals can be found but you need to be patient and network with the right people.

What's the biggest mistake you've made as an investor?

Letting a friend rent one of my properties. I never got paid. The money is gone and so is the friendship.

What do you like about being a landlord?

I love people.

What's the most memorable experience you've had as an investor?

Holding the check in my hand after my first sale.

What would you do differently if you could?

I wouldn't have let someone I know rent one of my properties.

What's the best deal you've ever done?

I bought a house for $180,000 and sold it for $270,000 after making a few changes.

What's your worst tenant story?

I had one renter who felt it was okay to pay late. I never made her pay late fees. That was a big mistake on my part.

What are your long-term goals? Did you have goals when you started investing, and have you achieved them?

I want to own ten rental houses when I retire. I don't want to manage any more than that, and the cash flow will be enough income to maintain the lifestyle I want.

Are you where you want to be?

No, I currently have only two rental properties. But they're great properties and I want to keep them.

What do you like and what do you not like about real estate?

I like getting a monthly paycheck. I don't really know how to do repairs, so that becomes a challenge and I do worry about something major happening. It was a very hot summer in 2011 and I got call after call about how the air conditioning units weren't working properly.

Has there been a book you liked or that helped you?

I've read almost every one of Donald Trump's books. I love him!

What does the future hold for you?

I want to buy more houses hopefully. Eventually I want to move to Ecuador and live by the ocean.

Single-family properties, multifamily, or commercial units— any thoughts?

Single-family are the best for me. They're easier to manage.

MICHAEL RAFF

Michael is the investor who sold me the commercial building which is now my office.

Please rate your level as investor, with one being a newbie and ten being a full-time investor.

I'm a five.

How and why did you get into real estate? How long have you been doing it?

I've been investing for five or six years. Before that I was a commercial broker.

What advice would you give to someone new to real estate investing?

Put money back into your investments, always have a reserve, and never quit studying and learning. It also depends on whether the person wants to flip, rent and hold, or both. Both have a unique schedule and direction. I found that renting was good for the long term, but flipping gave me quick results and cash, which is king in this business. A lot of times when you rent, your money is tied up in equity. Know the market.

What's the biggest mistake you've made as an investor?

Becoming friends with my tenants and not treating it as a business. I let my tenants slide on things, and this resulted in bad situations for all parties. Being a landlord doesn't make sense unless you own a certain amount of properties and have processes in place to handle the day-to-day issues. And you have to enforce those processes with your tenants.

What's your most memorable experience as a landlord?

One of my tenants put up more Christmas lights than Clark Griswold on my rental property in Edmond. The whole neighborhood was calling me. He had this huge display on a corner lot. He had music, lights, movement, the whole deal. I won't forget that one.

What would you do over if you had the chance?

I would have started earlier.

What's the best deal you've ever done?

The last three HUD homes I've purchased to flip all sold within two weeks, and I made 30 to 50 percent returns. It's hard to beat that.

Any bad tenant stories?

I had one tenant who was a non-payer and he was really dirty. Enough said.

What are your long-term goals? Did you have goals when you started, and have you achieved those?

My goal has always been to have enough properties and cash flow monthly to cover my living expenses.

What do you like and what do you dislike about investing in real estate?

I love finding the deals. I don't like the numbers side of it, but I deal with that because I have to. I use a partner in a lot of deals; he's a numbers and banking junkie, which really helps.

Has there been a book you liked or that helped you?

There have been many. I always read to keep pushing forward. I'm always looking for a new good book. I've heard good things about *Confessions of a Real Estate Entrepreneur* by James Randel, so that may be the next book I read.

What does the future hold for you?

My future is endless. I need to focus on my family and my health and not just real estate and deals. That's probably one of my biggest downfalls. That could be a book in itself. People who are successful in this business who haven't had it handed to them are built in a special way. A lot of the time they sacrifice in other areas such as their families or health.

Single-family units, multifamily units, or commercial properties—any thoughts?

It depends on how much money and what avenue you want to go. It costs more to get into commercial, and buildings will sit empty longer if they're single-tenant. Multifamily is a management game. I would say most people start with residential because it's priced favorably for someone to get started, and they don't know the commercial market (lease and sales rates) as well. Knowing the market is the golden key to success, regardless of which type of property you choose.

Michael can be reached at michaelpraff@gmail.com.

TAYLOR DAVIS

Please rate your level as investor, with one being a newbie and ten being a full-time investor.

I'm a six.

How and why did you get into real estate? How long have you been investing?

Almost four years ago I was working eighty-hour weeks at a small marketing company. I realized I could make twice as much for myself in real estate. This was just as the market started to crash. I started out as a Realtor, mostly because I didn't know any other way. I ran across an investor named Steven Earp, contacted him a few times, and he asked me to have coffee. We talked for a while and started working together on some deals. After a while we started N. R. Holdings and worked together.

What advice would you give to someone new to real estate investing?

The answer's always no unless you ask. Don't be afraid to ask. Don't be afraid of no. You'll hear a lot of rejection. Don't take it personally.

What's the biggest mistake you've made as an investor?

Getting complacent. After a few years, I got lazy with the business. Things were going well, and I became happy with the little business I'd built, but after a while the leads stopped coming in because I wasn't pursuing them. I let the pipeline run dry. I had to start it up all over to regain my momentum. Trust me, it's easier to keep good leads coming than stop getting them and starting over.

Why did you decide to become a landlord?

In the long term, it's good money and wise investing. Having other people pay your houses off while you continue build a property portfolio is everyone's dream.

What's your most memorable experience as a landlord or best deal?

Buying a house for $82,000, putting $3,000 in it, and selling it to a cash buyer for $125,000 less than a month later.

What would you do differently if you could?

I would have kept working hard at finding deals and put more money back into the deals I had.

Do you have any bad tenant stories?

I sold a property to a couple on a lease purchase agreement. They never paid, and had big dogs that tore up the place. And because it was a lease purchase, getting them out of the house was a nightmare.

What are your long-term goals?

To be managing my rental properties full-time when I'm thirty-five. I have one rental fully paid off, and I'm a full-time Realtor, so I'm getting there.

What do you like and what do you dislike about investing in real estate?

I love the business, but I hate the paperwork and taxes.

Has there been a particular book you liked, or that helped you?

I liked most of *Rich Dad, Poor Dad* and *The 4-Hour Work Week*.

What does the future hold for you?

Rentals.

Single-family, multifamily units, or commercial property—any thoughts?

Single and small multi for me, just because that's what I know well.

Taylor Davis can be reached at taylordavisrealestate.com.

MARSHALL GRAHAM

Rate your level as investor, with one being a newbie and ten being a full-time veteran.

I'm a five.

How and why did you get into real estate and how long have you been doing it?

I bought my first house just over a year and a half ago, the week I graduated from high school. I had launched my wedding photography business the year before. I was a high school graduate on the way to college, making a little more money than my high school teachers. I figured if I didn't start investing then (when I had virtually no overhead), it would be much more difficult down the road.

The first time I became interested in real estate was when you told me a little bit about your investments at the BSPI conference. After that I read *Creating Wealth* and *Nothing Down* and was sold on the idea.

What advice would you give to someone new to real estate investing?

Read, read, and then read more. Real estate investing is like reading. It isn't hard, you just have to learn how to do it.

What's the biggest mistake you've made as an investor?

Last December I had to evict my first tenants due to nonpayment. I decided I wanted to fix up a few things in the unit before renting it out again so I could raise the rent. However, up until that point, I didn't understand the concept of "winterizing" a house. I came back a week after evicting the tenant to start painting. We had just endured one of the worst ice storms in the history of the city, and as I opened the front door, I found a busted pipe in my kitchen. Water was shooting across the room. The apathetic neighbor stood on his front porch with a beer in his hand and told me he'd heard water running in my house for two days. I'm now a loyal supporter of turning off the water in a vacant house during the winter.

Why do you like being a landlord?

I love the idea of having a piece of property but letting someone else make the payments on it.

What would you do differently if you had the chance?

I would have been more firm with my first tenants. I was trying to be compassionate and lenient because I felt sorry for their kids. By the time I had to evict them I realized they were more concerned with liquor than keeping a roof over their kids' heads. It was a tough lesson.

What's the best deal you've done?

I'm currently renovating seven houses that I purchased for $3,500. That's total, not per house. I'll admit, they're small one-bedroom mill houses and might qualify me as a "slumlord." Some of the houses need major repairs such as patching floors, but a few of them just need a new coat of paint. Even though they aren't prime real estate, they'll rent out for $300 to $350 per month. That's a gross cap rate of around 700 percent.

What's your worst tenant story?

My first tenants were my worst. They already lived in the house when I bought it, and having them paying late or not at all was the least of my worries. They stayed in the house the maximum time allowed by the eviction process, and when they left they punched a few holes in the walls, left trash throughout the house, and even threw several tools I'd left in the closet into the dumpster and poured paint on them. I had the local sheriff come in to take a look and he proceeded to press charges. It was a nightmare.

What are your long-term goals?

My goal is to own fifty mobile homes by the time I'm twenty-five.

Did you have goals when you started, and have you achieved them?

My initial goal was to buy two homes within the first year. I bought nine.

How were you able to accomplish your goals?

I took the first step. And then the second.

What do you like and what do you dislike about being a real estate investor?

I love real estate when comparing it with other investments. It's superior in leverage, ability to buy below market value, tangibility, and much more. I don't like cleaning up after tenants.

Has there been a book you liked or that helped you?

There have been several—*FLIP: How to Find, Fix, and Sell Houses for Profit*; *Real Estate Riches*; *Creating Wealth*; *Nothing Down*; *Rich Dad, Poor Dad*; *Buy It, Rent It, Profit!*; and *The Millionaire Real Estate Investor*. You can't read too much.

What does your future hold?

Buying single-wide mobile homes this year. In my area I can buy them for around $5,000 and rent them out for $300 to $400 per month.

Single, multi, or commercial—any thoughts?

I like single-family homes because they more plentiful than multifamily and commercial properties. The majority of units in my area are single-family and they're easier to find and easier to sell.

Marshall Graham can be contacted at www.marshallgrahamphoto.com or at 864-907-9399.

ED O'TOOL

Rate your level as investor, with one being a newbie and ten being full-time.

I'm an eight. I spend the other 20 percent of my life as full-time dad for my kids.

I would like to know some of your background. How and why did you got into real estate? How long have you been investing?

I got into real estate about eight years ago because I always wanted to own and operate my own business. I also wanted a business I could run while working my full-time job with health insurance and a steady paycheck. Single-family real estate investing, at the time, had low barriers for entry and exit. This was appealing, as it was easy to start and fairly easy to quit if I decided I didn't want to do it.

What advice would you give someone just getting into real estate investing?

Read. Take advantage of the endless good resources on the web. Go to Biggerpockets.com and read and ask questions. Go to your local REIA and meet, network, and learn. Learning at your own pace, on your own schedule, is much better than having to learn quickly, in a reactive nature.

What's the biggest mistake you made as an investor?

Not establishing or consistently enforcing policies and procedures on simple things like rent collection, late fees, and property maintenance and repairs. It has caused lots of headaches. If you give people an inch, they're going to want more and more and more, and it never stops.

What do you enjoy about being a landlord?

I enjoy working with people and operating a business. This gives me the opportunity to both. I enjoy taking beat-down property and transforming it into one of the best in the neighborhood.

What's your most memorable experience as a landlord?

The first house I bought. How green and foolish I was! I knew very few people in the business and even less about what I was doing. I was fortunate to benefit from some generous help from a few friends and family members while I worked on the job at hand. It took nine months to get that house ready, as I thought I was saving money by doing the work myself. I ended up renting it to a nice family and they went from a two-bedroom trailer home with four kids to a nice, three-bedroom home with a basement and two bathrooms. They were able to buy the home a few years later. That experience was a source of pride and joy for me, having seen their living conditions go from limited to great, and knowing I was a big part of it. I would occasionally drive by the home when I needed inspiration or just to check on it. Unfortunately, during my last visit I noticed the house had no window treatments and there were papers in the window, indicating it was bank-owned. How sad.

What would you do over if you could?

I took a vacation from personal development and education. I turned my back on that part of the business in years one through eight. I failed to improve myself and to identify my flaws and faults. Even more importantly, I failed to collect ideas from people who were far more successful than I was. If I could do it over again, I would change that.

What was the best deal you've done so far?

The first house I bought, fixed up, and sold to the tenants. It was a very profitable deal. I had another deal where I bought a lot adjoining one of my rental properties for $500. That purchase increased the value of the property $5,000 to $10,000 in a weak market but $15,000 to $20,000 in a strong market. That was a pretty good investment.

What's your worst tenant story?

I rented a property to a crazy lady who was making ten to twenty repair requests a month. Things didn't need to be fixed, but she wanted them improved. The housing authority eventually terminated her lease and she became someone else's problem. It was tough but I got through it.

What are your long-term goals? Did you have goals when you started, and have you achieved those?

It's a moving target. Sometimes I want a hundred units, sometimes I want only thirty or forty that are paid for. I need to shift in how I operate my business so I'm not doing the $10-an-hour work, and so I'm strictly managing property.

Are you where you want to be?

Absolutely not at all. Part of the frustration is that the systems I have in place aren't working. I know what to do, and it aggravates me. Once I have those systems in place, my business will be so much easier. I can see the finish line, but I'm not there yet.

What do you like and what do you dislike about real estate?

It's a good long-term wealth builder and has good tax advantages. It's always a great topic of discussion. I can see that my retirement is being built. Plus, it's very flexible.

I don't like how far some of my properties are from my home. I live three hours away from several properties, and I loathe being away from my family. I have a fear of being sued.

Has there been a book you liked or that impacted you?

I enjoyed *From Janitor to Multimillionaire* by Rich Weese.

Single, multi, or commercial—any thoughts?

I prefer single. I don't own multiunits or commercial at this time.

What does the future hold for you?

When the time's right, I'm going to sell all my St. Louis property or hire an outstanding property manager.

Ed is from Springfield, MO, and can be reached at edwood79@hotmail. com. I had the privilege meeting Ed at an investors' conference about a year before I began writing this book. I admire him as a family man, as a wonderful investor, and as a great friend. His nature to give has made an impact in my life, and I hope his words will inspire you as well.

ZACH MCDORR

Tell me a little about yourself. How would you describe your real estate experience? How and why did you become a real estate investor?

I'm a newbie. My first taste of real estate came when I was a boy and my father bought two rental properties. The renovations required a lot of hot, dirty, and unpaid work by my brother and me. It was interesting to think that people were actually paying my father to live in his building, and I guess that's why I got into the business.

I learned that real estate is not without risk, though. While my father was negotiating to buy one building, the sewer line burst, and the owner had to pay $10,000 to fix the damage. If it had happened a few weeks later, my dad would have been stuck with the bill. He was also unlucky enough to buy the property at the top of a real estate bubble, hoping the price would go up. Instead the price crashed, and he paid $120,000 for a building that was worth only $85,000 three years later. These experiences soured my father on the real estate business, and today he still has only two rental properties, which he's constantly threatening to sell.

What advice would you give someone who's just getting started in investing?

Get educated. Read everything you can about real estate, especially the management part. Then find mentors who can give you advice. There are many people in the real estate business, and they've already made all the mistakes. Let them help you.

What's the biggest mistake you've made as an investor?

My biggest mistake involved contractors. My first two properties (and only two, so far) both needed renovation, and I hired the first contractor who came along. It turned out that the guy was really just a roofer, and farmed out the other work to questionable sources. I ended up with some really crummy, overpriced work, some of which I had to tear up and pay somebody else to redo. You should always do background checks and get references for any contractor. And ask your experienced real estate mentors who to use.

Why did you decide to become a landlord?

I decided to become a landlord because I like the idea of having other people working all day to make me money. It's a lot like collecting welfare, except I actually provide something of value in return for the money. I truly believe that passive income is the key to freedom in life.

What's the best deal you've done so far?

My best deal was on a three-bedroom house on one acre. It was listed for sale for $40,000, and I offered the seller $32,000. He took the deal right away, and the house has been a good money-maker so far.

What's your worst tenant story?

So far I've had only one tenant, and he's been pretty good. The only problem has been rent payment. He pays late one month, then a week early the next. The tenant always pays with a money order, which suggests he doesn't have a bank account. People who don't have bank accounts typically aren't very organized with their finances.

What are your long-term goals?

My long-term goal is to have twenty properties that are all paid for. This will take years of struggle, but those properties will provide me with more than enough income to live on. With the right property manager, I could even move back home to Maine.

Zach can be reached at zacmcdorr@gmail.com.

DICK BESHEAR, PRESIDENT, FIRST SECURITY BANK

How long has your bank been in business?

We've been in business since 1951, and were started by a family. I started out in the credit department compiling information for our loan officers. That's where I developed my experience and skills. It was a great training program for loan officers.

Why is it important for people to understand banks?

Understanding the banking system is necessary for anyone who wants to get ahead. Acquisition of capital is very important. A big deal for us is $800,000 or $900,000. I tend to refer to us as a micro bank. We're more customer-driven than many of the larger banks. We focus on "mom and pop" businesses that want to either build or expand.

Your bank services the local community and also invests in businesses. Are both sides of that profitable?

Our shareholders have told us it's important that we service the local community as well as the business deals we help finance. We have to find a way to make both those goals work.

I've told people about your bank and how well it works for me, but many investors don't believe what I tell them. They don't have the experience of dealing with an institution that's so open to dealing with a real estate investor. How did your bank become this way?

We're a small bank and know what our niche is. In our area of town, there aren't a lot of commercial businesses. I wish there were more, but that hasn't happened yet. So we had to look at what was available to us, and we knew that financing residential real estate would work. We've developed a lot of experience in lending to homeowners and real estate investors. Another area we've developed is church loans. We've done a lot of those over the years. People would be surprised at the number of commercial loans we've done.

One of the most important things we do is to develop a relationship with our customers and to understand them and their financials. Then we can, within reason, give them financial advice. Of course, we look for certain successful customers, and they share certain characteristics.

So every customer has a different situation?

It depends on their goals, as well as their financial strengths and weaknesses. Everybody has had challenges, like illness or divorce, and you have to understand your customers in order to give them the best chance to succeed.

Many of the new banking regulations are forcing community banks like ours to change. We're in the process of increasing our fees in order to cover the compliance costs and audit costs and the increased time it takes to stay within the new guidelines. But every bank has to do that. The basic business bank model is in transition.

What common mistakes do you see inexperienced borrowers make?

Not having adequate financial information, like tax returns, rent rolls, balance sheets, or financial sheets. Those are what the examiners want to see when customers come in. We also pay close attention to credit reports. Every once in a while we'll pull a credit report and match it to the information a borrower has given us on the application or financial statement. In real estate, you have to have your own capital to take some of the risk. People want to do this overnight, but it really doesn't work that way. The expensive mistakes come when people are first learning.

If you need to, hire professionals to make sure your taxes and financials are in order.

What are the obvious deal breakers?

When I'm looking at someone's financials and he has a lot of credit card debt, that tells me he has an issue. In some cases, people have used credit cards to finance remodeling property and that's somewhat understandable. But a high amount of credit card debt is a red flag to me. Credit cards are the easiest to acquire, and they're the easiest way to get in debt. If you have credit cards, make sure you make your payments on time.

We don't even look at credit scores. We look at when a person actually makes payments. If he starts making payments more than thirty days after the due date, we may not be able to do business with him. If he'll slow-pay someone else, he'll slow-pay us. And life's too short to deal with that.

When you've done due diligence and you see someone with accounts at multiple banks, does that bother you?

It's a credit consideration. One type of lending we wouldn't do for someone with multiple banks is a construction loan, regardless of whether it was residential or commercial. It's too easy to comingle the funds. If we were financing a permanent structure, as long as the numbers work out and he's making payments, it would probably work for us.

What about the serial entrepreneur?

I usually tell my customers to do what they know and to invest in themselves. Where I see people get into trouble is when they start investing in things they don't understand. At some point, those serial investors will have to pick one thing and stick with it.

What's the biggest change you've seen since you've been here?

One of the most recent laws that was passed was designed to handcuff the really big banks. But we're finding it has a lot of other restrictions that impact the entire industry, including mortgages. It's a lot tougher to make a home mortgage that it was a few years ago. I can't defend the institutions that were making some of the bad decisions, but I think some of the laws have gone too far.

We have an overdraft fee, where customers could pay us to cover certain checks. But we're not allowed to do a lot of those anymore. It's harder for average people to get loans, and that needs to change. If it doesn't, we may create a generation of renters and I think people need to have a stake or the pride of ownership. I travelled to Cuba, where most people rent. As a result, nobody takes care of anything. It's sad.

How does someone buy shares in your bank?

Our shares are privately traded. Historically, they've traded between shareholders.

RICHARD WEESE

Rate your level as investor, with one being a newbie and ten being full-time.

I'm a ten. I'm a full-time investor.

What advice would you give to someone just getting into real estate investing?

Continue to learn all you can as real estate continually changes.

What's the biggest mistake you've made as an investor?

Several years ago I was purchasing homes at a foreclosure sale on the steps of a Texas courthouse. In one sale, I purchased four different homes, and when the auction was over I visited each of them. I walked up to the front door of each house and explained to the occupant, either the owner or tenant, that I'd just purchased the home at foreclosure sale and offered "cash for keys" if he would leave quickly.

Upon visiting one of the homes, the occupant was obviously very agitated that I'd purchased the home. She wasn't aware that the home was even in foreclosure and asked that I return later that evening to speak with her husband. Before I returned, I went over all my paperwork, and to my surprise, I realized that her home wasn't the home I'd purchased at auction. It was actually the home next door.

I needed to return and explain to her and her husband what a terrible mistake I'd made and apologized for upsetting her so seriously. I did offer her several hundred dollars to take her family out for a nice meal to try and offset the concern that I'd placed upon her. I then marched next door to talk with the owner of the home that I'd actually purchased. It worked out very well, as the home that I actually purchased was larger, in better condition, and completely fenced. I consider myself a perfectionist, and this was obviously not one of my better moments.

What's your most memorable experience as a landlord?

My most memorable experience was when I exchanged my first property for a home, a Porsche, cash, and a note.

What would you do over if you could?

I would definitely spend more time with my wife and kids in the early years of my adventure in real estate. There's plenty of time to buy real estate in your lifetime, and it doesn't need to all occur in the first eight years.

What's the best deal you've done so far?

My best deal was an office building I bought early in my career. The price was $1,475,000, and I was able to negotiate a price with 10 percent down. The 10 percent down consisted of a reimbursement of my $50,000 commission, notes worth $60,000 secured by a property I already owned, and the balance from my parents and my in-laws. In less than one year, this brand-new building was 90 percent occupied and sold for $2,200,000 to a group of investors. This was nearly $700,000 profit on the down payment of $147,500. Remember, I'd used none of my money out of pocket for the down payment. I even decided to stay involved in the investment with the new partnership. Several years later, the building was sold again for $2,700,000, and I received a $60,000 selling commission plus my percentage of the profits for my ownership.

What are your long-term goals? Did you have goals when you started, and have you have achieved these?

I've had goals ever since my original investment in real estate. I've been very goal-oriented for my entire life. I feel that my goals were achieved much quicker than I'd ever anticipated for various reasons, including the fact I was living in a tremendous area of California during a boom and while inflation was running rampant, and I was able to take advantage of that.

Where are you now, in terms of your real estate career?

Due to my early success in real estate I was able to retire at age twenty-nine. I detailed the majority of these experiences in my book and have been very free with my information on Biggerpockets.com and in seminars I've given around the country. I currently own over 200 rentals, and my wife and I have owned over 1,000 single-family residences. I have no idea how many apartments we've owned. I receive a large amount of passive income on a monthly basis, and all my properties are managed by outside management companies.

What do you like and what do you not like about real estate investing?

I'm currently somewhat concerned about all the investors who are jumping back into real estate and doing flips or rehab projects. Personally, I believe the prices are being driven in an upward spiral that may create another false boom with a bumpy landing.

As I've grown older, I've become much more conservative and less of a risk taker. In the early days of investing in real estate, you have more time for a do-over if things go wrong. I'm not willing to risk in the current business environment.

Has there been a book you liked or that helped you?

There are two books I recommend to everyone, and neither of them is mine.

The first book I ever read on real estate was by William Nickerson and is called *How I Turned $1000 into a Million in Real Estate*. This book was redone several times, as the $1,000 turned into $10 million and more.

I also love the syllabus by Ric Edelman called *The Truth About Money*. It's a very easy book to read and will take financial illiterates and turn them into very knowledgeable investors. It's a good book to have your significant other or spouse read.

What does the future hold for you?

My wife and I spend a great deal of time traveling. We took a six-year period of time and traveled by recreational vehicle around the western states and into the western provinces of Canada, and we'll spend two months this summer doing the same thing. We've visited every continent, 105 foreign countries, and forty-seven of the fifty states. We'll visit the last three next summer. We've taken thirty-nine cruises as well as many trips within the United States.

I'm currently building homes both in south Texas and in south Utah. I have a sixty-four lot subdivision in south Texas which is approximately 50 percent complete, and I've built three spec homes in southern Utah in the past six months. I've purchased three additional lots for future homes to be constructed.

Single, multifamily, or commercial—any thoughts?

I'm much more of a believer in single-family residences or multifamily units. I've always been wary of purchasing commercial property. When the economy changes, a plumber, or insurance salesman, or real estate broker, or many other businesses can simply move out of the commercial property and into their home and continue running a business. There's always a need for having a roof over your head, and for this reason I lean towards residential. From 2009 to 2011, I lived in southern Florida and was shocked to see empty commercial property after empty commercial property. When I drove by those properties, I was extremely thankful I wasn't the owner making mortgage payments.

Author and investor Rich Weese can be reached at palmshores@ hotmail.com. You can also read more about him in his book, From Janitor to Multimillionaire, which is available at www. fromjanitortomultimillionaire.com, eBay, and on Kindle.

ERIC WILLIAMS

Rate your experience as an investor.

We went from zero experience and zero properties to sixty rentals in about five years. I was a full-time investor during that time.

I think real estate is a great business to be in. I learned a long time ago that they weren't making any new land, and that everyone needed a place to live. There aren't any bad neighborhoods, just different neighborhoods with different people. Cash flow was the best deal for me, but after a while I got tired of dealing with tenants and fixing toilets. I made a lot of money, which excited me, but I wasn't happy about the time commitment. Property managers are okay, but no one will manage them like you want to. I got frustrated when tenants weren't taking care of the property like I wanted them to.

How did you get into real estate investing?

I used to play basketball with one of my friends. I had to leave when we were done, but it seemed like he got to play all the time. We got into our cars one day and as I opened the door on my Volvo, I looked over at his brand-new Mercedes.

I asked him what he did and he told me he was into real estate. I had a job I was passionate about, but wanted to find a way to make more money and build a future.

My friend told me about what he did and how he did it, and I started reading as much as I could. I was reading an hour or an hour and a half a day.

I went out and found some money and bought my first property. I went after another deal but was told it had sold. A month later the Realtor called me back and said the financing had fallen through, so I was able to get it after all. I was hooked.

I met with a real estate agent who told me I could never get more than twenty houses. "The bank won't let you do it," she said. So I went out and bought sixty.

I think one thing that made me successful was the buying cycle. When other people were buying, I wasn't. And if they weren't buying, I was. That was key for me.

What advice would you give to someone new to the real estate investing game?

There's a difference between a pig and a hog. Hogs get slaughtered, and pigs get to keep eating. Don't get greedy, and take things slow. Do a little at a time. Watch your debt leveraging. Borrowing money sounds like a great idea, but if things turn on you, you're stuck with all that debt.

Keep your money close to you, and keep your debt low. It's slower, but in the long run you'll be in better shape.

What are the biggest mistakes you've made as an investor?

I put too much money into the first house I bought. I fixed it up like I was going to live in it, and thought the tenant was on the same page. But he wasn't. When he left, I still had to put money into it. I needed a new stove because it caught on fire and the roof was leaking, but he hadn't told me about it.

As a landlord, you have to put a certain amount of money into properties, but don't do it with the idea that you're doing it for the tenant. You're doing it for yourself, to protect your investment.

I know you're no longer in real estate investing. Would you get back in, or do anything differently?

We sold our last property three months ago. I would get back in if I could be involved in a project that was so big I couldn't be involved except to sit back and watch the numbers. I don't want to be involved in the day-to-day management. Plus, I wouldn't do the debt leverage. I would round up a group of investors, take only part ownership, and pay the investors off in five or six years. I'd also hire a property management company.

What was the best deal you ever made?

I bought a house next to a church for $6,000 and put in some carpet and paint. It included a single unit behind the house (a "shack in the back"), so I got two units. It was a money maker from day one.

What's your worst tenant story?

There wasn't one individual tenant. I was pretty good about being hands-off. Once a tenant moved in, I pretty much left them alone.

My problems came when a tenant left, and the worst one was the first one. I had rats and roaches to get rid of. She left her refrigerator but the electricity was off. Maggots were coming out of the fridge. As I pulled it out from the wall, there was an old biscuit behind it. When I touched it, roaches started flying out like crazy. I wanted to burn that house down. I'm surprised the house didn't explode from all the roach spray I used on that place. It was thirty degrees outside, but I left that place wide open while that spray did its work. I didn't care if anyone came in or not.

What did you like about being a landlord?

I liked that I was creating business and that I was securing a future for myself. I always smiled at the first of the month. That was a different time of my life. I don't know that I would be able to do that again.

What did you not like about real estate?

I enjoyed most of it. You owned a little piece of society. I didn't like the debt. When things start turning, they go down fast. I don't think there has ever been a debt-free business in the world that failed. But if you aren't careful, debt can kill you.

Did any book impact you?

I would recommend a few. I read about William Zeckendorf, who basically built the skyline of the United States. I learned a lot from reading that book. Also, I read about Daniel Burnham, who helped design and build Chicago. That was really inspiring. He said that small dreams will not make a man's heart pump, so always dream big. I never forgot that.

Single, multi, or commercial?

I think commercial is a safer hedge. Most businesses don't move, and it's easier to get money for bigger commercial deals. Single units are smaller deals, and sometimes it can be a bigger challenge to get them done. But, if you want to sell, it can be easier to move a single unit than a large commercial project.

You were savvy with banks. How did you build those relationships?

I had five or six banks. I don't know if they realized I had business at other banks. I just made sure I built a great relationship with the person who was doing the lending, and I always paid on time. I went by and talked to the bank every week, whether I needed something or not. Banks can be your friend, and they can tell you what a property is really worth, and you don't have to do any research. A bank is always going to be under on their appraisals, and that gave me great leverage when I negotiated.

I found banks by asking real estate agents. When I heard the same name over and over, I went in and introduced myself. I also found an insurance broker who loaned money. He didn't advertise, but he's been doing it for forty years. Those deals took only a day or two to get done. It was nice.

Eric Williams is from Houston, Texas,
and can be reached at dibinc05@gmail.com.

JASON HARTMAN

Could you tell us about your real estate investing background? When did you start?

I started investing in real estate at the ripe old age of twenty. I was in college at the time, and I've been investing in real estate since then. My company now helps people invest in properties all over the country. Our only job is to help investors. We don't deal with traditional homebuyers at all.

I have several companies now, including a publishing company. My main business is a real estate brokerage where we refer investors to local market specialists.

Do you still purchase any real estate?

Yes, I still invest for my portfolio. I'm not totally out of that game. Last year my partners and I purchased 139 units. I'm done flipping. I don't think it's where the real long-term money is. People who flip have spending money. People who buy and hold have real wealth.

Invest in places that make sense so you can live in places that don't make sense.

What's your basic advice to help people start investing?

I've been fortunate to talk to a lot of people about real estate. We have clients all over the world, and we own property all over the country. Foreign investors see American properties as an incredible value right now.

One mistake I see people make is that they overeducate themselves. They may spend twenty years learning how to do something but never actually do it. The real learning comes from doing. Just dive in, get your hands dirty, and you'll learn as you do it. It's really not complicated. It's a straightforward business. The laws and customs that govern people renting real estate have been around for centuries.

The thing that separates the people who build wealth from those who don't is *action*. In life, taking action is key. We run across so many people I call "seminar junkies." They're constantly "getting ready to get ready." They're constantly learning everything. You're never going to have it all figured out. Just jump in and do it. You'll learn as you go. On-the-job training is the best way to start.

One book I've tried to use in my business in the last few years is *Ready, Fire, Aim*, by Michael Masterson. Just cultivate a rational amount of carelessness. To get things done you just have to jump in and do it. Make stuff happen.

What mistakes have you made in real estate investing?

Do I have to pick just one? There have been a lot. In the last ten years I created something I call the "Ten Commandments of Successful Investing." It was a way to list the mistakes I've made, and the mistakes that thousands of other investors have made.

Commandment Number Three is, "Thou shalt maintain control." What it really means is, "Don't invest in other people's deals." This includes partnerships, pool deals, or anything where you're not a direct investor.

When you're not a direct investor, you leave yourself susceptible to three major problems. First, you might be investing with a crook. Second, you might be investing with an idiot. Finally, assuming they're honest and competent, they still take a huge management fee off the top of the deal. They get rich off of your dime.

Buy houses that you control, and let some time pass. They're the most tax-favored properties in America and produce great cash flow.

Another one of my commandments is Commandment Number Five, "Thou shalt not gamble." Property must make sense in terms of cash flow from the day you buy it, or you don't purchase. People who speculate or who bank on appreciation in the future almost always lose.

I also tell people, "That shalt be area agnostic." Don't become too attached to any one area. I spent most of my life in Southern California. That area doesn't make any sense from a real estate investment perspective. I've heard people tell this crazy rule: "Only invest in the area where you live." The problem is that you may not live in the right place. Even if you do live in a good market, "Thou shalt diversify."

But you have to be careful to not overdiversify. If someone were to buy nine houses, I would recommend buying them in three different cities. That way, you've diversified your location, even if you haven't diversified your asset classes.

Are you a landlord, or do you entrust management companies?

I do both. I used to always tell people to have a management company. What our real estate company does now is find local market specialists in markets we like. The specialists buy properties at auctions or through banking relationships. They rehab the properties and get them rented so our investors can buy the property. We recommend a property management company, and the client can hire whoever they want or they can have no property manager.

Until about three years ago, I had managers for my portfolio. But I became disappointed with managers. At one of my properties in San Antonio, Texas, my property manager wrote me a letter telling me he was getting out of the business. I was busy and had an assistant looking at finding someone. But nothing got done by the first of the next month. Suddenly, a rent check showed up with a note from a tenant. "Hi, my name is Tony. I rent your property in San Antonio. I'll just send the rent check to this address. Is that okay?"

Sometimes doing nothing is the best business move. I've been self-managing that property ever since. What's even more amazing is that I've never seen the property. I've never met the tenant. If you told me five years ago that I could self-manage a property I'd never seen, I would have answered that you were crazy. I now teach a class on how to self-manage long-distance properties. It works well for me.

With self-management, the costs have gone down dramatically. I think the management company really served only as a middleman and never heard from the tenants unless there was a problem. When there's a problem now, the tenants call me, and if it's something small, I find a handyman or the tenants fix it themselves. I may regret self-management one day, but it's worked great so far. Management companies will tell you it's not possible to do it that way, but I'm actually doing it, and so are many of my clients. You can still hire a Realtor or company to lease out the property, but you can manage the property from a distance.

You have a lot of irons in the fire. How do you stay focused on one of your businesses?

I don't. I'm not very focused. I have it set up so that I have several companies with different purposes. They complement each other, and one of my companies helps educate investors, which forces me to stay sharp. If I wasn't involved in that business I would be even less focused that I am now.

Is there anything you regret or would do over again?

One of my regrets is not buying more properties. I was way too light when I was purchasing. I regret selling some of them. I should have kept more of the properties. I wish I would have started investing on a nationwide basis sooner. That would have been a very, very good move.

What's the best deal you ever made?

When I was in college I bought a property from a client and paid little down. I made almost an infinite return. The same was true on my second deal, when I bought a condo for $100,000 and sold it eleven months later for $160,000. I put 10 percent down, but it wasn't even my money. It was my grandmother's and I paid her back.

The best deal I have right now is a 125-unit apartment complex in Scottsdale, Arizona. I bought the note with partners and then we foreclosed on the note. We rehabbed the property and have rented it out. We paid $4.9 million and put some money into it, but it's easily worth $6.5 million already. That was a nice deal. We'll keep that for a while, and when it really starts producing I think it will be a home run.

What's your worst tenant story?

My worst tenant stories have come at the hands of property managers. One property manager in South Carolina was really difficult to deal with. She threw up every obstacle she could. I had a property that was located next to a college and wanted to rent to students on a room-by-room basis. The manager wouldn't cooperate at any level. When tenants would make simple requests such as requesting a discount if they moved in during the middle of the month, the manager would turn the tenant away. It was a terrible experience.

Have you achieved the goals you set for yourself?

I'm happy with my real estate career. I could have done better, and there are still great things in my future.

Owning income-producing property is the most historically proven asset class. It's simple, tried and true, and it just works.

What do you like and what do you dislike about investing in real estate?

I like housing. I don't invest in retail or commercial. Everybody needs a place to live, and that can never be outsourced. Housing is the place to be, whether it's a single-family house or apartments. I love single-family homes. Some studies show that our country will add over 100 million people in the future, and they're all going to need a place to live.

The only problem is that if you have over twenty units, they can be hard to manage. And that's when you might start looking at apartments.

Are there any books that have helped you?

I like Robert Kiyosaki's books and my own books. *Creating Wealth* by Robert Allen really influenced me.

Any final thoughts?

We're coming on a time with the global economy and the game is changing. When you invest in properties, you're really investing in packaged commodities. The wood, the concrete, the steel, and all the energy it took to make the property are part of the package. The ultimate investing equation is to buy the packaged commodities below the cost of construction with a thirty-year mortgage and then outsource the debt service to a tenant. That's a virtually guaranteed way to build real wealth that appreciates.

Visit jasonhartman.com to learn more about Jason
and the services he offers.

Part Six

Fish or Cut Bait

*Success is not final, failure is not fatal;
it is the courage to continue that counts.*

Winston Churchill

So now you know my story, as well as the basic outline of the stories of several other real estate investors. And you've been given a lot of practical information and advice.

Hopefully, you learned from this book. If you're a newbie, I hope it opened your eyes to what you can do and how you can use real estate to create freedom. If you're a seasoned investor, I hope it inspired you to make bigger and better deals.

But there are two main lessons I wanted you to learn.

First, *your freedom is in your hands.* It may not be easy, but you have the power to change your life and to create a lifestyle most people only dream of. If you want to take the easy way out and live the same life you have now, that's your choice. If you keep complaining but never doing, you can't blame it on me. From this day forward, if you don't take any action, the only person responsible is the one you see when you look in the mirror. I did my part and you're holding it in your hands. It's time to either fish or cut bait.

The second lesson I want you to remember is to *never, ever, ever, give up*. You're going to have challenges. It doesn't matter how much you've accomplished or what you've already overcome. There are going to be bumps in the road and hurdles you have to clear. Always keep moving forward, even if the most you can do is take one small step. When you do that, you'll never go backwards again.

Get to work and find your next property.

And may your next deal always be your best deal.

Part Seven

A Glossary of Real Estate Terms

When I started investing in real estate, I bought and studied every book I could find. I wasn't messing around with my new career. I was going to do everything I could to succeed. If there's a book involving real estate investing, the odds are I've read it or it's on my "to read" list.

One thing I noticed about the books I read was that none of them had a complete glossary of real estate terms. Some of the lists I read were good, but none of them was exhaustive. So when I decided to write my own book, I made it a priority to create the best glossary of real estate terms in the industry.

The following is a list of common real estate terms you should become familiar with when you start investing in rental properties. Keep this list in a convenient place so you can refer to it when you need it. Study it at night or when you have free time.

*

1031 exchange: An IRS provision which allows you to buy and sell qualified property within designated time frames while deferring any capital gains.

A

Abandonment: The voluntary and intentional surrender of property rights, with no intention of reclaiming them or vesting them in another person. Nonuse in and of itself is not necessarily abandonment.

Abstract: A written history of the ownership of a property, showing transfers in ownership and any encumbrances, such as mortgages or liens.

Abstract of title: A compilation of the recorded documents relating to a specific parcel of land. Title attorneys refer to abstracts of title and give opinions as to the condition of title. In some states it's called a "preliminary title report."

Abutter: Property that abuts, joins at a border or boundary, or is contiguous to another parcel of property, where no other land, road, or street intervenes.

Accelerated clause: A provision in a loan that grants the lender the right to demand payment of the entire outstanding balance on a home loan if the borrower breaches the terms of the mortgage or other specified events occur. The terms of the acceleration must be clearly spelled out in the mortgage.

Acceptance: The consent of the person receiving an offer to be bound by the terms of the offer. The acceptance must be communicated to the offerer and, when dealing with real estate, must be in writing to be enforceable. A buyer has the right to revoke any offer before a seller's acceptance.

Accession: Acquiring title to improvements to real property by annexing fixtures or accreting alluvial deposits.

Accrued depreciation: The difference between the present value of improvements and the reproduction or replacement costs, as valued on the appraisal date.

Acknowledgment: A formal declaration made before a notary public or authorized official at the time a person executes a document. The acknowledgment states that the person signing the document is signing voluntarily and that he understands the nature of the instrument he's signing.

Acquisition: The act of becoming the owner of real estate.

Acre: A tract of land equaling 43,560 square feet, 4,840 square yards, 160 square rods, or 208.71 feet by 208.71 feet.

Acre-foot of water: The amount of water that would cover one acre of land one foot deep. Approximately 43,560 cubic feet.

Act of God: A destructive act of nature that cannot be caused by human involvement, such as rain, lightning, floods, earthquakes, or hurricanes. Many contracts allow the parties to delay completion of their required performance (or vitiate the agreement completely) if an Act of God intervenes.

Ad valorem tax: A tax based on the value of the object or thing subject to taxation. Property taxes are the most common example.

Adjustable period/adjustment period: The time frame between interest rate changes on adjustable rate mortgages (ARMs).

Adjustable Rate Mortgage (ARM): A mortgage that permits the lender to adjust the interest rate on the basis of changes in a specified index. The interest rate may move up or down, depending on the change to the index. The changes can be made only at times specified in the mortgage.

Adjuster: Someone who investigates insurance claims and recommends an appropriate settlement amount.

Administrator: A person appointed by a judge to manage and settle the estate of a person who died intestate (without a will).

Adverse possession: Acquiring title to real property owned by someone else, after engaging in open, notorious, hostile, and continuous possession for a period of time set by statute. It's sometimes referred to as "squatter's rights." However, the possessor doesn't have a marketable title until he obtains and records a judicial decree quieting title.

Affidavit: A sworn, written declaration made before an authorized official.

Agent: A professional who sells insurance policies.

Agreement/agreement of sale: A contract for the sale and purchase of property between a seller and a buyer.

Air rights: The right to build upon, occupy, or use, in the manner and degree permitted, the space above the ground corresponding with the boundaries of a tract of real estate.

Alienation: The transfer of real property from one person to another. When someone sells property, he's alienating himself from it.

All-inclusive deed of trust: *See* wraparound mortgage.

All perils deductible: A dollar amount beyond which an insurance company begins to pay for a loss.

ALTA: American Land Title Association.

Amenities: Benefits generated and received through the exercise of rights to real property, tangible and intangible, and not necessarily money.

Amortization: Repayment of a loan in equal periodic installments that include both principal and interest.

Amortization period: The time frame for recovering the financial investment in a project.

Amortize: To reduce a debt by making regular, periodic payments of both principal and interest.

Amortized loan: A loan paid in equal installments during its term.

Annexation: Attaching, adding, or joining two things, generally a subordinate thing to a principal thing. This usually refers to two parcels of land, particularly when one a large city annexes another.

Annual Percentage Rate (APR): The total finance charge, including interest, loan fees, and points. These items are expressed as a percentage of the loan amount.

Appraisal: A written estimate, created by a qualified appraiser, of real estate value. An appraisal meets the standards of various agencies (such as FHA, VA, and FHMA) and is based on factors such as the recent sales of comparable homes in the same area.

Appraised value: The value of property at a specific time, based on facts regarding the property such as location and any improvements to the property.

Appraiser/valuer: A person qualified by education, training, and/or experience who estimates the value of real property and personal property.

Appreciation: An increase in the value of property. The opposite of depreciation.

Appurtenance: Something annexed to another thing that passes as incident to it. Rights of way, easements, and structures such as barns are often referred to as appurtenances.

Arrears: Payment not made on or before its due date.

Asking price: The listed price for a particular piece of property. This is a starting point for negotiations, and the sale price may be higher or lower than the asking price.

Assessed valuation: A determination of property values for the purpose of taxation set as established by a governmental agency.

Assessed value: The value of property according to a tax assessor. Property taxes are based on the assessed value of the property.

Assessment: A specific tax on real estate to pay for public improvements, including streets and sewers.

Assets: All things owned by a person or business. Assets include personal property, real property, and intangible property.

Assignment of contract: Selling, transferring, and/or assigning rights under an agreement.

Assignment of mortgage: Assigning collateral that secures a debt obligation.

Assumable loan/mortgage: A loan where the buyer assumes responsibility for an existing mortgage. The buyer pays the balance on the same terms as the seller negotiated with the bank. Also known as assumption of mortgage.

Attachment: The legal process of seizing property of another by levy or judicial order, and holding or liquidating it to satisfy the judgment or lien.

Attorney-in-fact: A person authorized to act for another person as granted by a power of attorney.

Auction: A public sale of a property, where the property is sold to the highest bidder. Some auctions are "with reserve" where the seller sets a minimum price. If the bidding doesn't meet or exceed the minimum, the seller isn't legally required to sell the property. Other auctions are "without reserve" (also known as "absolute") where the seller is required to sell the property for the highest bid.

Audit: An examination of records to verify accuracy and adequacy performed by someone who has the necessary education, training, and experience.

B

Balloon mortgage: An agreement calling for periodic payments that don't fully amortize the face amount of the note prior to maturity. At the end of the note, the full balance of the principal becomes due. Due to the large size of the payment, it's called a "balloon."

Balloon payment: The large, lump sum principal payment due at the end of a balloon mortgage.

Base map: A map with established and accepted reference points (such as state or county lines) on which land ownership can be plotted.

Baseline and meridian: Established lines used by surveyors to locate and describe land. This system (used in most states) creates a reliable and authoritative way to set the boundaries of property.

Beneficiary: A person who receives the proceeds or benefits from a will or trust.

Bequeath: To leave personal property to another under the terms of a will.

Bill of sale: A document used to transfer the ownership of personal property.

Binder: An agreement to purchase real estate given with earnest money. It's a symbol of good faith and acknowledges the buyer's intent to purchase the property.

Biweekly payment mortgage: A mortgage whereby payments are made every two weeks instead of once a month. This technique saves the buyer a substantial amount in interest payments.

Blanket mortgage: A mortgage which finances more than one piece of property.

Bodily injury: Physical damage to a person.

Bond: Any obligation under seal. A real estate bond is a written obligation issued under the security of a mortgage or a trust deed.

Breach of contract: The failure of any party to a contract to meet any of his obligations under the contract without legal justification.

Bridge loan: A loan to help buyers who close on a new home before the sale of their current home. The loan "bridges" the time when they pay two mortgages.

Broker: A person who's paid to bring parties together for the purpose of doing business.

Building code: Regulations controlling the design and construction of buildings. They're usually created and enforced by city or state agencies, and many of them even dictate what type of material may be used.

Buydown: A Veterans Administration loan plan available in a few new housing developments, where the builder agrees to pay part of the mortgage for the first few years.

Buyer's agent: A broker licensed to negotiate and transact real estate sales on behalf of a buyer. The buyer's broker doesn't have an agent relationship with the seller.

Buyer's market: A time when the demand for property is less than the supply. Buyers have choices of many properties, and the negotiating advantage shifts to the buyers.

C

Cap: A limit on how much the interest rate or monthly payment can vary in an adjustable rate mortgage.

Capitalization rate/cap rate: A percentage ratio determined by dividing net income from investment and the value of the investment. Often referred to as "return on" and "return of" capital.

Cash flow: Revenues minus expenses over a given period of time. The king of real estate investing.

Cash reserves: An amount of cash many lenders require buyers to have in the bank after purchasing a home. It's typically enough to cover two mortgage payments in the event of a financial emergency.

Cash value/actual cash value: The money an asset would bring on the open market if sold immediately.

Caveat emptor: Latin phrase meaning, "Let the buyer beware." The buyer has the burden of inspecting property to make sure it meets his standards. Once he buys it, he takes it "as is."

CC&Rs: Covenants, conditions, and restrictions. Restrictions that control the use of a property. Many neighborhood associations have strict CC&Rs that limit what can be done in the neighborhood.

Certificate of reasonable value (CRV): A document detailing the maximum value and loan amount for a VA guaranteed loan.

Certificate of title: A description of property issued by an abstract company or attorney stating that the seller legally holds the property.

Chain: A surveyor's unit of measure equaling sixty-six feet.

Chain of title: The chronological order of ownership of a tract of land from the original owner to the present owner.

Chattel: Personal, tangible, and movable property. Chattel isn't normally part of a real estate transaction.

Civil action: Actions enforcing or protecting legal rights. All actions that aren't brought in criminal courts (including administrative actions) are civil.

Civil rights assurance: A provision that no person will be discriminated against or excluded from opportunities on the basis of being a member of a protected class, including race, color, age, sex, religion, handicap, and national origin.

Clear title: A title free and clear of encumbrances.

Closing: A meeting where the sale of a property is finalized. The deal isn't closed until the buyer signs the mortgage documents and pays closing costs.

Closing costs: Money due at closing to cover items such as document processing fees, appraisal reports, and credit report fees.

Closing statement: A disclosure statement outlining the funds received and expected at the closing of the escrow, including deposits, taxes, and insurance.

Cloud on title: Any claim, encumbrance, or condition that affects the owner's right to clear title of real property.

Coinsurance: A division of risk between an insurer and insured.

Collateral/collateral security: Any asset that guarantees the repayment of a loan. In the event the borrower isn't able to repay the loan, the collateral is sold and the proceeds are applied to the loan balance.

Collateral heir: A beneficiary who's not from the direct line of the deceased (such as a child), but from a collateral line. These include brothers and sisters, aunts and uncles, nephews and nieces, and cousins of the deceased.

Color of title/apparent title: A fact which appears, on its face, to support the claim of ownership but because of a legal defect falls short of establishing title.

Commission: The fee charged by a broker or agent for providing real estate services, such as helping buyers find and purchase property.

Commitment: A written promise to make or insure a loan for a specified amount and on specified terms.

Commitment of funds: Reservation of funds for a specific purpose, based on an estimate, and before there's a binding contract.

Common element/common area: In a condominium or apartment, land and areas of buildings used by all owners or tenants for mutual convenience and safety.

Common expense: In a condominium, operation expenses for the benefit or necessity of all the owners.

Community property: Property accumulated during the course of a marriage and owned in common by both spouses.

Comparable: Properties used as comparisons in appraisal reports, substantially equivalent to the subject property by selling price, rental income, or similar objective measure. Comparables help determine the value of the property.

Compensable interest: Interest or right of parties that can be compensated by insurance or other legal remedy.

Compound interest: Interest paid on the original principal as well as the interest accrued.

Concession: A benefit or discount offered by a party to close a deal.

Condemnation: The process by which real property of a private owner is taken for public use under the right of public domain, after the owner has been compensated fairly.

Condition subsequent: A condition, which, if it occurs, will defeat an existing estate in real property or terminate an existing legal obligation.

Conditional agreement/conditional commitment/conditional sale contract: A legally binding contract subject to conditions detailed in the agreement being satisfied. Common conditions include that the buyer sell his home by a set date or that he arrange financing by a set date. The seller may be required to do something by a specified date, such as painting the house or repairing known damage.

Condominium: Fee ownership of a unit in multiunit building. Each unit owner owns a proportionate share of common areas.

Consideration: Anything of value given to induce another to enter into a contract. Consideration includes money, services, a promise, or the agreement to forbear from exercising a legal right. Consideration is what the parties give each other to create a contract.

Constructive eviction: An act by the landlord which deprives the tenant of the beneficial use and occupancy of the property.

Constructive notice/legal notice: The conclusive presumption that all persons have knowledge of the contents of a recorded instrument, such as a deed or encumbrance.

Contamination: The presence of biological, radioactive, toxic, or hazardous substances at levels that present a public hazard or exceed applicable standards.

Contingency: An event defined in a purchase agreement that must occur before a contract is binding. A common example is a contract contingent on the buyer obtaining financing.

Contract: An agreement between at least two parties, either oral or written, to do or not do certain things. The parties must agree on the terms of the contract and each must give consideration.

Contract for deed/installment land contract/owner-carry sale: An agreement where the buyer makes payments in a manner similar to a mortgage and has equitable title, and can use the property for any and all legal purposes. However, the seller retains legal title to the property until the contract is paid off.

Contract of sale: A written agreement setting out the terms and conditions for the sale or purchase of a property. It's the purchase document a winning buyer signs at an auction.

Contract rent: Payment allowing the renter use of property as detailed in the lease.

Conventional loan: A mortgage loan issued by a bank, credit union, or private investor, and not insured or guaranteed by a government agency.

Conversion clause: A provision in some ARMs allowing the parties to convert an ARM to a fixed-rate loan. The conversion normally happens only after the first adjustment period, and the new fixed rate is set at the prevailing interest rate.

Conveyance: Transferring title to real property via a written instrument, such as a deed.

Cooperative: A multiunit building owned by a corporation or business trust. Occupancy rights are granted to shareholders based on the value of their units.

Cosigner: A party willing to assume the risk for a buyer whose credit is insufficient to make the purchase on his own. In the event the buyer is unable to make payment, the cosigner is legally responsible for the payments and balance.

Cost of reproduction: The cost of duplicating a property with the same or similar materials as of a certain date or period.

Courses and distances: A method of describing real property using a starting point and the direction and lengths of lines to be run. Similar, if not identical, to metes and bounds description.

Covenant: A written agreement in a deed which sets terms and conditions on what parties may do on or with a certain property, or which restricts or forbids certain uses of the property.

Credit report: A historical list of your use of credit and your ability or willingness to pay on time. Many lenders use a credit report as the main basis in determining whether to loan money.

Curtilage: The land surrounding a dwelling that extends the property boundaries. The area may be fenced or include other structures such as garages and stand-alone workshops.

D

Damages: Compensation (usually money) recovered through the courts by any person who has suffered injury to person, property, or rights by the act of another.

Debt coverage ratio (DCR): The ratio of a property's net operating income to its annual debt service. If the ratio is 1.0, it means the property is only paying the bills and not making a profit.

Debt service: Payment on a debt for interest and retirement of principal.

Debt-to-income ratio: The amount of debt held by a person or business relative to income. Lenders typically want borrowers to have a ration ranging from 33 to 40 percent.

Declaration of taking: A document issued by a government agency as part of the condemnation process. Once the declaration is filed in court with a deposit of estimated compensation, title is transferred to the condemner.

Deductible: The amount an insured must pay before an insurance company will begin to cover a loss.

Deed: A legal, written instrument which conveys some right, title, or interest in real estate from one person to another.

Deed of trust: A written instrument which transfers title to land to a trustee as security for a debt or other obligation.

Deed restriction: A provision or covenant in a deed controlling, limiting, or restricting the use of the land.

Default: Failure to perform a required legal duty at the required time or in the required manner. In real estate terms, it's the failure to make a mortgage or rent payment on the due date.

Deferred maintenance: Existing requirements for repairs and rehabilitation that are being delayed or deferred until a later date.

Deficiency: The difference between the amount owed to a lender and the proceeds received from a foreclosure sale. The lender may be able to obtain a deficiency judgment against the borrower for the difference.

Delinquency: Failing to pay a mortgage payment on time.

Deposit: A percentage of the purchase price paid to bind the sale of real estate.

Depreciation: A decrease in the value of real property caused by deterioration, loss of market value, or obsolescence. In accounting terms, it's a write-off of a portion of the value of the assets.

Descent: The process by which one person, upon death of another, inherits real estate as an heir at law. Descent is tightly controlled by state statutes.

Deterioration: Impairment or worsening of condition. One of the causes of depreciation, which reflects a loss of property value, caused by wear and tear, disintegration, use in service, and the elements.

Devise: The transfer of real property under a will. The deceased is the devisor and the heir or beneficiary is the devisee. Where there's no will, the real property "descends" to the heirs according to state statute.

Discount: A sum paid to obtain preferred FHA and VA mortgages.

Discount points: A loan fee charged by lenders. One point equals 1 percent of the loan amount.

Dispossess: To deprive a person of possession, use, or enjoyment of real property.

Documentary tax stamps: Official stamps affixed to a deed for the amount of transfer tax. Some states don't use tax stamps.

Double closing: A closing wherein a property is bought and sold, then to another buyer sold simultaneously.

Dower: A common law estate in land given to the wife from her husband's real property upon his death. A dower consisted of a life estate in one third of the real estate owned by the husband during the marriage.

Down payment: A percentage of the purchase price the buyer provides in cash up front at the time of the sale.

Due diligence: The detailed analysis and risk review of an impending transaction. Due diligence is commonly undertaken by a prospective buyer prior to acquiring a business to ensure that he's aware of any potential problems with a property.

Due on sale clause: An acceleration clause requiring full payment of a mortgage or deed of trust when the property changes ownership or the title is transferred.

Duress: Forcing a person to take action or to be inactive against his will.

E

Earnest money: A cash deposit made by a purchaser of real estate as evidence of good faith and to acknowledge that the parties have reached an agreement.

Easement: A privilege or right which one person has to use or enjoy the land of another. For example, municipalities have easements to enter property to access sewers.

Easement appurtenant/pertaining appurtenant: An easement attached to, accompanying, and passing with a greater interest. It has no existence other than its relationship to the greater one.

Economic life: The period over which a property will yield a return on the investment.

Ejectment: An action to regain possession of real property, with damages for an unlawful retention.

Elevation: The distance above or below a set point.

Eminent domain: The right of the government to take private property for necessary public use, with just compensation paid to the owner. By using eminent domain, the state may acquire property for projects such as streets, parks, public buildings, and public right-of-ways.

Encroachment: The building of a structure or any improvements partly or wholly intruding or trespassing upon the property of another.

Encumbrance: Any claim, lien, charge, easement, restriction, or liability attached to and binding upon real property which may lessen the value of the property. Encumbrances can be put into two different categories. First, those that affect the title, including judgments, mortgages, and liens used to secure a debt or obligation. Second, those that affect the physical condition or ability to use the property such as restrictions, encroachments, covenants, and easements.

Engineering feasibility study: Evaluation of proposed construction to determine whether the project is economically, structurally, and environmentally feasible.

Environmental assessment: A written evaluation to determine the potential environmental impact of proposed construction.

Equitable title: The buyer's interest in property under an installment land contract.

Equity: The value of real estate over and above any encumbrances or liens against it. The difference between the market value of property and what's owed on the property.

Erosion: The natural diminishment of land through processes of nature, such as rain, streams, and wind.

Escalation clause: A clause which increases the amount of monthly rent when a specific event occurs.

Escheat: When property reverts to the state after a person dies without heirs.

Escrow: A procedure where a third party holds property or money for the benefit of buyers and sellers pending the happening of a contingent event.

Escrow payment: A portion of a buyer's monthly mortgage payment held in trust by the lender to pay for items as they become due, such as taxes and insurance.

Estate: The extent or degree of a person's ownership in real property.

Estate for life: An interest in property held by the tenant for his own life or the life or lives of one or more other persons as designated in the document creating the estate.

Estate for years/tenancy for years: An interest in property for a set period of time, for one day or greater.

Estate from period to period: An interest in property with no set termination date. The rent is set at a certain amount per week, month, or year.

Estate in reversion: An estate that reverts to the grantor after the termination of another estate or after a contingency.

Estoppel: A legal doctrine precluding a person from asserting rights that are inconsistent with a previous position or representation, or arguing facts after a court has ruled on them.

Eviction: The act of depriving a person possession of property pursuant to a judgment of the court. This happens to tenants who don't pay their rent.

Exchange: Disposal of any interest in property by exchanging it for another interest of equal value without the use of cash.

Exclusive listing/sole listing: A written contract giving a real estate agent the exclusive right to sell a certain property for a specified period of time.

Executor: The individual or institution designated in a will to settle the estate of the testator.

Expert witness: A person with sufficient knowledge, education, experience, or skill to enable him to give an opinion on facts in dispute.

F

Fair Credit Reporting Act: A consumer protection law regulating the disclosure of consumer credit reports by credit reporting agencies. The act also establishes procedures for correcting mistakes on one's credit record.

Fair market value/market value: The price property would sell for if it were placed on the market and sold within a reasonable period.

Fannie Mae: A nickname for the Federal National Mortgage Corporation (FNMA), a corporation chartered by Congress which supports the secondary mortgages insured by the FHA and guaranteed by the VA, as well as conventional loans issued by banks and credit unions.

Federal Housing Administration (FHA): An agency of the U.S. Department of Housing and Urban Development (HUD) which insures residential mortgage loans made by private lenders. The FHA sets standards for construction and mortgage underwriting, but it doesn't plan or construct housing or lend money for housing projects.

Federal National Mortgage Association: Popularly known as Fannie Mae, it's a corporation chartered by Congress which supports the secondary mortgage market. Fannie Mae purchases and sells residential mortgages insured by the FHA or guaranteed by the VA, as well as conventional loans issued by banks and credit unions.

Federal Reserve System/the Fed: The central bank of the United States, comprised of twelve regional member banks. It was created by Congress and establishes policies that control or moderate interest rates.

Fee: An inheritable estate in land.

Fee simple/fee simple absolute: The most comprehensive ownership of real property. The owner has unrestricted, absolute power over the property and can dispose of it as he pleases. It is sometimes referred to simply as "the fee."

Fee tail: An estate or interest in land which cannot be conveyed by the owner. The property must descend to the heirs of the holder. Most states have abolished fee tail.

FHA/Federal Housing Administration: A federal agency chartered by Congress to expand and strengthen home ownership by encouraging private, long-term, low–down payment mortgage financing.

FHA-insured mortgage: A mortgage issued under FHA regulations.

Finance charge: The total cost a borrower must pay to obtain credit. The amount of interest a borrower must pay on a loan.

First mortgage: A mortgage superior in right to any other mortgage on the property.

Fittings: Objects which can be removed from a structure without causing damage to it, as opposed to fixtures, which once attached become part of the property.

Fixed-rate mortgage: A loan with a fixed interest rate for the duration of the loan. Compare these to adjustable rate mortgages.

Fixtures: Items that are affixed to real property and cannot be removed without causing damage to the property. Fixtures become a part of real property.

Flip: To sell a property quickly after purchasing it for the purpose of making a quick profit.

Foreclosure: A legal procedure whereby mortgaged property is sold to pay the debt following default in payments or terms.

Forfeit: A legal proceeding where a person is forced to relinquish money, property, or the right to property because he engaged in criminal, negligent, or improper action. The property lost is called a forfeiture.

Formula: The manner by which interest rates are calculated on adjustable rate mortgages. Add the margin to the index to get the interest rate.

Fraud: An intentional misrepresentation of truth to deceive another person, with the intent to cause the person to act in a way that causes him harm.

Freddie Mac: The Federal Home Loan Mortgage Corporation (FHLMC), a federally chartered corporation which supports the secondary mortgage market. Freddie Mac purchases and sells conventional home mortgages.

Freehold: An estate owned in fee simple for an indefinite time period.

Functional obsolescence: A decrease in the value of an improvement due to functional inadequacies, often caused by age or poor design, such as wiring or plumbing that's out of code.

G

General lien: A lien which attaches to any and all property owned by the debtor, except property specified as exempt by statute.

General warranty: A covenant in a deed whereby the grantor agrees to protect the grantee against any claims regarding the chain of title.

Good faith estimate: A lender's estimate of any and all closing costs and the monthly payment.

Graduated lease: A lease that provides for a fluctuating rental rate, often based upon future determination or contingencies.

Graduated payment mortgage: A loan where the borrower pays only a portion of the interest accrued each month during the first few years of the loan. The payments increase gradually to a predetermined rate during the first few years until they reach the amount necessary to amortize the loan during the course of the mortgage.

Graduated rental system: A concession lease in which the lessee's rental rate fluctuates in accordance with the ratio of his gross income to gross fixed assets. Most of these leases also establish a nonrefundable fixed minimum rental (FMR), and the rent payment cannot be below this amount.

Grant: Conveying or transferring real property. The operative words in a conveyance of real estate are to "grant, bargain, and sell." The owner (seller or grantor) delivers the grant (or title) to the grantee (or buyer).

Grantor/grantee index: The most common document recording and indexing system. All documents transferring property or an interest related to property, such as deeds, easements, and mortgages, are recorded by the grantor's last name in the grantor index and cross-indexed by the grantee's last name in the grantee index.

Gross income: The projected annual revenue from operation of a business before any expenses or taxes are paid.

Gross rent multiplier: The ratio of sales price to monthly rental income for single-family residential properties.

Ground lease: A lease to use land for a defined period.

H

Habendum clause: A clause in a deed with "to have and to hold" language which defines or limits the quantity of the estate granted.

Hail and wind deductible: A 1 to 2 percent deductible you pay in addition to your regular deductible to be covered for hail and wind damage.

Hectare: A measure of surface area equaling 10,000 square meters or 2.471 acres.

Hereditaments: Every class of inheritable property, including real, personal, corporeal, and incorporeal.

High waterline: The high waterline at ordinary tides.

Holdover tenant: A tenant who remains in possession of leased property after his lease has expired.

Home inspection: A thorough inspection that evaluates the structural and mechanical condition of a property.

Home inspection report: A report written by a qualified inspector regarding a property's overall condition, including an evaluation of the structural and mechanical systems.

Home warranty policy: Insurance that covers small repairs to the home, including electrical and plumbing. Most home warranty policies last only one year.

Homeowners' association (HOA): An organization of homeowners in a development, condominium, or subdivision. The purpose of the association is to maintain, preserve, and enhance the property, particularly common areas enjoyed by all owners.

Homeowner's insurance: A policy that covers damage to the policyholder's residence. Most lenders require the mortgagee to have homeowner's insurance.

Homestead: A home used as a personal residence. In many jurisdictions there's a homestead exemption, and most liens (except tax liens) cannot be filed against the property.

I

Impound account: An account held by a lender for the payment of taxes or insurance. Also known as an "escrow" account.

Improvements: A significant, permanently attached addition to land, such as a building or a driveway. Repairs or replacements will not count as improvements.

Income property: Property (residential or commercial) owned primarily for the monthly cash flow it will provide.

Indemnify: To protect another party against loss or to keep another party free from damage.

Index: The measure of interest rate changes that determine adjustments in ARMs.

Inflation: A rise in the cost of goods, services, or housing.

Installed building equipment: Equipment and fixtures required to make a building usable for its intended purpose which are attached as a permanent part of the structure. Loading docks, overhead cranes, and elevators are examples.

Installment contract/land contract: An installment contract for the purchase of real estate. Title isn't transferred to the buyer until all the payments (or a specified portion) are made. If the buyer defaults, the property and all the payments are forfeited.

Instrument: A written document creating, limiting, or denying rights of parties.

Interest rate: The fee lenders charge borrowers, which is determined as a percentage of the amount borrowed and amortized over the life of the loan.

Internal rate of return (IRR): The rate of return that would make the present value of all future cash flows plus the final market value of a property equal to the current market value of the property. The higher the IRR, the better the opportunity.

Intestate: A person who dies without a valid will.

Investment property: Property that isn't occupied by the owner but by a tenant who provides positive cash flow to the owner.

Involuntary lien: A lien imposed against property without the consent of the owner, such as a tax lien.

J

Joint and several: An agreement which binds two or more persons individually and jointly. If the parties default, they can be sued individually or collectively.

Joint tenancy: Ownership of real property by two or more persons, where every party has an equal interest. It includes the right of survivorship, whereby upon the death of a party his interest passes to the survivors.

Judgment: A court decree determining the rights and liabilities of the parties in a lawsuit.

Junior lien/junior mortgage: A lien placed upon property that has a lesser priority than another lien on the same property.

Jurisdiction: The authority to legislate within a defined area or over a particular subject matter.

Just compensation: Market value the government is required to pay for any real estate taken under eminent domain.

L

Land management: Programs detailing how to use, improve, and maintain land for the maximum public benefit.

Land surveying: Identifying or marking a particular parcel of land by a professional surveyor or engineer.

Landlord: A person who rents property to others.

Late charge: A fee charged by a lender or landlord when a mortgage or rent payment isn't made on time.

Lease: A written document which allows a person to use property for a specified period of time in return for an agreed amount of rent.

Lease purchase: A lease in conjunction with purchase agreement that allows the tenant to take possession of the property prior to the close of escrow.

Leasehold: The interest or estate a lessee holds in the real property he's leasing.

Legal description: A document containing a detailed description of a particular parcel of land, including the boundaries, which meets the legal standards for the jurisdiction in which the land is located.

Lessee: A person who's renting property from a landlord.

Lesser interests: Any interest in land other than fee simple.

Lessor: The owner of property leased to someone else. Generally, the lessor is also the landlord.

Leverage: Owning or controlling properties valued at more than the direct capital invested in them. Mortgaged property is sometimes referred to as being leveraged.

Liability: Any debt or obligation owed to another.

Liability limits: The maximum amount payable as a benefit under an insurance policy.

License: A revocable authority to enter or use another person's land or property which doesn't grant an estate in the property.

Lien: A claim or hold placed upon the property of another as a security for debt.

Life cap: The total amount adjustable mortgage interest rates and monthly payments can vary during the duration of a loan. Different from the periodic cap, which limits the extent to which your interest rate can fluctuate during a predetermined adjustment period.

Limited liability company (LLC): A business structure that provides liability protection and, under the right circumstances, tax advantages for its owners.

Link: A unit of measure used by surveyors equaling 7.92 inches. One hundred links equals one chain or 66.6 feet.

Lis pendens: A public notice declaring an action at law is pending which may affect the title to specific lands.

Listing authority: A provision in a contract between an owner of the property and the real estate company selling the house. The authority details the length of the agency, any commission to be paid to the company, any costs the company charges, and whether the listing is exclusive, tender, auction, or general.

Littoral rights: Granted to an owner of land with a shoreline contiguous to a sea or lake which allows him to use and enjoy the shore without a change in its position created by artificial interference.

Loan commitment: A written promise loan for a specified amount on specific terms.

Loan to value ratio (LTV): The ratio between the mortgage loan principal and the property's appraised value.

Lock-in: A written agreement where the lender guarantees a specified interest rate if a mortgage closes within set time frame.

Locus: Legal term referring to a particular parcel of land.

Loss: Injury or damage that occurs to a person covered by an insurance policy.

M

Margin: The number of percentage points lenders add to the index rate to calculate the ARM interest rate.

Market price/market value: The price at which a reasonable buyer and a reasonable seller (both free from any outside pressure) would be willing to buy and sell the property.

Marketable title/merchantable title: A title free from encumbrances, liens, or reasonable doubt of defect which can be readily sold or mortgaged to a reasonably prudent purchaser.

Mechanics' lien: A lien which secures payment to material men, contractors, and mechanics for materials and services used to repair, improve, or maintain real property.

Meeting of minds: The mutual intention of two persons to enter into a contract of their own free will.

Member Appraisal Institute (MAI): A designation given to members of the Appraisal Institute, a professional association which certifies appraisers.

Metes and bounds: A system of land description which identifies property by specifying the shape and boundary dimensions of the parcel. The description starts at a well-marked point and follows the boundaries of the land by courses and metes (distances and compass directions) and bounds (landmarks and monuments) and returns to the true point of beginning. The description must enclose the property by returning to the point of beginning, or it's defective.

Mineral rights: The right to extract minerals from land which doesn't grant an easement on the surface land. Any right to enter the land and drill or mine for the minerals must be acquired from the person who owns the surface rights.

Monument/monuments description: A natural or man-made fixed, permanent object used as a reference point for surveying or to establish ownership boundaries for a particular tract of land.

Mortgage: A voluntary lien pledging a particular property as security for repayment of a loan.

Mortgage banker/direct lender: An entity that loans its own money for mortgages, sells those loans to long-term investors, and services the loans for the investor until they're paid in full.

Mortgage broker: A person who buys mortgages wholesale from lenders and then sells them to buyers, or who negotiates loans from lenders on behalf of borrowers.

Mortgage insurance: Insurance that covers the lender against loss caused by a buyer's default.

Mortgage insurance premium (MIP): The amount paid by a mortgagor for mortgage insurance.

Mortgagee: The lender or one to whom a mortgage is made.

Mortgagor: The borrower or one who makes a mortgage.

Multiple Listing Service (MLS): A cooperative, collective listing used by real estate agents which details homes for sale.

Multiple use: Managing natural resources to achieve optimum use and enjoyment in a manner which balances environmental, ecological, and aesthetic values.

N

Natural resources: Products or environments found in nature, including soil, air, water, and plants.

Navigation servitude: The public's right to use navigable waters.

Negative amortization: When monthly payments fail to cover the interest costs of a mortgage or loan. Any uncovered interest is added to the balance of the loan.

Negotiable: A promissory note (including a check) or similar instrument where title to the instrument, and the money it represents, can be transferred by endorsement and delivery by the holder. Some negotiable instruments (such as bearer bonds) do not require endorsement and can be transferred by delivery only.

Negotiation: The process or "give and take" by which parties attempt to reach a mutually satisfying agreement.

Net income: Income minus expenses. It's determined by subtracting all expenses from all revenues. It should be compared to gross income or gross revenue.

Net lease: An agreement where the lessee pays all property expenses, such as taxes, insurance, and maintenance, in addition to rent.

Net rents: Rent income after all operating expenses are deducted, but before mortgage debt payments are subtracted.

Net worth: The value of a person's assets, including cash, after deduction of the value of all liabilities.

Nominee: A person who's appointed to act in the place of another, such as a trustee or agent.

Nonrecourse debt: A debt that limits the lender's legal remedy to filing a claim against the collateral. In the event of a default, the lender cannot file a claim against the borrower individually.

Nonusable condition: A condition relating to property or structures which are unserviceable because they've deteriorated beyond the point where they can reasonably or efficiently be restored, or because they're in a condition that puts the health and safety of personnel in jeopardy.

Notary public: A person authorized by law to acknowledge and certify documents and signatures as valid.

Note/promissory note: A written promise to pay a specified debt within a specified time frame.

Notice to quit: A written notice from a landlord to a tenant directing the tenant to vacate the premises. Landlords are generally required to deliver notices to quit before a tenant can be lawfully evicted.

O

Obligation: Funds reserved for specific, known requirements, such as the amount due under a contract or set aside as a realistic estimate of costs.

Obligor: One who places himself under a legal obligation. The person hold holds the obligation is an obligee.

Obsolescence: The loss of property value due to structural, economic, or social changes.

Off the plan: To purchase a property before it's completed after having reviewed the plans.

Offer: The expressed intent by one party to form a contract with another party under the terms and conditions conveyed in the offer.

Offset statement: A statement issued by the owner of property or by the owner of a lien encumbering the property, detailing the present status of the lien.

Open-end mortgage: A mortgage that permits the mortgagor to borrow against the property after the loan has been reduced with no condition that the mortgage be rewritten.

Option: One party's right to act or to refuse to act without the permission of another.

Order of possession: A court order in a condemnation action which allows the government to possess and use lands.

Origination fee: A fee paid to a lender when establishing a loan, which is normally a percentage of the value of the loan.

Outstanding rights: Existing encumbrances, obligations, or liens on property. The government may condemn property subject to any outstanding rights or it may eliminate them.

Over-improvement: Improvement to land that isn't necessary or that cannot be justified from a financial perspective.

P

Partial taking: Taking part, but not all, of a property for public use, under power of eminent domain with just compensation.

Partition: A legal action which divides real property owned jointly by two or more persons. Partition is generally reserved for situations where multiple people own a property but cannot agree on what to do with it. Partitioning the property gives each person an equal share of the property, and he's free to do with it what he pleases.

Partnership: A business relationship by which individuals can jointly own property, sharing equally in the expenses and income.

Passed in: When property offered at an auction doesn't sell because the highest bid fails to meet the reserve price.

Percentage lease: A lease whereby rent is a percentage of gross or net income from sales or services. Such a lease often guarantees a minimum or maximum rent, regardless of business volume.

Performance mortgage: A mortgage or deed of trust which secures performance of an obligation other than a promissory note, such as an option.

Periodic cap: A limit placed on the amount the interest rate in an adjustable rate mortgage can fluctuate during the adjustment period.

Permanent construction: A structure suitable and appropriate to serve a specified purpose for at least twenty-five years with no more than routine or minimal maintenance.

Permit: A privilege granted to use real property for a specified purpose which is revocable at will and which conveys no possessory interest.

Personal property: All physical objects of a personal or movable nature which a person can own, not including real estate.

PITI: The four parts of a monthly mortgage payment: principal, interest, taxes, and insurance.

Planned unit development (PUD): Property developed at the same or slightly greater overall density than conventional developments, with improvements often clustered between open, common areas.

Plat: A detailed map of a town, section, or subdivision, showing the locations and boundaries of individual properties.

Plot: A particular, specific tract or piece of land.

Point: A fee or charge equal to 1 percent of the principal amount of the loan. One point is therefore 1 percent of the subject loan.

Point of commencement: A surveying term describing an established point from which a true point of beginning is identified.

Possessory interest: The right to use and possess real property.

Power of attorney: An instrument authorizing someone to act on another person's behalf. The power can be limited to a certain time period, can cover only certain issues, or it can cover every aspect of a person's life.

Premium: The periodic payment made to an insurer to provide insurance for a specified period of time.

Prepayment penalty: A penalty for paying off the balance of a mortgage or deed of trust note before it's due.

Prescription: Acquiring a right in property (but not the property itself), such as an easement or right-of-way, by means of adverse use of the property that's continuous and uninterrupted for the prescriptive period. It's similar to adverse possession, but title to the property never changes.

Price: The amount paid in legal tender, goods, or services for goods, property, or services.

Prime rate: The interest rate banks charge to preferred customers.

Principal: The amount of a loan or the balance remaining on a loan.

Private mortgage insurance (PMI): Insurance (also known as "mortgage guaranty insurance") which protects lenders against loss if a borrower defaults on a mortgage.

Probate sale: The auction of a home after the death of a homeowner, and the proceeds from the sale of property are divided among heirs or sold to pay debts. The sale is organized by the executor of the estate and is overseen by a probate court judge.

Property: The rights or interests a person has in the thing he owns or is allowed to use. Property includes the right to possess, to use, to encumber, to transfer, and to exclude.

Property damage: Physical damage to property caused by the negligence, recklessness, or intention of a person.

Property tax: An assessment placed on property based on the value of the property. The revenues generated fund public works, such as roads and sewers.

Prorate: To divide in proportionate shares. At closing, items such as property taxes, interest, rents, and other items are prorated so the buyer pays a percentage of these fees based upon when he takes possession of the property.

Public domain lands/public lands: Land owned and administered by the national government which isn't reserved for any specific purpose.

Punch list: A "to do" list or list of things that need to be completed on a particular project.

Purchase money mortgage: A mortgage granted on the same land and concurrently with the conveyance which is used to secure the unpaid balance of the purchase price.

Q

Qualified fee: An estate in fee simple encumbered by limitations imposed by the grantor.

Quiet enjoyment: The right of a grantee or tenant to enjoy possession of the premises without interference.

Quiet title: A court action brought to establish title, to clarify who's the rightful owner of property, and to remove any cloud on the title.

Quitclaim deed: A deed of conveyance where the grantee gives up any claim he may have in the property specified in the deed.

R

Range: A specified strip of land six miles wide, which runs in a north-south direction.

Real estate agent: A person licensed to negotiate and transact the sale or lease of real estate on behalf of the property owner or the buyer. Agents are generally paid by commissions.

Real estate investment trust (REIT): A security that sells like a stock. REITs invest in real estate directly, either through owning properties or mortgages.

Real Estate Settlement Procedures Act (RESPA): A federal law requiring the disclosure of certain costs in the sale of residential property financed by federally insured lenders.

Real property: Land and anything built on or affixed to it.

Realtor: A member of the National Association of Realtors.

Realty: Real property or real estate.

Recapture clause: A clause which gives the landlord the right to terminate a lease if certain conditions or standards aren't met. In a percentage lease, the landlord has the right to recapture if a defined minimum volume of business is not maintained.

Recordation/recording: The act of filing a document, such as a deed or mortgage, in the office of the county recorder.

Redemption: The right of an owner or lien holder to redeem property during the foreclosure period or after the property has been sold for taxes.

Refinance: To apply for a new mortgage loan to receive more favorable terms.

Related furnishings: Property which isn't fixed to or part of a building, such as furniture, furnishings, and equipment.

Release: An instrument releasing a right, claim, or privilege, such as a lien or encumbrance.

Release of lien: The discharge of property from a lien, such as a judgment, mortgage, or claim.

Relocatable building: A building designed and intended to be readily moved, assembled, disassembled, stored, and reused, such as a trailer.

Remainder: An estate which vests immediately after the termination of a prior estate, such as a life estate, which is created at the same time and by the same instrument as the other estate.

Rent: The compensation received by the owner of real estate from a tenant.

Renter's insurance: A policy that covers an individual's personal belongings while he resides in rental property.

Replacement costs: The cost of a replacing a building, while ensuring equivalent utility, using modern materials, and eliminating any deficiencies.

Reproduction costs: The cost of building an exact duplicate of a structure, including any deficiencies.

Reprogramming: Transferring funds from one appropriation account to another, for purposes different than the original appropriation.

Requisitions on title: Requests from the buyer for additional information regarding the title of the property.

Rescission of contracts: Cancelling, revoking, or repealing contracts by the mutual consent of the parties or by cause.

Reservation: A right reserved to the owner in the sale or lease of property.

Residual estate: The balance of a testator's estate after deducting the debts, bequests, and devises.

Restriction: A limitation upon the use, occupancy, or development of real estate, placed by covenant in deeds or by public legislative action.

Restrictive covenant: A clause in a deed limiting the use, occupancy, or development of land.

Reversion/reversionary interest: The residue of an estate left to the grantor which commences after the determination of some particular estate granted by him.

Revocation: The recall of a power or authority previously conferred.

Right of entry: A written instrument which grants authority to enter on certain premises to perform specified acts, but does not grant an estate or interest in the property.

Right of survivorship: A trait of joint tenancy by which the surviving joint tenants are awarded all right, title, and interest of the deceased joint tenant without the need for probate proceedings.

Right-of-way: The right or privilege to pass over a designated portion of the property of another. Right-of-ways may be private (such as an easement) or public (such as the right to use highways and streets).

Riparian owner: One who owns land which abuts a river or watercourse.

Riparian rights: The right of a landowner to use water on, under, or adjacent to his land, for general purposes, and to access navigable waters.

S

Sale-leaseback: An agreement where the owner of property wishes to sell the property but retain occupancy by leasing it from the buyer.

Sales contract: A contract by which a buyer and a seller agree to the terms of the sale of property.

Satisfaction of mortgage: An instrument recording and acknowledging full payment for an indebtedness secured by a mortgage. It releases the encumbrance on the property created by the mortgage.

Seal: An embossed impression on paper authenticating a document or signature, usually issued by notary publics or corporate officers.

Seasoning of title: A seller's history of ownership in connection with the sale and financing of a specific piece of property.

Second mortgage/secondary financing: A loan secured by a mortgage or trust deed, which is junior or subordinate to a first mortgage or deed of trust.

Section: An area of measure equaling one square mile or 640 acres. A section is 1/36th of a township.

Secured loan: A loan which is guaranteed with security, such as real property, an automobile, or business equipment.

Security instrument: A document under which collateral is pledged, such as a mortgage or financing agreement.

Security interest: An interest in or encumbrance on personal property or fixtures, obtained to ensure payment of an obligation.

Sedimentation ranges: Upstream range lines used for examining data on erosion or sediment buildup.

Seisin: Actual possession of property by one who claims rightful ownership of a freehold interest.

Seller's market: A time frame when the demand for property is greater than the supply, which grants opportunities for sellers to ask higher selling prices.

Semipermanent construction: A structure appropriate for a specific purpose for a limited period (five to twenty-five years), which requires a moderate to high level of maintenance.

Separate property: Property owned by a spouse which is not community property, such as property that was acquired prior to the marriage or as a gift or devise during the marriage.

Servitude: A burden on one estate to the benefit or advantage of another.

Settlement statement: A financial statement rendered to the buyer and seller at the time of a real estate transaction which accounts for all funds received or expended.

Severalty ownership: Sole ownership, ownership by one person only.

Severance damages: Payment to an owner of real property for the diminution in value of a remainder area in a partial acquisition. The damage is generally caused by the acquisition or by construction of improvements.

Sheriff's sale: A sale of property held by court order to satisfy a judgment or tax lien.

Simple interest: One method of calculating interest paid on a loan. It's determined by multiplying the interest rate by the principal amount of the loan, then dividing by the payment period.

Sinking fund: A fund in which equal monthly or annual deposits accumulate with simple interest to a predetermined amount at a calculated time. The fund is used for paying a debt or replacing improvements.

Site: A parcel or tract of land, sufficiently improved to be used as a building lot or for other similar purposes.

Sole/exclusive agency: An agreement which precludes all other real estate agents from working on the disposal of a specified property.

Special condition: A condition that must be met before a contract is legally binding, such as a home inspection or that the buyer be approved for financing.

Special warranty deed: A deed in which the grantor warrants or guarantees the title only against defects arising during his ownership of the property. It does not warrant or guarantee against defects existing before he owned the property.

Specific performance: A legal remedy which compels a person to perform or carry out the terms of a valid, existing contract.

Statute of frauds: A law which requires certain contracts (including those for the sale of land) to be in writing or they're not enforceable.

Subdivision: Any land which is divided or is proposed to be divided for the purpose of creating two or more lots, parcels, units, or interests.

Subject to/subject to mortgage: Transferring title to property encumbered by a mortgage lien without paying off the debt. The seller is not released from his obligation to pay the existing mortgage.

Subletting: An arrangement where one tenant leases to another.

Subordinate: To make subject to, junior to, or inferior to.

Subordination clause: A clause in a mortgage or lease which places the rights of the holder secondary or subordinate to a subsequent encumbrance.

Subordination of collateral: To reduce a lien to a junior or inferior position.

Subprime loan: A loan that doesn't conform to Federal National Mortgage Association (FNMA) lending guidelines and requirements.

Subrogation: Substituting one person for another in regard to a legal right, interest, or obligation, such as when a mortgage holder sells his rights and interest in the mortgage to another.

Substitution of collateral: To substitute one piece of collateral for another.

Subsurface rights: Ownership rights to water, minerals, gas, oil, and natural substances lying beneath the surface of a tract of real estate.

Surety: One who guarantees or ensures the performance of another.

Surface rights: Ownership rights in a tract of real estate limited to the surface. They do not include air above the property (air rights) or minerals below the surface (subsurface rights).

Surrender: The cancellation of a lease by mutual consent of both parties.

Survey: The act by which the boundaries of a piece of land are measured. The drawing or report showing the precise legal boundaries of a piece of property.

T

Tacking: When an adverse possessor has passed his rights to another. The time for the first possessor passes to the second possessor.

Tax deductible: Payments or purchases a person may deduct against his federal and state taxable income.

Tax deed: A deed given by the government when property has been purchased by a member of the public, when the property has been sold because the owner failed to pay taxes.

Tax lien: A government claim for unpaid real estate tax encumbering the title of property.

Tax sale: A sale of property, usually at a public auction, for nonpayment of assessed taxes.

Teaser rate: An introductory, lower mortgage rate offered on adjustable rate mortgages.

Temporary construction: A building suitable and appropriate to fill a need for a short period (less than five years) without regard to maintenance or upkeep.

Tenancy by the entirety: Joint ownership between a husband and wife. The tenancy is created at the time of conveyance, is severed by divorce, and the property goes in entirety to the survivor upon the death of the other party.

Tenancy in common: Co-ownership of real property between two or more people, each entitled to possession according to his proportionate share without the right of survivorship. Each owner may sell or otherwise transfer ownership of his share. When one of the owners dies, his share passes to his heirs.

Tenant: One who holds or possesses land by any kind of title, either in fee, for life, for years, or at will. A person who rents and occupies lands or buildings which belong to another, under the terms of a lease.

Tenant at sufferance: A tenant who possesses lands by lawful title but keeps them after his lease has expired without acquiring any title to the property. He's allowed to remain in possession of the property at the will of the landlord, who can end the tenant's right to occupy at any time.

Tenant at will: A license to use or occupy lands and structures at the will of owner with no fixed term. The tenancy can be terminated at will by the owner.

Tenure in land: The manner by which an estate in lands is held.

Term: The length of time for which an estate is granted, or the period which the lessee is granted to occupy the premises.

Termination: The end of a lease or contract before the scheduled or contracted time, which may be due to the default of one of the parties or by mutual agreement.

Termination at will: An agreement which allows either party to terminate or rescind the agreement at any time for any or no reason.

Termination for cause: Termination of a grant, lease, contract, or other right to use property because of a lessee's violation of a condition of the grant or agreement.

Testate: Having a valid will.

Title: A legal instrument which proves a person's right to ownership of property.

Title insurance: A policy which protects or indemnifies a party against loss or damage due to defects in the title of a specific property.

Title search: Researching or checking the title of a property to ensure the seller is the legal owner of the property and that there are no other claims, encumbrances, or outstanding liens.

Topographic map/topo: A map showing physical features and relative elevations of the area surveyed with the use of contour lines.

Township: A territorial subdivision measuring six miles long, six miles wide, and containing thirty-six sections, each of which is one square mile.

Tract: A specific area of land contained in one description.

Trade fixtures: Articles of personal property affixed to real property which are necessary to the carrying on of a trade or business and are removable by the owner without damage to the real property.

True point of beginning: A surveying term referring to the point from which a legal description of property begins and ends.

Trust deed/deed of trust: A deed conveying land to a trustee as collateral or security for the payment of a debt. When the debt is satisfied, the deed of trust is released. If there's a default, the trustee has the power to sell the land and use the proceeds to pay the debt.

Trustee: One who holds property in trust for another.

Truth in Lending Act: A federal law requiring lenders to fully disclose, in writing, the terms and conditions of a mortgage, including the annual percentage rate and any charges associated with the mortgage.

U

Unconditional agreement: A legal contract that binds both the purchaser and the seller to complete a transaction on an agreed date at an agreed price. It isn't subject to any conditions and commits both parties to transferring the property.

Under-improvement: Improvements or changes inadequate to support the highest and best use of the property. These include building a house that's smaller, less expensive, or of inferior quality to other houses in the neighborhood.

Underwriting: Evaluating a loan application to determine the risk involved for the lender.

Undue influence: Taking unfair advantage of another's weakness in mind, distress, or necessity for the purpose of fraud or to gain an unfair or unethical advantage.

Usury: Charging an interest rate greater than that permitted by law.

Utility: The usefulness of a property and whether it satisfactorily serves in its intended purpose.

Utilization inspection: An inspection of property to determine if it's being put to its optimum use.

V

VA loan: A mortgage issued by a private lender that's partially guaranteed by the Department of Veterans Affairs (VA).

Vacancy: A rental property that's unoccupied or empty.

Valid: Legally sufficient or meeting the requirements of law.

Valuation: A written analysis, prepared by a qualified valuer, detailing the estimated value of a property.

Value: The quantity of goods or money which could be received in exchange for the thing being valued. The present worth of all the rights and benefits of owning a property.

Vendee: A purchaser or buyer.

Vendor: The seller.

Veterans Affairs (VA): A federal agency that administers benefit programs facilitating the adjustment of veterans returning to civilian life, including a home loan guaranty program.

Void: An agreement which is unenforceable and has no force or effect.

Voidable: An agreement which is capable of becoming void but is not void unless one of the parties asserts a right to make it so.

Voluntary lien: A lien placed upon property with the consent of the owner, such as a mortgage.

W

Waiver: The voluntary renunciation, abandonment, or surrender of a right, claim, or privilege.

Warranty deed: A deed where the grantor covenants that he owns the property without any liens or encumbrances and will protect the grantee against any claims regarding the title.

Waste: Willful destruction of any part of the property which would injure or prejudice a landlord's reversionary right.

Waterline: A measurement of the ebb and flow of tides, which can vary. The high waterline is the highest point on the shore the tide normally rises. The low waterline is the lowest point of the tide.

Wetlands: Land areas sufficiently inundated by surface or groundwater which can support vegetable or animal life requiring hydric soils for growth and reproduction.

Wildlife management: Applying scientific and technical principles to wildlife populations and habitats for the purpose of growing and maintaining them for ecological, scientific, or recreational purposes.

Wish list: The criteria for your perfect home.

Withdrawn lands/withdrawn public lands: Public domain land held back for a special governmental purpose or to benefit an agency by reservation, withdrawal, or other restriction.

Wraparound mortgage: A seller's existing mortgage that is assumed by the lender as secondary financing (in addition to a new mortgage) for buying property. Also known as a "wrap."

Z

Zoning: Governmental restrictions on the nature and extent to which property can be used, typically referring to the ability of local authorities to restrict certain types of development in certain areas.

Letters and Forms

These letters and forms are to help you build your business:

Lease Signing Checklist Form

Welcome Letter

FYI Letter

Pest Letter

Renters Insurance Letter

Deposit Received Form

Lease Addendum for Lease Extension Renewal Form

Letter of Intent to Purchase

Pre-Qualify a Renter

You do have permission to copy and edit the letters and forms for your real estate business.

■ ■ ■

8 NE 48th Street | Oklahoma City, OK 73105 | 405-633-1008

www.thesavvylandlordbook.com | info@thesavvylandlordbook.com

Lease Signing Checklist

1. _____Tenant application(s)
2. _____Tenant paid application fee
3. _____Tenant copy of driver's license or state ID card
4. _____Tenant background results
5. _____2 copies of lease
6. _____1 copy of move in check list (Tenant will initial and receive a copy)
7. _____1 copy of FAQ Sheet (Tenant will initial and receive a copy)
8. _____1 copy of Utilities phone numbers
9. _____1 copy of Important numbers
10. _____1 copy of Pest Control letter
11. _____1 copy of Welcome letter
12. _____1 copy of Renters Insurance letter
13. _____Property Photos/Video
14. _____Collect Lock Box
15. _____Air Filter (Show Tenant how to install new filter)
16. _____Eviction Process (Explain the process, then have Tenant sign & date)
17. _____Appliance Agreement
18. _____Monies Owed (Pro-Rated Rent, use as Receipt)
19. _____Work Order (What needs to be address immediately)
20. _____Collect 'For Rent' sign

LEASE SIGNING CHECKLIST FORM

■ ■ ■

8 NE 48th Street | Oklahoma City, OK 73105 | 405-633-1008

www.thesavvylandlordbook.com | info@thesavvylandlordbook.com

Dear Resident,

Welcome and thank you for choosing PROPERTY MANAGEMENT to take care of your housing needs! We hope that you and your family will view your new residence as not just a house but a home. This information packet is provided to help make your move a little bit easier as you get adjusted to the new area. Enclosed are important phone numbers and general information about services. We hope that you find the information useful and that you keep the packet in a convenient spot for easy reference. As you settle into your new home, if you have any questions, please do not hesitate to contact us through our web page at www.WEBSITE.com. Once again, thanks for choosing PROPERTY MANAGEMENT .

Sincerely,

Property Manager

WELCOME LETTER

. . .

8 NE 48th Street | Oklahoma City, OK 73105 | 405-633-1008

www.thesavvylandlordbook.com | info@thesavvylandlordbook.com

FYI

If you need to speak with someone in the office the number is XXX-XXX-XXXX or email us at info@WEBSITE.com

We do not allow parking on the grass.

We do not spray for pests once you take possession of the property.

If something breaks in the home contact us and we will send someone out to assess the issue and fix it.

If you are directly or indirectly responsible for any damage to the home excluding natural disasters or natural ware and tear on the property you will be charged for the repair.

If something should cause your food to spoil or damage to your possessions we are not monetarily responsible to replace any of those items renters insurance is highly suggested.

Int_____ Int_____ Int_____

FYI LETTER

■ ■ ■

8 NE 48th Street | Oklahoma City, OK 73105 | 405-633-1008

www.thesavvylandlordbook.com | info@thesavvylandlordbook.com

Dear Resident,

We at PROPERTY MANAGEMENT would like to welcome you to your new home. We make sure all of our properties are pest free prior to a new tenant's arrival. We do not spray the properties throughout the course of the year. It is your responsibility to maintain a clean dwelling to keep the property pest free. We are excited you have chosen PROPERTY MANAGEMENT for your housing needs and hope you enjoy your new home.

Thank you,

Property Manager

PEST LETTER

. . .

8 NE 48th Street | Oklahoma City, OK 73105 | 405-633-1008
www.thesavvylandlordbook.com | info@thesavvylandlordbook.com

Dear Resident,

The following letter is about the benefit of having renters insurance. We at PROPERTY MANAGEMENT strongly suggest you invest in protecting your property. There are many different companies that offer this as a single policy or you can call your car insurance carrier and they may be able to add it to your current policy.

You may not own the place where you live, but you still need insurance protection. Renters insurance is for anyone who rents a home, be it a house or an apartment. Renters insurance can protect your personal property against fire, theft and vandalism.

Renters insurance doesn't just help provide coverage for everyday necessities like furniture and clothes, it also helps protect theft-prone valuables like your laptop and bike - wherever you take them.

In the event of a disaster which leaves your home uninhabitable; Allstate, Shelter, and State Farm cover the increased costs of a place to live until you can move back in.

Property Manager

RENTERS INSURANCE LETTER

∎ ∎ ∎

8 NE 48th Street | Oklahoma City, OK 73105 | 405-633-1008

www.thesavvylandlordbook.com | info@thesavvylandlordbook.com

Deposit Received

Property:_____ City:_____ State:_____

Prospective Tenant(s):_____

PROPERTY MANAGEMENT has collected the deposit in the amount of $_____ from the prospective tenant(s) as a non-refundable fee to purchase an Intent to Rent on the property listed above.

Upon signing of this document PROPERTY MANAGEMENT will remove said property from public offering and will hold the property for the prospective tenant to produce the "amount due" monies needed to complete the rental agreement.

PROPERTY MANAGEMENT will "hold" the property for no longer than _____ days. If prospective tenant fails to fulfill said task within ____days after signing this document, a fee for lost rents, administrative cost, advertising, and holding cost will be assessed to prospective tenant(s) in the amount equal to amount collected to date.

All parties understand this document is not a rental agreement and no possession is permitted until an entire rental agreement has been properly signed and completed.

Property Manager   Prospective Tenant(s)

_____Date_____ _____Date_____
                             _____Date_____

DEPOSIT RECEIVED FORM

■ ■ ■

the savvy LANDLORD™

8 NE 48th Street | Oklahoma City, OK 73105 | 405-633-1008

www.thesavvylandlordbook.com | info@thesavvylandlordbook.com

THIS ADDENDUM is a modification to the existing Lease Agreement dated

This extension made this date, _____, by and between PROPERTY MANAGEMENT as owner/agent, and _____ as resident: The parties hereby have previously entered into a lease regarding the premises located at _____. The term of that lease shall expire on _____.

1.   The term of the lease shall now be extended as follows:

2.   The rental during the extended term shall be as follows: (please circle one): (Please note, resident, pays a higher rental rate for flexibility of having a shorter term and pays a lower rental rate for agreeing to stay for a longer term. If the resident vacates sooner than the time period agreed to below, resident agrees to pay a lease cancellation fee of (2 months rent). Please check one of the options below.
____   I wish to extend the lease for 12 months with a monthly rental rate of $575.00
____   I wish to extend the lease for 6 months with a monthly rental rate of $625.00
____   I wish to lease on a month to month basis at a monthly rental rate of $675.00
Rent will be due in advance of the first day of each month of the extended term.

3.   Upon execution hereof, the Lease Extension Agreement, this addendum shall become an integral part of the lease. All other terms and provisions of the lease shall remain in full force and effect.

Resident's signature _____ Date _____

Resident's signature _____ Date _____

Owner/Manager's signature _____ Date _____

____ If resident will not renew existing lease on premises noted above, and will vacate the property on or before expiration date of lease as noted above please check here and sign below.

Resident's signature _____ Date _____

Resident's signature _____ Date _____

Owner/Manager's signature _____ Date _____

LEASE ADDENDUM FOR LEASE EXTENSION RENEWAL FORM

■ ■ ■

the
savvy
LANDLORD™

8 NE 48th Street | Oklahoma City, OK 73105 | 405-633-1008

www.thesavvylandlordbook.com | info@thesavvylandlordbook.com

Selling Realtor
Broker Company Nam
Address, City, State 12345

re: Letter of Intent to Purchase

Mr. Selling Realtor,

My client would like to make a group offer on a set of properties listed by Broker Company Name.

The properties involved are:

- MLS 486899 4009 Crabtree Cove, Midwest City, OK
- MLS 486904 1617 Melinda Ln, Midwest City, OK
- MLS 486907 914 Holly Dr, Midwest City, OK
- MLS 486915 1004 Jasmine Ln, Midwest City, OK

My client offers $115,000 Cash for all 4 properties, in their current condition with tenants in place. All deposit money will be credited at closing. Rents collected will be pro-rated to the end of the month of closing and credits to buyer at closing. Seller forfeits any unpaid rents.

Closing can be completed as soon as title work is completed, estimated 14 days or less from execution of contract.

Current property management services will be terminated on or before closing date and all fees due the property management company will be paid in full by seller.

Buyer is fully qualified and has proof of funds, available upon agreement in principle or execution of Purchase Contract.

Please advise if this offer is acceptable and if so, I will submit a fully executed Purchase Contract and supporting proof of funds documents for seller's signature, and we can open escrow.

Regards,

Great Investor Realtor

LETTER OF INTENT TO PURCHASE

∎ ∎ ∎

8 NE 48th Street | Oklahoma City, OK 73105 | 405-633-1008

www.thesavvylandlordbook.com | info@thesavvylandlordbook.com

Address: _____

Hello _____,

We have received your inquiry about the home at _____!

The home is a brick 3 bed, 1 bath in a great neighborhood, in _____ Schools.
Brand New Kitchen Floor, New Paint, CH&A, W&D
$600.00 Rent (12 Month Lease)
$500 Deposit

When do you want to move it?
Will you be living by yourself, if not how many people will be living with you?
Have you driven by the property?
When would you like to view the home?

If you are serious about this home please fill out the online application so we can
start the process:
www.WEBSITE.com/new

Other homes we have available:
www.WEBSITE.com/

Thank you

Property Manager
Address, City, State 12345
XXX-XXX-XXXX Office | XXX-XXX-XXXX Fax
www.WEBSITE.com/

PRE-QUALIFY A RENTER

■   ■   ■

Thank You.

There are so many important people in my life, I can't begin to list everyone who has touched me. I do apologize if I make a mistake and forgot to mention you. This book would not be a reality if it wasn't for my loving family and their encouragement, my dear wife Shannez' and my mother Linda for being by my side through the entire process. I would like to thank everyone who has contributed to this dream project, so here we go - Walter B. Jenkins for grace and leadership, Elizabeth Hunt for art direction, Jason Grotelueschen for input, Thomas Womack for editing, Eric Weber for interior layout, Gary Tompkins for formatting & typesetting, Lisa Ham and Jeri Segard for proof reading, Dean Wendt for his voice, John Day for insight, and Coach Greg Salciccioli for pushing me.

I would like to the thank all the interviewees for giving me their time and wisdom.

For those that have encouraged and supported me through the years:

Devin Long	Donny Ho	Linda Hamilton
Steven Earp	Greg Drury	Britt Cordon
Ken & Sharlene Monier	Dutch Revenboer	Roy Barrett
Zac McDorr	Kenny Malabag	Carol Britton
Ben Shrewsbury	Dewey Beene	Sean Pruitt
Ed O'Toole	Jim & Trish Garcia	Marc McIntosh
Bryon Hanawalt	Marty Wolf	

Team:

Delton Brown	Lucky the plumber
Mitch Salfridge	First Security Bank
Alvin Smith	Vickie & Robert at B&B Sales
Bille Presnell	Pam Schrader at Old Republic Title
Alvin Harbert	Josh at Wolf Mechanical
Jake Long	Russell & Mitch at Carpet Depot
Becky Ferguson	Tiffiney McMillan at Premier Locators
Phyllis Henize	

■ ■ ■

About the Authors

Steven R. VanCauwenbergh was raised by his single mother in a one-bedroom apartment in New Jersey. He grew up with one simple dream. He wanted to live in a house. Steven took that dream, rolled up his sleeves, and has purchased more than 50 income producing homes since 1999. Steven attended high school in California, then moved to Oklahoma to attend college, and quickly started his first business. While creating several successful businesses, he met and married his wife Shannez' who is a constant support and strength to him. They have two children, Kennedy Grace & Maxwell James. Steven lives an energetic and abundant life thanks to the freedom his real estate investments have created. He enjoys educating and guiding others to financial freedom.

Walter B. Jenkins is the proud father of international hockey sensation Katie Jenkins. Before beginning his career as a writer and speaker, Walter was an attorney and sports agent. He now helps people turn their ideas into great books. In his spare time he enjoys studying tae kwon do, scuba diving, riding his bike, and training his German shepherd, Jake the wonder dog. Learn more at www.walterbjenkins.com.

■ ■ ■